ENTERING THE
RIVER NAKED

ENTERING THE RIVER NAKED

Field Notes from the Feminine Wild

ANN SHANNON

PrayerDancer Press
Portland, OR

Grateful acknowledgement is made for permission to reprint:

Lines from "Call", "Water Woman", and "Passover Remembered" reprinted from *Womanpriest: A Personal Odyssey (Revised Edition)*, by Alla Renée Bozarth. Copyright © 1988 by Alla Renée Bozarth. With permission from Alla Renée Bozarth. This book can be ordered at: bearblessings.com

Lines from "Novaya Zemlya" *and* "Passover Remembered" reprinted from *Stars In Your Bones: Emerging Signposts on Our Spiritual Journeys* by Alla Bozarth. Copyright © 1990 by Alla Bozarth. With permission from Alla Bozarth.

Abridged quotation from *Hymn of the Universe* by Pierre Teilhard de Chardin, translated by Gerald Vann, O.P. English translation copyright © 1965 by William Collins Sons & Co., Ltd. With permission from Georges Borchardt, Inc., Literary Agency.

Quote from "O Canada" reprinted from *Diesel*, by Patrick Califia, formerly Pat Califia. Copyright © 1997 by Patrick Califia. With permission from Patrick Califia. (Having gone through a gender transition, this author now publishes under the name Patrick Califia.)

Abridged quotation from *Woman and Nature: The Roaring Inside Her*, by Susan Griffin. Copyright © 1978 by Susan Griffin. With permission from Counterpoint Press.

Excerpts from pp. 29 and 92, *Talking With Angels: Budaliget*, 1943 by Gitta Mallasz; translated by Robert Hinshaw Copyright © 1988 by Daimon Verlag (Einsiedeln, Switzerland). With permission from Robert Hinshaw, Daimon Verlag.

"Turning-Point," and "Dove that ventured outside," translation copyright © 1982 by Stephen Mitchell; from SELECTED POETRY OF RAINER MARIA RILKE by Rainer Maria Rilke, edited and translated by Stephen Mitchell. Used by permission of Random House, an imprint and division of Penguin Random House LLC. All rights reserved. Any third party use of this material, outside of this publication, is prohibited. Interested parties must apply directly to Penguin Random House LLC for permission.

Printed in the United States of America
First Printing, 2018

Published by PrayerDancer Press
Portland, OR
prayerdancerpress.com

ISBN 978-1-7323315-0-1

Cover Photos: Linda Cook Photography; Shutterstock

Typesetting services by BOOKOW.COM

To the purely generative feminine fire,
in her endlessly brilliant, ecstatic dance
of birth and incarnation.

CONTENTS

PREFACE

September 17, 2018

Why now? Twenty-four years later?

There has been a ripening to time.

While some of us are choking on wildfire smoke for months at a time, others are inundated by off-the-charts, out-of-season flooding from superstorms. In the Great Outbreak of 2018, those in the South and Mid-West U.S. saw 782 twisters touching down (93 were EF4s or EF5s). The limits of any society cut off from Nature and the feminine are getting real. The Age of Extinctions is accelerating, and we are on the list.

Unless…

The world has never been more needful than it is today of Woman. Woman, bedded down with Nature. Woman, given to the wisdom and energies of Nature running freely through her. Woman, given to the instincts of her heart, rising in Her power as an incarnation of Nature.

If there is anything I know from my struggles and triumphs as a woman, it is this: at our core, each of us is an extension of the Cosmic Mother Herself. We may not have the slightest inkling of it. Still, all of the force and resources of Creation's birthing capacities stand behind us. They are within us, reaching through us individually and collectively, waiting to be claimed and brought to bear on all that we ache to give birth to in our own lives and in the world.

Each of us has the potential to embody that larger Woman Self. She holds the key to every conundrum we wrestle with. And She reveals Herself to us, quietly, intimately, often rapturously, in Nature.

My stumbling life has thrown me back, time and time again, to the bottom of things. With everything else emptied out and stripped away, I find myself reduced to formless being. But I am never alone there. I am always met and held, soothed and renewed, in deep and tender ways as I rest, with nowhere else to go, in what feels like a vast sea of being.

"There is field, out beyond….I will meet you there." Rumi says. And I have been privileged to find myself there. This is the ground of all being. The Womb of Creation. It is a Feminine field. A birthing field. It is the primordial field of Nature's arising – the source of my being and yours, of all women's and all men's. It is the ground of being of every creature and plant, every mountain and stone. It is a mythic field, inherently transformational, always expansive, and full of mystery.

That mythic field may have been buried and forgotten in today's world. But it remains the fertile repository of that god-like *"strength which, in old days, moved earth and heaven."* (Tennyson, "Ulysses") And it is reaching for the surface through every circumstance of your life and mine.

What, I wonder, less than mythic orders of being could begin to equip us in addressing the personal and global upheavals confronting us today? What less than the primal force of Creation living through us, could burst out into life with the magnetism and energy required to shift the axis around we are all so wildly spinning? Where else is that capacity going to come from?

My life in the forest tells me that Nature will sing us back there if we go to Her often enough. So will dropping down through the substance of our lives, allowing the relentless stirrings of our heart to lead us home to what is sacred and essential.

Both pathways carry us into the taproot of that Feminine Field. If we are present to that womb of all being in us – if we give it rein and space enough – it will reveal itself. It will weave its life – its ways of knowing and being and working – into the fiber of our being. Its primal sweetness will come bounding deliciously back, encoding itself anew in our DNA. It will revivify all that has been drained out of us, and open orders of being that are light-years beyond our comprehension.

This is the Great Mother of the Universe, with her inherently transformative, creative juices alive and coursing through our own veins. As the lifeblood of our aspiration, She is eager to work through our hands, to sing through our lives and voices, to the world.

Calling us to leave all smallness behind, She unbridles the mythic powers of the Feminine in the most personal, tender, and unexpected ways when we re-root ourselves in Nature. And She is calling us all to rise, in concert with one another, to catalyze one another in lifting ourselves and humanity out of the mire.

There are so many of us who know this now, who are owning Nature's Life, the Great Mother's Life, as our life. Many are doing important, beautiful, critical work. But every hand is needed. Every voice. Every song. Each of us has our own way, our own unique role to play in calling others who are on their way to this beautiful reality and all that it can give birth to.

So I give you my song, long and lovingly tended. It always belonged to Her. It actually had very little to do with me.

There is such wonder in meeting another woman's life. In that ground where your struggle meets mine, setting fire to my heart, your transformation feeds my own. Then we are in that sacred field again, meeting in a mirrored dance of emergence. So I pray for a new body of work, our very own genre within women's memoir – the stories of my sisters who are out there, mapping their own new and wild terrain. None of us live just for ourselves. Let's create a chorus, calling to others as we go.

Finally, I suggest we reframe how we emotionally hold and language the planetary crisis we are facing today. This is Life, exposing all that is unworkable in no uncertain terms. It is Nature, all of Creation, calling humanity back to Her and Her informing harmonies. Back to what sustains us. This is the Universe, calling us back to Joy.

Our hearts ache to be restored to a vision all of us can share. One that celebrates the preciousness of every human being. One that works to ensure the well-being of every life. Let's go there together, daring to forge all that is wanting, waiting, and possible. The great turning of a planet does not have to be as killing and heavy as we presuppose with the Cosmic winds of Nature rising under our wings. She seeds galaxies, for God's sake – billions upon billions of them!

What could be more joyful than to have our lives billowing out with the whispered inspirations of Creation Itself? What could be more ecstatic than to ride ever-new currents of the Great Ascendant Arc of Being and Becoming, as Nature labors, through us, to bring forth a more flourishing world?

With love to you and our Great Mother,

Ann Shannon

Chapter I

A VOICE IN THE MIST

*Each of us, whatever the circumstances of our lives,
has a place within where we stand in the presence
of the absolute goodness of our own heart;
Where excellence flows through us
with the power of a sacred river;
Where beauty whispers our name
and calls us home to Infinity.*

*Our human task is to discover that place,
to return to it often, whatever the obstacles,
to root ourselves in its mysteries,
and seek after its visions.*

There was a period during the early eighties when I had the unshakable, not-quite physical sense of something calling to me. Initially, it had an ephemeral, voice-like quality that seemed to come from a great distance away. Over several months, my day-to-day life became imbued with the gentle, intriguing nudge of its insistence. Whether I was ploughing through paperwork at the law office where I was a legal secretary, feeding the ducks with my daughters at our neighborhood park, or waiting in the checkout line at the grocery store, it was there, lingering in the background. I was constantly straining to hear it.

I developed the habit of turning to look over my left shoulder, stretching my neck like a crane, trying to catch sight of what might lie just beyond my seeing and hearing. It is not that I actually expected to see or hear anything. I realized this was not an actual sound. But it was so haunting, so bordering on the physical, so pervasively present amid the constant stream of my daily activities as a working supermom, that the impulse to treat it as real was irresistible.

Gradually, a recurrent image took hold... of making my way through a dense fog, struggling to find my way to whatever was calling to me from beyond thick, grey veils of mist. All of my senses became involved. They finally trained themselves on a faint, light-like thread emerging out of the mist on the ground in front of me. This was not a voice. It wasn't even a sound. Within the light was a quality of goodness that felt both compelling and familiar. It was so subtle as to be almost imperceptible, yet it was exquisitely distilled, crystalline and pure. Settling into its elusive, enigmatic qualities, the feeling grew to certainty that I had experienced this light before, long ago – perhaps in the unnameable, remote distance of another lifetime, or in another dimension. This was absolute goodness, the goodness so deep that it lies below all thought, behind the created world, within the deepest reaches of the heart, at the source and center of all existence and form.

Those months of listening were precious and pivotal. The voice calling to me, and the thread of light that it led to, were reminding me of what my life is about. They were urging me to find my way back to the absolute goodness that my heart longs for, to spend my life bridging the distance between that seemingly removed, hidden world and this terrifying, often painful, visible one.

The journals that follow are markings in the mist following that slender thread of light which, through those months, laid claim to me. Its emanations deepened the already mystical center orienting my life. It led me over time into the subtle heart of nature and the feminine Divine and, ultimately, to the forested foothills of the Sierra Nevada mountains, where I often walked the woods each night until dawn.

—◆•◆—

Chapter II

INTIMATIONS, LIGHT AND DARK

1988

There is a new sound
of roaring voices
in the deep
and light-shattered
rushes in the heavens.

The mountains are coming alive,
the fire-kindled mountains,
moving again to reshape the earth.

ALLA RENÉE BOZARTH, "Call,"
Womanpriest: A Personal Odyssey

M Y experience of the house is that of an ongoing battle with chaos. I am swimming upstream, against a river of physical decay that is fraught with rapids. The weight and pressure of the currents are slamming against me, constantly hitting me, washing me under, knocking me back. This is a life and death struggle. I am reeling and disoriented. The river whispers in taunting echoes, behind the thrashing currents, "You are never going to make it. Give up."

Every mountainous pile of clean, unfolded laundry cascading back onto the floor in the basement, each unmade bed and unswept floor, every stack of unsorted mail, each dirty, crusting dish and pan in the sink hits me with the force of a jagged, slicing rock. Every step I take, every turn I make going from one room to the next, exhausted from another day of dealing with a petulant attorney, slaps me in the face with yet another task left undone, another wave of defeat.

I am swirling down, deeper down, darker down ... into a thick, muddy bottom that sucks all courage and strength out of me.

—◆•◆—

Maybe all of life is swimming upstream. And it is an entrenched, stubborn delusion to think it could ever be anything but pressing into the storm, against the constant weight of forces that would reduce me to the base elements that I struggle to hold at bay.

Triumph. That is what I have sought. Some final, irreversible increment. An accomplishment so undeniable that it would put me forever out of danger of being overtaken by all that overwhelms me. Because that triumph has never been achieved, when my strength wanes, I plummet. I drown, again and again, in the fear that all is lost, that the dark forces will swallow me whole, devour all that I have fought so long and hard against.

For this moment at least I can see clearly. A final victory is not possible in the dialectic between life and death. There is no final, decisive battle to be fought. There is no way to win, no place to finally rest. Whatever I manage to achieve is only for this moment, precisely because life is always throwing down a new gauntlet, driving me into new, uncharted terrain.

I thought there was a place to get to, one where I would finally be secure from the possibility of defeat. I have fought, and I have fought hard. I have also never been strong enough to hold the ground gained. I yield it at the first impulse.

———•●•———

A part of me remembers what it was to live in the forest. To walk under trees towering with mystery. To greet the rain with spinning, open arms and welcome it to my tongue as a brother. To lie bare-skinned on silken animal pelts, on the burnished arm of a lover, beneath a black and crystal night. To know cat and mist, deer and leaf, fire and wind as mother and sister, teacher and friend. To gather sun-warmed berries along the clearing of a mountainside and to fish beneath the roar of mighty waters journeying home.

A part of me aches for that life, remembering what it was to breathe the pulsing powers of the Earth with every step and sight and sound, and feel her mythic, sweet caress upon my brow and limbs.

———•●•———

Dream: Through a Sacred Wood:

I am being carried through a sacred wood in a horse-drawn carriage. The coach is round, tapering toward the bottom. Its wood is a highly polished, reddish-brown cherry. The trees on both sides of the single-lane dirt road grow together overhead, forming an arch that stretches from one end of the road to the other. The woods are still, silent, and deep and go on forever.

I am looking out of the window at an ancient burial ground. The bodies lie on the ground in one long, distinctively configured, single row of bodies laid side-by-side, end-to-opposite-end, head-to-foot-to-head-to-foot. They stretch as far as I can see in both directions for the entire distance of the road. The arms of each body are folded, crossed at the heart, with palms down on the breasts. The legs are up, bent at the knees, with the feet flat on the ground beside the head of each previous and successive body.

These are all skeletons, just bone, and very, very old. They are covered in a simple, rotting white-turned-to-grey cloth. Their hair, however, continues to grow, flowing in densely textured, deep, river-like currents that form a thick carpet covering the forest floor. I lean out, taken in by the intricate, exquisite detail of these waves. The numinous energy of this still-growing sea of hair fills the forest and every cell of my body.

REFLECTIONS ON THE DREAM:

The tone of the dream is one of entering an unfathomably sacred realm. I know instantly on waking that these bodies are all women. They are the ancient mothers and grandmothers with whom I have come to identify in the textures and struggles, strengths, joys, and sorrows of my life as a woman and mother.

The arched road reminds me of the birth canal. The body of the coach is shaped like a cherry and is reminiscent of both the pregnant womb and the heart. Its color is a mixture of blood, the blood we shed and the blood of all that we sacrifice in order to give birth, and of the Earth which gives birth to us. Somehow I know that travel along this single lane road moves in only one direction, like time.

The arrangement of the bodies is distinctive, obviously conscious. It is mystifying until I realize that the position of the legs is the birth position. Laid head to foot to head to foot, the bodies physically represent the eternal mother/daughter lineage: generation after generation of woman being delivered, head first, from the pelvis of her mother.

There is something elemental and holy about these now-only-bone bodies. They speak of the sacredness of what remains from the lives women have lived through time: an unbroken chain of love and sacrifice, passion and birth, given through an endless stream of blood and strength, pain and nettled commitment, at intensely personal costs we can never comprehend or appreciate, so the promise and beauty of life on this planet can one day be fulfilled.

This forest is the sacred burial ground of all the generations of women who have ever lived. Having given all that they were to lift life up for the next generation, they have something to offer me and the quality of my life. They are reaching out to me and to all women. They are telling us of a vast ocean of textured, nourishing energy flowing out to us, individually and collectively, from the living residual – the still-growing hair – of what they gave birth to in their own spirits. They seek to reinforce and strengthen us and the feminine in the world today.

They are asking me to consciously celebrate, to draw on that living residual. They are asking us to explore our connection to the wealth of their spirits as a collective mythological dimension, an inexhaustible reservoir of our own and our shared woman-nature. They point to the cumulative, collective inheritance of soul and consciousness in all women, one that is more accessible and real than we can imagine. They are a part of the time stream, the shared ground of being, of all women. These bones, what endures, and the numinous energy emitted from by their still-growing hair, offer us their collective strength and wisdom. The passion grown in their lives is a living resource that is in service to our efforts to heal our own lives and the life of our world.

—•◦•—

Call to the Forest Floor

Shadows flicker into firelight,
Memories flame into visions.
   The ancients are stirring,
    rumbling like mountains
    from beyond the mist.

Gathering mysteries,
  they call to her
   from the sacred burial ground
    of the primeval wood,

The Priestess of the Sacred Tree,
    the Womb Goddess and Nurturer,
        the Mothers and Grandmothers of old.

Whispering in the indistinguishable rhythms
    of a softly murmuring brook,
They walk beside her,
    catching her as she stumbles
  along the steep and jagged, darkened path.

In the courage and tenacity
  of the love they have sown,
they tell the forgotten secrets,
building a body-bridge
through which the spirits and dreams
of ancient generations of women
speak their love
to tomorrow's woman-flesh.

Casting the seed to future generations of women,
Past,
    Present,
        Future,
Bound one to another,
    In one another,
      Through one another,
Laced,
  life to life,
    body to body,
      heart to heart,
        soul to soul,
          generation to generation,

and back again,
in the music of grace.

In the fierceness of love's naked will
to triumph over all the obstacles,
she catches the light in a child's eyes.

Lifting the world
with her opened belly, heart and hands,
she cradles the new life burning
its wide, hungry eyes
into her being.

Does she know who she is, Woman?
Does it ever occur to her?

The ancients will tell her,
as they call her to the forest floor
to dance with shadows and with fire.

There, in the firelight and the dancing,
they will teach her how to flow
beyond the boundaries of her flesh,
out past the edges of her knowing,
into the luminous folds of the deep.

There, in the firelight and the dancing,
they will kneel beside her at the eternal altar,
to drink the unconsuming fire.
Then, in the relentless rhythms of her dreams,
they will call her home again
to breathe to fire
the smoldering embers of Life's buried flame.

—•••—

SPRING, 1988

Uncertainty spins like a vortex driving through my middle. She is my daughter! My precious one! The light of her smile has warmed my dreams and lit the distant hills. Now there is only this harsh whirling, this eating fear that she is lost to me. Or worse, that she may ultimately become lost to herself.

She spits ugly, writhing expletives that slit my heart. But I am not innocent of hate and rage. Ours is a mirrored dance, pulsating with a mutual, mutilating madness.

Where is the willingness to overcome the terror of this darkness? Will she ever know how much I love her, despite my raging? Can I let her go? How far? Dare I count on the strength of love and the good to return her, someday, to me and to herself?

Questions spin wildly, searching for a center... a door... a touch... some gentle miracle to heal the anger, to create space for forgiveness. I pursue her, crazed, unrecognizable even to myself, because I am afraid to leave the darkness unattended and unredeemed. I panic in the darkness because I have lived in its shadow and know its power to consume.

—•••—

I call to her inwardly, across the futile, absorbing distance. *I have always, and will always love you. I had to read your diary.* And I will never regret it.

The danger you are in was a relentless, tearing wound stabbing through my middle. I could not risk ignoring it any longer. And I was not wrong. You are too young, too innocent, too wounded by my failings as a mother to comprehend the danger or the impact of the damage that would follow in its wake. Go ahead, hate me forever if you must.

He will not have you! I will not let you fall into this pit.

—•••—

REFLECTIONS AFTER READING TEILHARD DE CHARDIN

*"In the new humanity which is begotten today, the Word prolongs
the unending act of [Its] own birth.... All matter is ... incarnate."*

—Teilhard de Chardin, *The Hymn of the Universe*

It is staggering to realize that the life I live today, in the smallest triumph I
manage to bring forth from my attempts to lift it, is the finger of Genesis
extending itself out through space and time.

How can we humans begin to grasp the implications of that? How do
we let it in, that our everyday lives carry that great, primal burst of light,
with all of its creative import, forward? ... that the force of all creation is in
us, behind us, reaching through us, seeking to move itself to some higher
ground through the focal point of our body and consciousness, through
every stubborn issue we grapple with in our daily lives?

How do we gain more direct access to the magnitude of the resources,
the energy and power, beauty and sustenance which that offers us? Does
creation speak to us and through us in a different language, one too-long-
forgotten?

We live in the distorted, limiting dimensionality of the world we inherit
and circumscribe with human language and thought. What might we
discover if we looked to other, deeper, more encompassing roots of the
wisdom encoded in, and flowing through, the life all around us? ...The
large and small of it, the near and far of it?

The immense beauty, the import and scale of the real truth is lost to us.
We have constructed a culture that does not know, foregoing the larger
force of creation which stands behind us, which would pour into our lives
the vast, generative forces of a cosmic fire that still actively burns through
a universe in a constant state of gestation and birth.

———•◦•———

Every time I can remember to do it over the past week, I take a minute or
two or five to consciously open my body to the creative forces which made

the sun and sky, clouds and trees and stars. My body transforms into a kind of satellite dish, scanning the great round of the heavens and the Earth for whatever unknowable diffusion of energy, light and encouragement the universe might be beaming out to me. Every cell opens, hungry and absorbent.

It's quite ecstatic. Definitely a rush.

As every cell tingles with delight during these energy baths, there seem to be distinct channels through which the energies pour. Through the top of my head. Through healthy-sized circles in the arches of both feet and the palms of my hands. Through my pelvis and heart. Awash in cleansing and shimmering fountains of light, with my spine vibrating and singing like a tuning fork, it is as if I have been touched by that unknowable source from which the universe seeks to shape my life into some new, exquisite expression of itself.

I have experienced unfathomable wells of goodness calling to me, in me, flowing through me before. I have felt the Divine, the good claiming me, yes. But I wasn't prepared for this order of magnitude: the full, infinite impulse of creation flowing through, underlying, in, and available to me.

I can only glimpse it, saying, *Yes, Yes, a thousand times, Yes. Take me. Use me. Mold me into what I know not.*

For an instant I surrender, letting go to be forged into the forms, movements and purposes of this wonder.

—••—

For this my human heart is formed: to consciously receive and celebrate, to offer myself into the directionality, momentum and purposes of the creative force moving through my life, as it comes to me from within thousands of unseen dimensions, moving 20 billion years and countless life forms forward. The great moment of Genesis is active and alive, pressing from above and below and within me, with all its energy focused, intensely circling, swirling and dancing, rising.

—••—

VISITING MY FAMILY IN ARKANSAS

God, how I love these people. The power of the love that flows between us courses through my chest with the solid force and brilliance of lightning as we sit around the dining room table telling stories and secrets. As we laugh and share jokes. As we stumble through fierce minefields of intense, emotionally held opinions. As we share an intimate glance or a light touch that goes beyond what we know how to say in words.

Family. Bound one to another. Connected by a love that is stronger than our differences. By a love that is more resilient than our intermittent harshness and judgments of each other. By a love that is more enduring, more persistent, than the periods of darkness that have overtaken us, each in our own turn, and hidden us from one another. By a love that returns us, over whatever expanse of time, to one another.

I am grateful for all of it. For the terror and the failures as well as the splendor and the strength. For the blindness, pain, and struggles as well as the tenderness. But most of all, for the love that circles to complete itself and us, drawing each of us gently and patiently in, to forgiveness and to its own shimmering essence.

—●•●—

Each night, after Stewart and the girls have gone to bed, I come upstairs to the attic to look out over the city, with its trees and houses silhouetted against the clear night sky. The city lights shimmer like an inviting bed of stars, a fresh, pure galaxy perched between the tree tops, drawing me into itself. The beauty of the world is too much too bear. Its absolute goodness is laid out, held up for me to see. It is dancing on my skin and reaching inside me.

In infinitely hued nuances of shadow and form, the world speaks, ever silently, gently insisting on the goodness from which we all come and which we are meant to claim.

I have to weep. What have we humans done with this beauty? How and why do we so blindly ignore and mutilate it? I remember at 13, watching my parents rage at each other. One after the other on the attack, while the other was on the defensive. Faces contorted, voices exploding with guttural ferocity, coffee thrown to the ceiling, and once, my father handing a loaded gun to Mother, daring her to shoot him. They switched roles reflexively, as if on cue, the instant the other softened. It was an involuntary, unforgiving dance. *Why?* I asked, time and time again. *What kind of sadistic God creates us, then abandons us to be devoured by these monstrous forces that rise up from nowhere to bat us about and swallow human beings whole?* Like the good Catholic girl I was, I prayed. I prayed and prayed, for years, to St. Jude, the patron saint of hopeless cases, asking why.

And now this revelation, this unbearable answer.

The Divine is all around us calling, a living, giving sea into which we are born. The darkness is ours, the price and symptom of our forgetting who we are and where we come from.

———•••———

My mind and heart naturally leaps to the universal at play in my predicaments and suffering. I instinctively drive for the depth of what we share and are confounded by as human beings, craving a more comprehensive understanding that will make it easier to bear. I suspect the root of that comes from being the oldest girl of eight children born into a more than slightly troubled marriage, and part of my large, closely knit, Catholic extended family.

We lived next door to my maternal grandparents in Shreveport until I was seven. Danta (Mama's father) helped Daddy build our little postage stamp of a one-bedroom house before my sister Martha was born. Mama's sisters and brothers (except for her youngest brother, who was a priest) came over with their entire family after Mass every Sunday for dinner. They stayed all day.

While the adults visited, we kids played hide-and-seek. We ran through the high grass of the adjoining fields and through Gramma's rose bushes in the side-yard. We played under our house, had watermelon fights, oogled at the Jersey cows at the dairy across our little tarred street, and squealed through the sprinkler. (Summers are long, hot and humid in Louisiana.)

We regularly spent nights with one cousin or another. Our cousins were our best friends. Our only friends.

Thursday was the men's poker night. Penny ante.

Our pleasantly cherubic, 4 foot, 11 inch matriarch and Great Mother, the heart and hearth of the clan, was Gramma. There was an immutable constancy to everything about her, from the endless meals she served, to the clothes she wore. Meals at Gramma's were not potluck. She was always in the kitchen. Peeling. Chopping. Stirring. Mashing. Seasoning. Roasting. Baking. Frying. Never rushing. Seemingly content. Standing at the sink or the stove, day-in and day-out, in the same box-like, faded blue print, bib apron, she quietly poured her love out to us all in the only way she knew how. Searing pot roasts in her heavy aluminum, Dutch oven before nestling it into a savory bed of onions, garlic, carrots and potatoes. Lifting the lid to stir the green beans, filling the kitchen with the aroma of steamed bacon. Plucking the feathers of the chickens Danta had killed Saturday afternoon. (I can still see one running in headless circles, spouting a fountain of blood after having its neck wrung).

One or more aunts visited almost every day. Family dramas and angst were hashed out at the dining room table over coffee. Breasts were beaten. Tears were shed. This family, at least for a time, was a world unto itself, the river of life itself, overflowing of familial love. But undertows, riptides, were there in the shadows.

I can still see Mama sitting in her drab housedress, rolling the spit-dampened, now-bare tip of her wooden pen into an ashtray to gather ashes. She ate ashes for hours at a time, and had long ago chewed the black paint from the tip of her pen. Sometimes, though, she just sat there silent and bewildered, lost in pain too deep to name, silently crying. The helplessness and vulnerability in her eyes, the child-like innocence in her face pierced me. They stung like a cord of tiny needles squeezing through my chest, calling me, reminding me of fathomless realms of suffering that lie hidden, below the surface, at the heart of things.

At my cousin Sandy's, her dad often came barreling down on her in fits of contorted rage. In the summer, there was a slightly electric aura of anticipation surrounding her mother each morning as she fussed over her makeup and hair, and got irritable at being interrupted. She was getting ready to go out, to 'the club.'

Marjorie would stand next to Sandy – purse on her arm, jewelry flashing – for one final review of the list of jobs she had written down for Sandy to do. It was a long list: there were meals to cook, laundry to fold, floors to sweep, 'or else' ... all while saddled with the responsibility for four younger brothers. And Marjorie never left without the warning: "If your Dad calls, whatever you do, don't tell him where I am or how long I have been gone."

Sandy was 12. The weight of her burden and dread was crushing. Her dad always called. Panic was palpable in her doomed attempts to cover for her mother.

The whole human race was present in our not-so-little microcosm of a family. Somehow, that was registering, imprinting itself on me. Now my mind automatically leaps to the whole, to the universal that is reflected in and beyond my personal conundrums. That is as reflexive as breathing, as the in-breath is coupled to the out-breath. I have been trying to understand, to come to terms with all of it, since I was 11.

—••—

Sitting in the attic at night, looking out of its tall windows has become my nightly retreat. As I look over the treetops, I can't stop hungering. My hunger has always been my ally, a friend who points my way home whenever I have gotten lost. There is a sense of being led, of knowing that I am on a path, that it is taking me somewhere I can trust.

But there is so much to be burned out of me first. I wonder, though. Is it possible to wholly long for the Divine while surrendering to the wisdom of its delay in revealing itself? Is it possible to hold both sides of the paradox in one's heart at once?

—••—

Chapter III

LONGING FOR THE HOMELAND

1989-1990

"How do I survive where I do not belong?"

PATRICK CALIFIA, "O Canada"

THERE is a sense of dis-ease underlying my days. It fills my evenings and nights. Despite all the openings that have been unfolding, the core of my fear inevitably resurfaces. Today, it's anxiousness about how to proceed in this unknown territory of light. An irresistible impulse to control. To direct. To steer. To master. As if there is something to do with it, rather than to simply wait on it. I cannot let go. I can't trust the good to keep coming without manipulation. Or is it that I cannot trust myself?

The final simplicity is that I am afraid. Afraid I will lose this precious light, this tender opening, the exquisite radiance imploding inside me. I am afraid of life without this treasure.

———•••———

Once, walking through the woods at the beach when I was tired, I curled myself into the inviting, open neck of a huge old-growth fir. I had read years earlier how Native Americans leaned against trees to borrow the tree's energy while on long-distance runs.

Leaning the full length of my body hungrily along the inverted curvature formed by two massive, six-foot tall roots shooting vertically down into the ground, I nestled my back against the thickly-ridged, porous bark of its trunk. The fathomless peace of the tree enfolded me. This was a being sharing its inner life with me. With its immense arms around me, in an instant I felt what it was to stand for centuries in living stillness. To be rooted in the dark and moist, giving richness of the Earth. The Earth's silent, fertile goodness flowed up through the veins of my trunk reaching for the sky, out through my branches, and into the fingertips of my leaves. Surrounded by hushed, cushioning layers of green, the wind blew like singing angels through my hair. As this knowing filled my body, I broke into sobs, full of loneliness for the forest which is my home.

———•••———

Reading *The Way of the Shaman* has made me homesick. It is stirring memories lost in the mist. I am at home in darkness because it is familiar terrain, terrain I have come to love. Terrain that is healing and comforting.

I long for the fluid, rich, mythic energies that emerge from the shadowy deeps. They are part of the memory of my soul. They are written into my body. I have longed for return, to live out the fullness of my life in those deeps ... in the sweet, fertile soil of a darkness which moves with pregnancy, birth and delicate luminosity.

Something is stirring at the edges of reality, in the long, greying shadows of the forest floor. Pounding with the fierce steadiness of a drum. Calling my name. It casts images in the firelight of old dreams, then reaches into the soft hollow of my belly and pulls hard, twisting loose the sweet, ancient memories buried in that place where body meets soul.

Leave the wound open and gaping.

Let the blood of my aching pour forth, spilling its essence into the womb of the sacred wood. Let it find its way home, to be gathered by the spirits of the mothers and grandmothers.

Beneath a night sky filled with crystals and tree tops, they sit in a circle of fire. They are waiting... silent... part of the Earth. They pass the cup of forgotten wisdom to one who has returned to them. She drinks. They pass the pipe. The old ones tell stories. They drum, calling her to join them in song and dance, teaching her to draw the ecstatic energies of the Earth up through her body, through her feet and hands and pelvis, until she melts into stillness, silence and prayer. She looks into the circle of their eyes. The light there bridges through her heart, arcing into the distance of the horizon.

—◆◆—

SITTING WITH STEWART'S MOTHER IN THE HOSPITAL

Her shallow, sometimes erratic breathing punctuates the stillness. She is more comfortable today. Her thin, angular, wasting body is no longer in crisis. She hovers at the edge of life more placidly now.

I love being with her. In the space of her dying, I can stroke her soft, cool skin, rub her legs, look into her eyes, and whisper my love with tender abandon. The quiet embrace of death lingers around her, waiting patiently for its own time, its own way, its own space, as it moves closer.

During the middle of the night, somewhere in the still half-light between the worlds, I sit next to her meditating. I wonder, "Where is she?" Without pausing to question the possibility of knowing, I sink more deeply inward to see. Reaching out to feel for her is as natural as reaching out to take her hand. I am there, within her within... in a space of pure, softly shimmering white light, immersed in sweet and tender joy so intense and real that it startles me back into everyday consciousness.

This is a sacred place. A place to be entered with an open heart and an unfettered mind. A place whispering to those who listen.

She stands at the gate.

———•••———

There is so much to handle getting the house ready to sell. It's overwhelming. How do I manage myself as well? How do I keep an inner focus? How do I unify it while I juggle scraping and painting, rehanging switch plates and curtains, installing insulation, scouring floors and cleaning gutters?

Sandwiching sixteen years of deferred maintenance into the tiny, pressured crevices of time hiding between the everyday needs of house and family while working full time, lonely questions float in the dark around me. *Where is he? Why is all of this left to me?*

I go on with my frantic, doomed attempts at being wonder woman. I pray for the ability to find some way to hold it all as one. I appeal for grace and light and the ability to find my way to something higher.

The world, doing things in the world, has always fragmented me. I get caught in a spiral of hammering anxieties doing the simplest of tasks. Mounting panic drives me from one unfinished task to another, until my attention splinters like glass and I drop off in exhaustion and defeat. When I am pushing ahead, I have the sensitivity and compassion of an elephant at full charge, and do about as much damage to anyone in my path.

This is a fearful thing to pray for: *Shatter all that keeps me driven, anxious and afraid. Burn it out of me.*

———•••———

This is my life. How it has been. No lies. No pretenses. No recriminations. Just the way it is. Lots of aspirations, hunger, longing for beauty and light. Lots of ugliness, anger and resentment, failure to fulfill those longings. Lots of indulgence, slipping into what is small and unworthy. Lots of circles. Lots of ruts. Lots of cookies and ice cream. Lots of digging myself out, desperately hammering, cutting the space open again to construct a new window-in-time through which to crawl out into life gain, after casually walking away from the last one given to me. The question is, how do I accept the humanity of it, the understandableness of it, and at the same time confront it in a way that is a demarcation from the past? One that leads to change?

My whole life is a prayer... a lifting up,
  a seeking of redemption.
   ...the betrayals,
    ...the self-degradations and shame,
     ...the fears,
      ...the resentments,
the long, dark nights of desperation.

It was all a prayer...
a pounding against the walls of the heart.

———•◦•———

Sometimes I feel the whole length of time stretching from beginning to end, as one intense, unrelenting cry of separation. It is an endless cry of loneliness so shrill it is unbearable. I can't help but feel that if I could enter that cry, if I could surrender to it, if I could experience the pain of it fully, everything would shatter, perhaps the universe itself would burst open, and there would be nothing but light.

———•◦•———

Against the cold, hard bottom of the world,
I cry out to You.
Pinned beneath the weight and darkness of our separation,
a dense, unbearable loneliness
presses its relentless aching down on me.

I will not stop crying. I will not stop calling.

My crying is from the beginning,
from the first instant of creation,
when, torn from the flesh of your Divinity
in that searing, unwilling moment of brilliance,
You hurled me, alone and afraid,
into the vast, echoing chasm
of time and forgetting.

Mine is a newborn's scream,
howling its insistence for its mother.

I will not be comforted.

Without your touch, your breath,
your cradling arms around me,
without your light and life inside me,
I will pierce the universe with my calling,
crying until time shatters.

———•◦•———

I have decided to go to church this morning, for the first time in years.

I gave up on traditional Christianity when I hadn't found the devotion I was searching for at the Presbyterian Church we attended. They were nice enough people. There was a sense of community that offered a place to give. The music delivered me into the heart of my aspirations. And there was always some treasure to take home from the sermon. All of which was good. Still, something was missing. I was hungry for a church life that served as its main meal the process through which to gain and deepen my direct experience of the Divine.

My primary complaint against Christianity is that it spends itself preening on its beliefs, like a rooster fluffing its feathers. I am certain that Jesus is immeasurably sabotaged by his own promoters in this, since the problem with beliefs is that they are inherently lifeless abstractions, if not insufferable ego trips, that we bludgeon ourselves and others to death with. Beliefs are at best a substitute for the real, immediate, living experience of the Divine (or Jesus, if you are Christian) within us.

We have ended up with a tragically degenerated, desperate imitation of authentic religious life, a masturbated pretense by which we try to excite ourselves into salvation: if I pronounce I am saved by Jesus often enough and loudly enough, if I remind myself and you that I am Christian convincingly enough, if I concentrate on the sins of those out there and vehemently condemn the rest of unsaved humanity viciously enough to scare them into becoming Christian, maybe I will start to feel saved. Maybe some of the edge of my fear, guilt and shame – of my shriveled heart and outright meanness – will disappear, and I will feel safe again.

Of course, that is the extreme side of Christianity, and Presbyterians are anything but extreme. Theirs is a milder, kinder, and infinitely more palatable brand of Christianity than the one that rankles me so deeply.

Still, I felt ridiculous when I was the only person weeping in prayer every Sunday before services began. (I was usually the only one praying at all, though it doesn't speak well of me to have noticed.) Everyone else sat quietly open-eyed, waiting, casually looking around, nodding to or visiting with others who were on their way to their seats.

Understand, I weep reflexively and uncontrollably, though I am discreet and have mastered silent sobbing, just walking into the sanctified space of a church. I have ever since I was a teenager. One Sunday, after a particularly intense catharsis, a woman followed me out of Mass to the bathroom to see if I was O.K.

I was 18.

It was embarrassing.

Trying to understand the phenomenon of those tears later that week in group therapy, I decided it was guilt, and that simply not going to Mass any more was the way to solve the problem. But I am 42 now and it still happens, whatever church I happen to stumble into, despite the fact that I don't feel guilty in the same way or about the same things.

No, the source of this weeping is much deeper than guilt. I have finally isolated it. It is an unbearable, timeless and unspeakable longing, an implacable homesickness for the Divine – which is where, deep down, I know I belong, though you might never know that from my behavior.

The final break with "church" came for me when I realized our minister didn't have any kind of prayer life. I was talking with him about prayer, and was stunned when he said that Divinity school had not taught prayer or emphasized maintaining a prayer life during the course of his ministry. Besides that, he didn't have time to pray.

Now that was astounding. It simply set me on my butt, wondering. What spiritual counsel could he or any Christian minister possibly give me without an inner life of their own? It obviously wasn't this minister's, or even the Presbyterian Church's fault. It was, however, patently clear that whatever the problem might be, it was too deep for me to stick around while they worked it out. Christianity could do without me.

So here I am, six years later, going to a very alternative church. My friend Mary, whom I dearly love and respect, has recently gone to work at the Song of the Rose Cafe here in Portland. It's a vegetarian restaurant owned by some devotees of an Indian spiritual teacher named Yogananda. He wrote *Autobiography of a Yogi*, which I read almost twenty years ago. Yogananda died in 1952, but his teachings live on, stressing meditation as the primary tool for inner communion and reunion with the Divine.

Mary has been impressed with the depth and purity of devotion of everyone she has met who is a follower of Yogananda. Since I trust her judgment implicitly, I am two steps behind her in going to see for myself if this could be an avenue for my own spirit.

The service is held in a room above the New Renaissance Bookshop here in Portland. I go up the narrow staircase and am greeted by a woman with shoulder length, loosely curled blonde hair and huge, kind green eyes. She smiles at me like an old friend, hands me a program, and shows me a room filled with rows of folding chairs. Against the wall at the front of the room is a narrow altar covered with a white, brocaded silk cloth. Two tall, diamond shaped glass oil lamps are lit on each side of the altar. In the center, an elegantly brass-trimmed, white capis, lotus candleholder glows golden below framed pictures of five "masters" which hang on the wall. Highest and center is Jesus. I recognize the photo of Yogananda on the far right, since it is the same photo that was on the cover of *Autobiography of a Yogi*. I do not know who the other three[1] are.

I bow to Yogananda, instinctively honoring him since this is his place of worship. Sitting to meditate, I have the sensation of a delicate stream of light gently arcing from Yogananda's heart in the photo to my own. The light has a healing quality ... an almost unbearably personal tenderness. It is a stream of pure white radiance, subtle, yet brilliant and sweet. I see it whether my eyes are open or closed. Mostly, my eyes are closed.

It is so good to be here. I have journeyed such a long way to get here. I cry, as always, weeping throughout the entire service. Only this time, the tears flow out of relief and gratitude for this light pouring into me.

"Who are you?" I wonder, asking Yogananda, "How is it that you receive me with this kind of tenderness, as if reaching into the pain of my whole life?" The stream of light continues filling my body, soothing every aching, hurt, lonely and discouraged hole in me.

———•••———

[1] Ananda, I later learn from Mary, honors these five Masters as the source of their spiritual path: Jesus, who appeared to the Great Himalayan Master Babaji asking him to send a teacher to the West to teach inner communion through meditation; Babaji, formerly incarnated as Krishna; Lahiri Mahasihia, Babaji's foremost disciple, and to whom Babaji taught the ancient technique of Kriya Yoga; Sri Yukteswar, Lahiri's foremost disciple and the guru of Yogananda; and Yogananda, who was sent to the U.S. in response to Jesus' apparition request to Babaji.

Chapter IV

SEEDS OF THE UNDREAMED

1989-1990

...all things are fashioned oddly,
The joints of the universe are mysteriously hinged.

Do not, therefore, attempt
to name things too clearly
or imagine the crystal vision
you see to be precisely itself.

All things are born
and flow again
in realms of the magi.

ALLA RENÉE BOZARTH, "Novaya Zemlya"
Stars in Our Bones: Emerging Signposts on Our Spiritual Journeys

For three weeks now, I have been having a recurrent dream: Yogananda is standing at my bedside all night long, pouring the same, pure and tender white light that came from his picture at church into me. My body is being filled with it. Every organ, every cell, is swimming in white light, being soothed and blessed with a subtleness of attention and care I have never felt before.

Maybe there is something to this guru thing.

———◆•◆———

Sacrament of Water, Salmon Street Springs, Portland

I am the brilliant white light flashing in the fountain at night, surging with the naked urgency of an overfull heart. Hurling myself wildly up from the center, I call to brown and freckle-faced children and to lovers to come from their park benches and soak themselves in the uncontrolled joy of my spilled passion; to stretch with me and pierce a starless night sky.

The full moon rises over the river behind me. A Tri-Met bus makes its way over the Hawthorne Bridge as cars hum their way off into the distance along Front Avenue. A girl in a white sailor dress walks coyly into my circle. A small army of eight-year-old boys ventures in and out and in again: dancing, squealing, tasting, spinning. They catch the sweet fire of my joy in their eyes and carry my crystalline flame back to their mothers, who sit nearby, watching.

———◆•◆———

Summer

I am a friend to trees and leaves and sunlight,
   to breezes and rivers,
      to stars and the deep black of the night sky,
         to clouds and roses and green grass,
to water and dirt and bugs,

to fountains and pink silk shirts, to notebooks and pens,
to my deck, where I sit watching evening fall.

I am a friend to music, to violin and guitar and flute,
    to this house, my husband's favorite chair,
        and the sink I can't keep clean of dirty dishes.

I am a friend to the sounds of children playing,
    to slamming screen doors and ringing doorbells,
        to the carpet my dog has soiled too often,
            to the stained-glass windows my mother-in-law had made;
        to my living room that wants more light and fresh air,
and the flower pots that keep me company in the moonlight.

I am a friend to evening falling,
    more soul-mate than a friend,
        to white clouds turning gold-fired-lavender and rose,
    making my heart sink deep and thick
with longing and remembering.

I am the blue of the sky,
        the clean field and vivid line of the snow covered mountain
            shimmering pink at sunset.

I am the sweet, cool singing of the wind on skin and cheek,
    the invisible glistening
        within the damp, dark smell of the fruiting earth,

I am these things.
As certainly as the sun shines and the wind blows.
They are in me and I am in them.
    We are one essence,
            one heart flowing

through all reality
changing shape and color and form.

One source,
　One being,
　　All emerging,
　　　Flowing into and out of one another,
　　　　Reflecting to one another
　　　　　the true, hidden, common essence
　of our ancestry and our home.

　Wind, you are my brother,
　　Sky, you are my friend.
　　Sun, you are my teacher,
　whispering the forgotten secrets,
the forgotten knowing,
　of the common language
we have forgotten how to share.

You are more than an event,
　more than a pleasure,
　　more than something to soothe myself with
　　　at the end of a difficult day.

You are part of me calling me back to myself.
Speaking in a tongue of pure mystery and beauty,
　a language I have missed,
a language I have ached and cried for.

I am that, I am.

———◦•◦———

I never tire of watching trees. I am captivated by their floating leaves changing shapes and colors in the light. They are a mystery I have been trying to penetrate all my life. How can they be so beautiful? So abundant with soothing revelation, so full of nuance, so new at every second? They are a comforter in times of stress. An inspiration. A remembrance.

Speak to me. Tell me your secrets.

You seem to know so much that I do not. You convey so much with your being – your gentle, silent being. Soak into me with your ocean-like rustling waves that rise and fall.

Sweet wonder, I take your sacrament into the altar of my heart and float with you on the breeze.

———◆•◆———

I cannot be satisfied with answering phones and typing letters to sheriffs. The screaming inside me will not be stilled. It pours through my arms and neck with a stubborn insistence... hammering away like a church bell calling me to prayer.

Matins... in the dark, cool halls of the monastery, I see shadows, veiled figures surrendered in resonant, circular chanting that drives them deeper into the center.

I am the monk at prayer, absorbing the eternal echoes of the soul's song, its longing for God and eternity.

And I am dying at this black-and-amber screen with its soft clicks, lost in hour-after-hour of scratching my way through a reality that is empty and means nothing to me.

I want to shred every piece of paper that comes across my desk, set fire to it, and throw myself into the flames rather than spend the rest of my life with dead pieces of paper marking my days. The halls of the soul call me and call me and call me back to an earlier, simpler time, when my whole life was spent in devotion and prayer.

Is this a memory? Am I caught out of time, in a place that is strange to me?

This place runs on a different rhythm, and on terms that leave me lost and lonely.

Do not abandon me here in this alien land where I am dry and hungry, desperate and shrill. Lead me home again.

———•••———

If I can breathe in the evening air, only for a minute, I'll be O.K. Something of my striving comes to rest as it soaks in the peace of trees set against the darkening sky. There is a peace that lies behind all form and color, past the smells and sweetness. It is a presence that reaches in to caress my striving, anxious heart. This is becoming my little ritual: to let the air and sky and face of the morning or evening embrace me for a moment with its peace as I stand beside my open car door, before coming or going.

I breathe it in, full of wonder.

———•••———

On a bench beneath the elm trees next to the library, before going in to work

For all my years of trying, I have never understood the mystery of trees or how they move me. But I can invite them to enter me. I can ask them to be in me. That is my real prayer: to take in the beauty of the world around me so completely that it becomes my breath, my blood and bones and heart, the very rhythm and essence of my life and what is inside me.

———•••———

Full of longings, I drink in the freshness of pristine white clouds against deep, virginal blue. As the sun sinks, their intense, glimmering-gold edges set me to burning. Then rising tides of rustling leaves carry me drifting, beyond the shores of knowing, where veiled, nameless memories wash warm and tingling on my skin.

———•••———

What if the freshness of the wind flowed in our veins and the clarity of blue sky sang in our bodies? What if the lushness of trees swelling in the wind filled our lives with their ever changing nuances of life and light, shade and form?

Would they come to us that way if we asked often enough? If we sought their counsel long enough? What if we laid ourselves open to them, asking for their being to imprint itself in us until it was our own?

Today it seemed possible. It seemed as if they heard my prayer and came into me. And I could feel the joy of their life, their being, inside me.

———•••———

I sit in the stillness of a cool summer evening, with luminous grey and white clouds overhead turning rose and iridescent gold amid patches of blue. The deepening stillness of the evening calls me. I sink, floating as quietly as the clouds above me, with my heart changing color and hue and form as often and as silently as they do. I am floating in stillness. Alive. Moving. With the hand of the deep on my heart. Lost in the fluid majesty of an ever-changing sky.

Jealous of the clouds' iridescence, I try to capture their essence in my eyes and heart, to savor the taste of their light upon my tongue. A part of me knows that the clouds, the evening, the golden sky turning brilliant and soft all at once, the leaves floating so gently they break my heart open, have secrets to tell me. I drink them in with my eyes, and all the while my heart is falling down, farther and farther down, into the center of things, into a knowing that is at once stillness and a whirlwind of passion and longing to drink this sweetness, this distilled essence that lies at the heart of all things.

———•••———

AFTERNOON AT THE RIVER

There, beneath the river, beneath the birds fluttering, beneath my own longings, there is a fullness that reveals itself. It stands brightly and simply in the silence, holding all form, all life, all perfection. To drink from this spring is to know all things while knowing nothing, and to be satisfied.

I ask the clouds to enter my heart, to teach me their silence, to imprint in me the gentleness and ease and grace with which they allow themselves to be moved and changed. They are without resistance, free floating in the currents of their destiny, and they make me hungry for freedom, for the ability to let go, to follow the ebbs and eddies, the currents of my own life without fear or judgment.

For a moment I am lost in cloud-nature. I am free, surrendered to all that is.

AFTERNOON AT RIVERFRONT PARK

Looking out at the river, its magic is growing inside me, taking root in my body like a newly formed life. It has planted itself in me over time, over the years I have come to sit here on summer evenings to escape my driven life and watch light flickering across the water.

The river has put itself inside me. It has washed over me and come inside me, like the soothing evening air that I breathe in, full of a sweetness that shakes me to a quivering tenderness.

I am full of questions by the river. I try in vain to comprehend the beauty around me. The being of the wind. The moist, giving sweetness of the grass. The diamond-white brilliance of the moon.

Somewhere between pulsing ridges of waves, I slip into the fabric of all that is living. Breathing at last with life's own rhythms, I melt into the oneness of a God that cannot be separated from the creation She breathes Her own self into.

I choose to look for God in manifested forms. To see and taste and feel the dancing rhythms of the Divine at play in laughing children running through the changing shapes of a fountain. In the shining, clean spine of a lighted bridge silhouetted against a black night sky. I want to see God's face smiling in beauty that breaks my heart open, and that tingles with radiance coming to life inside me.

We have forgotten to look for God in this world. The Divine is all around us, calling.

—••—

The moon has called me outside the past few nights. I sit facing her on the cold, painted cement steps of our small front porch, crowded between the flower pots and iron railing, hushing our whining cat to silence. Then I withdraw into the moonlight washing over me. Like the gentlest of rains, she soaks through my skin. My face and arms, shoulders and chest become porous openings to a shower of light bathing every cell of muscle and bone. White light streams brilliant through my forehead, dissolving in delicate, effervescent rivulets that break into quiet explosions of healing somewhere at the bottom of me.

For a moment, I cannot distinguish myself from the moonlight, or the moonlight from God. Then, when I get up to go in to bed, I dream of God coming through my forehead and flooding my body in streams of white light.

—••—

Late afternoon on the deck

Rain patters softly on the roof overhead. Listening to the quiet below the sound, my breathing settles down into a deeper place. I am falling. Falling backward into rest. With the grey sky and tender young leaves sprouting above me in the clean, moist, quiet air, I am falling. Falling back into silence and rest.

It is good to rest in a hurried world... to lie for hours in the grass looking at leaves, listening to birds. Watching rain fall softly to the earth from a grey sky, it is possible to fall beneath the rain, beneath the Earth and sky.

If I rest there long enough, surrendering my driven modern life into the arms of the Earth, I begin to hear my own heart beating to her rhythms. I remember how to breathe again with her breath... and feel safe again.

—••—

There is a part of me that is called back into being by the rhythmic textures of the wind. Drawn to the surface from the buried, long-forgotten deeps, it bursts into joyful resurgence in my body, relieved, like a neglected child who has waited too long to be seen and celebrated for the beauty she holds in her heart.

What have we neglected in the modern world? What have we denied existence to? When we allow ourselves to be buried in dead lives, what is the real cost of being removed from all that is beautiful? Who will uncover the promise of the new world that waits for us, hidden within the heartbeat of the Earth?

Amid stirring leaves that seem to rise up with repressed hope and the clattering of three disharmonious birds, two starlings chasing a crow, I come outside to read.

Finally, a day to myself. Enough missed opportunities, given away for no good reason to habit and mundane trips chauffeuring fully grown daughters where they could damn well take the bus. I come out to the back yard, to sit on the deck beneath the leafing shade of a maple tree. With George Winston playing beside me, I am reading *Women of the 14th Moon*.

It sets me stirring, heating the mysteries of blood until I feel the richness of other women's lives flowing into and nourishing my own through an almost visible, luminous umbilical cord. Ancient, moving shadow-forms of all that we share descend in a warm, enveloping mist.

There is a dark place inside me where we share everything as women, all the promises of fertility that ache to burst from our wombs and into life celebrating. My womanhood has been full of the sorrow and pain and wisdom of all women through time. I am pregnant with the collective inheritance of what we have borne in our bodies, on our shoulders and backs, and in our hearts – all those dark, heavy mysteries which seek to resolve themselves in some future woman's life.

It is all in me. But there is also a need to bear and taste its giving fruit – an implacable hunger for a wildly exuberant triumph of spirit that will hold the power and beauty of the feminine forward and revealed. There is a need in my heart to honor the enormity of who we are, to see that and celebrate it with others, claiming the majesty, the full measure of the treasure that we were born into, and of the legacy we carry through life to the next generation, whether or not we ever bear children.

How do we do that? By sharing the yet-unspoken depth of our own woman's life experience? By calling ourselves awake to the process of giving birth to what women have been trying to give birth to throughout time, even if it is only in ourselves? Life. Life in its fullness. Life in its magnificently realized beauty and possibility. Life that looks back, all the way back, to the beginning. Life that experiences all the pangs of birth, the cosmic impulse to bring forth whole and pure and brilliant, reaching out to all that is unborn with the light and life and force of exploding galaxies.

Sometimes I feel that impulse, the power of its pushing in the dark red depths of my belly, rising up to course through my spine and leap into the future. Then I know. There is no greater joy than to be a woman, to have the birthing energy of the universe coursing through me from beginning to end, body and soul, heart and mind.

A dear friend and mentor asked the other day, *How is it that you get so lost, when you have seen and tasted the light in all the ways that you have?* It's a critical question. How could she understand that cavernous place inside me that is so cut off from even the faint possibility of light? When I am in that place, fear has its way and swallows me whole.

Yes, there is that fearful part of me. That part that cannot let go. That part of me, once it seizes hold, cannot find the floodgates or where to open them. And there is also that part that is purely creative, a place where the eternal knowings rise like mountains, where the creative force of the universe flows through me. Yet, as often as I find myself in either place,

I haven't found the path between them. It's like being thrown from one world into another one.

———◆•◆———

Sometimes in prayer, I feel the great rumble of all that wants to be born in all the worlds rising up from the bottom of me. Shooting like a great column of fire and light, with the force of a Cosmic wind, it reaches and roars unimpeded, sending its raw ecstasy rushing through my body.

We are all the incarnation if we only knew it. Men as well as women. If we could allow ourselves time enough to be alone and experience the immensity of our longings. But this world, this killing modern world with its endless demands and encroaching horrors, conspires to deny us access to the rich, mythic source and nourishing currents of our existence.

I choose to come home to grass and to the dark, fertile secrets of the Earth.

I will root myself in the fluid richness of my mother's touch, choosing to stare bewildered at cool, fragrant layers of green leaves turning from dark to emerald in sunlight and wind, until I become the wind and light and ever-mutating hues of green.

———◆•◆———

It is a beautiful, sunny September day. The sky is blue. The wind is blowing the elegantly tipped leaves of the oriental maple outside my living room window. The afternoon sun is turning golden on the house across the street. My daughter Lisa is asleep on the couch. Traffic purrs softly in the distance. I hear a dog barking, a child clapping, a fan whirring from my bedroom. The hallway door clicks softly as the wind shifts outside.

Behind it all is silence. Peace. A peace that sinks into me.

———◆•◆———

Fall Afternoon, Macleay Park

Scattering gold and green brilliance
high on the slopes of a hill,
the forest gives its light.

Banks of leaves rise,
Like angels sharing tales of grace,
Throwing their wild beauty into life.

What magic flame waits to burn in our lives?
What bright wonders
might leap from our ecstasy
to rush into the world
beating like a thousand calling drums,
   if we learned to dance,
surrendered,
   to the shearing force,
      of our own heart's inner fire?

———•◦•———

A day for myself in the dappled brilliance of a clear fall day on an old park
bench.

   I sit facing the steeply rising eastern canyon, where banks of trees cas-
cade green and gold. Looking south into the body of the forest, a towering
elm's singular, dark spine is accentuated by the intense, vivid gold circle of
the afternoon sun dropping below its leaf line.

   Burn. Burn into me with the clarity and sweet fierceness of this light.

   This is the unspeakable brilliance with which You descend in my soul,
boldly announcing Yourself, burning the new world, the new way, the new
being, into me. You pierce through my spine with the newly born, the fully
alive. The old is gone, scattered by the light, even if only for this moment.

   There is nothing to do but receive this golden-white brilliance, to welcome it, to rest in the fierce joy with which it claims me.

There are angels in the forest. Today, I see them in the intense gold and green glow bursting from leaves. I hear them in the high pitched, lonely calls of birds I cannot see. Walking along the wooded path beside a meandering streambed, I know I am surrounded by whole communities of beings, old and wise and friendly.

In the soft, unending grace of floating leaves and changing light, the sun turns leaves to liquid, golden fire. Standing with my back against a massive old-growth fir, looking up into the layers of life all around me, I wonder. *Is it You? Or does this just remind me of You?*

With the hand of Your beauty all around me, reaching, leaning, swirling, falling, in angles and rushing patterns that have the fullness of river, I can only pray for Your song, Your life, Your way, to be in me.

The moon is high in the sky tonight. Full and brilliant. Floating among high, sheer, pure white clouds that remind me of angels. The world, life itself, seems clearer on these cold, dry winter nights. I wrap myself in the thick, luxuriant warmth of my wool coat as the wind whips its wild exhilaration. In a great, living arch beneath the moon, the sky becomes a sacred chamber through which I am called to ascend. And the moon is an opening into the source of all light.

What is real here? What is imagining?

This is real: the brilliant sweetness of the moonlight is the same light I see at the inner altar. It is the same light I see in the deepest communion of meditation and prayer. When I see it hanging in every molecule of the night sky and feel it falling like grace on my shoulders, my body knows it to be the same and goes flying. Every cell opens to receive a night saturated with light.

We think we know what the moon is. And knowing, we deny ourselves its magic, inner reality.

Indigenous cultures are closer to the real truth.

—•••—

While out to dinner with a small group of church friends at a nearby cafe, for an instant a space opens. I notice the light in K's eyes as he laughs. The light that he is touches the being I am. I have an inkling, an infinitessimally small glimpse into the enormity of what human beings share when our lives touch.

As we step outside together into the sharp cold of a foggy winter night to walk home, I go ahead of everyone else. Wrapped in timeless and vast, opening inner space, there is nothing in all the wide world except the sacramentally clean, dark forms of the trees beside me and the peace of setting my foot down. In the soothing, resonant sound of my shoes gently striking the pavement in the quiet of a misted night, I want to walk forever until I learn how to be inside a simple step.

—•••—

Chapter V

CRASHING AT THE FORK
BETWEEN THE WORLDS

1990–1992

...now, go and do the heart–work
on the images imprisoned within you.

RAINER MARIA RILKE, "Turning-point"
Ahead of All Parting: The Selected Poetry and Prose of Rainer Maria Rilke

DREAM:

I am walking with Julie and Stewart, up high. The path is level, though we are on top of a mountain. It is dusk, darkening quickly. The green of the trees is deeply shadowed. It's raining furiously. I decide to take my chances and descend. Stewart and Julie stay on the upper path, walking off into the distance as I cut at a 45 degree angle going down the mountainside.

The rain is coming down in lashing waves, giving way to torrential floods. I am struggling to keep from being swept away. Driving my hands into the completely saturated ground, I try to find something to hang on to below ground, but there is nothing. The watery soil can barely hold the thin grass and slips through my fingers. It cannot hold me.

I notice a small book, about 2-1/2 inches square, in my hand. I am trying to hold on to it because I realize it will somehow help me.

REFLECTIONS ON THE DREAM:

Waking up I am unnerved, sensing the dream is foreshadowing a particularly difficult time ahead. I associate the torrents of water and how they are washing me down the hill with the intense emotions which have been released in recent months. Since taking a class at Ananda Church in September, I have been using a powerful mantra[1] for breaking through obstacles. The minister explained that each of us has seeds of karma that are stored in our energetic spine. The mantra releases them. I have flippantly ignored the warning she gave before teaching us the mantra, "This is extremely powerful. Use it only as a last resort, after you have exhausted all other ways of working with a problem."

I have used the mantra almost constantly, every time I confront a stubborn old pattern. In other words, every day, all day.

For some time now I have sensed danger. Like a silent alarm is sounding, warning the mantra is too much for me, only to then ignore the need

---

[1] mantra, in the Hindu tradition, is a sequence of Sanskrit words, often including a Divine name, that carries Divine vibrations which quiet the mind and resonate in the mind and heart to bring about spiritual transformation

for caution. Using the rationale, *I have been working on this for over 20 years*, in response to countless old, thorny issues that have plagued me with their resistance to change, I have recklessly plowed ahead.

In the last month or so, after only three repetitions of the mantra, it feels as if a strong wind tunnel is blowing up through my spine. By twelve to twenty rounds, the intensity is unbearable and I have to stop.

The theory behind the mantra is obviously no abstraction. The emotional core of whatever issue the mantra was used in reference to erupts, exploding with relentless force from the unconscious into undeniably confronting circumstances in my daily life. Everything but the need for change gets stripped away. It's like getting beaten senseless. You wake up in a mess on the floor, badly shaken, but you grasp, with unmistakable clarity, the urgency of getting the hell out of there.

Initially, I started noticing the onset of a series of crises hitting me about three weeks after having used the mantra in hopes of a breakthrough on an issue. More recently, the time frame has shrunk to days. Now the crisis comes within hours.

I've been cavalier in dismissing the danger signs, telling myself I don't care what the cost of the pain is, if it will crash me through whatever keeps me from having the life I really want. The dream is warning me of what lies ahead. I am vulnerable to being totally swept away by the emotional storms I have unleashed with the mantra.

The little book in the dream is the exact shape and size of Yogananda's *Scientific Healing Affirmations*. It is as if the dream is telling me to hold on to Yogananda's healing affirmations, that they are the only thing strong enough to hold onto through the storms ahead.

—••—

DREAM:

I am standing beside a river that is a torrent of rushing floodwaters. Its swollen waters are a roiling fury of massive rapids. A huge, primitive raft – made of freshly stripped, raw logs that are bound together by loosely tied, coarse rope – is careening roughly over the savage currents. The raft covers the entire expanse of the river. Three tiny, very frail Vietnamese peasants (two women and a man) at the back of the raft are powerless. They are hanging on for their lives as the raft is thrown wildly up and down, slamming them around in the process.

Down the river, I see the raft is headed for certain disaster. The river forks just ahead into a Y, the arms of which are half as wide as the base, and neither side of which is wide enough for the pitifully constructed raft.

REFLECTIONS ON THE DREAM:

I wake awash in foreboding. The three helpless peasants who are so obviously ill-equipped are aspects of me. The straight line of the river forking into a Y reminds me of the spine, splitting at the base of the skull into the two hemispheres of the brain. The river is moving with annihilating force. Its rushing tumult is a perfect depiction of the energies I have experienced in my body in recent months, those loosed by overuse of the obstacle mantra throughout the fall. I feel stupid for having used the mantra again last week after the clear warning given by the flood-down-the-mountainside dream.

This dream is shouting at me. I am in for a brutal crash, one I could very well not survive. All I can do is hang on for dear life – like those helpless, ineffectual peasants, at the mercy of powers infinitely greater than they have the capacity to control.

I resolve never to use the obstacle mantra again and begin praying, with a renewed sense of humbled vulnerability, for the ability to make it through whatever lies ahead.

——◆•◆——

Today I freelanced for the first time at the law firm of Garvey, Schubert & Barer. The afternoon was disastrous. Their WordPerfect network is set up so differently than the one at my old firm. I didn't know how to get in and out of documents. The fear was shrill. Humiliating. All equipment is frightening, foreign stuff to me. New machines are terrifying. It feels as if at any minute they will explode in my face and leave me standing naked, utterly exposed in my incompetence.

When I sent a fax in the morning, going from a copier I didn't know how to use to a telecopy that quit in midstream, I went to another copier. I made all the photocopies, put them in their envelopes and returned the originals to their respective files. Then I realized I had never re-sent the malfunctioned fax. It was as if electric currents were traveling down my arms and legs, hitting with a jolt at the center of my torso.

At moments like those, I am reeling, disoriented. I struggle to regain my shattered focus, but it is like drawing the dead, resistant weight of a horse from the outer edges of my shattered nerve endings. The dispelled shreds of attention and energy, which I gather from the shaken edges of myself, come reluctantly, and only with Herculean effort, back to the center in which I am struggling to regroup myself.

There is something chemical that happens in my brain at these points. I am on the edge, trying with everything I can muster to calm down and think clearly. But the harder I try, the weirder, physically and chemically, I feel. It is as if I am on a strong drug, and every nerve ending is taut while I am trying to fight through a dense fog for any clarity at all. The tension and fear develop an intensifying torque. I feel more and more incompetent as I struggle harder and harder to hold myself together.

Today I prayed for help several times, without relief. Walking back to the copier searching for one set of documents that I had misplaced and still needed to send to the client, I thought, "No wonder I can't make myself do this anymore! It's like signing on to be tortured for eight hours. How could anyone face this day after day?"

While today was the worst of it, the most intense end of the pendulum in intensity, it wasn't unusual. There are many days I spend in just that state, trying to keep track of a thousand threads of detail, terrified of not being able to, then losing hold. I come home feeling like I've been beaten senseless.

How could I have done this for eight years? No wonder it has taken such a toll on me. No wonder I have gained forty-three pounds and can't face it any more. What is a wonder is that I can do it at all.

I am tired of fighting. So very tired. I can't sort it out. I try to lock on to You. I remind myself that You are there, that You are real, and that this relentless panic is what is unreal. I don't feel sane anymore.

There is no place I feel safe or that You are with me as I go through this. You come and go between the storms of my fear. It's just me and my demons, with me struggling to find a rope to hang on to in the lashing waters of the storm.

The demons are winning.

I am living through the deluge of the dreams I had after Christmas.

In *Scientific Healing Affirmations*, Yogananda instructs us to sort through what is true and false, to repel the illusions, the uncertainties and weakness by taking refuge in the higher truth of our oneness with the infinite resources of the Divine. For whatever reason, though, I am not strong enough to hold the force of what assaults me at bay. I cannot find the place within on which to stand against all that overwhelms me. Affirming *No! I won't let this sweep me away,* just doesn't work.

The way of the world and my own mind are killing me.

MORNING MEDITATION

Recurrent image:

I am huddling, like a child, squeezed tightly in the lighted column of the spine. The gnawing demons of my fear are waiting hungrily outside, like a pack of wild dogs. They have treed me, like an animal. Their snarling teeth are bared; they are in a growling frenzy, spitting and dripping saliva, leaping at me as they wait for me to emerge. I drive deep into the spine and the light, calling to You – and Your reality comes and goes as my will to pierce through to You rises and quickly falls away again.

—•••—

The world is crashing, splintering into me with shard-like teeth. Every time I think there is some little opening, it explodes in my face in an hour or in a day or two, cutting more deeply than ever into me. Nothing in my life works. Tonight it was an argument with Lisa and Stewart. There is nothing to hold onto except You – and You are only a memory that I cannot resurrect with my limp will: dry dust in my dry heart.

How many times will I ask to die before You grant me my wish? I have dug my way into the deeps so many times over these last two years. For what: Clarity? Resolution? An opening? A breath of hope? A reason to breathe at all? For how long? An hour? Three hours today, before the next wave slams the breath out of me and leaves a greater, deeper, darker emptiness than ever before.

The recovery periods get shorter, shallower. The fragmentation comes quicker. The ground is shakier. Today my whole body was shaking, for hours. I couldn't figure out why. Toxic thoughts ran like quicksilver through me, holding on to nothing, not even each other, scattering their lightning-like, acidic fingers through every vein and cell. Darting here, I try to grab on to some twig, to dig my fingers into some little piece of soggy ground, anything solid to hold onto; but there is nothing. A little spasm that lifts the heart and then dies off as quickly as it begins.

I wanted to just walk off the face of the earth tonight. Just walk off the edge and fall forever into the darkness I can't escape, in a final surrender of my vain efforts to put more space between me and the darkness that won't surrender its pursuit of me.

Is that why You made the earth round? We would all walk willingly off the edge at so many points in a lifetime – every generation, trying to escape its own particularly configured pain leading to the final, leaping edge of madness.

—•••—

Chapter VI

BEYOND THE FATHER

1992–1994

...It is we sleeping women,
waking up in a darkened world,
cutting the chains from off our bodies
with our teeth, stretching our lives
over the slow earth,
seeing, moving, breathing in the vigor
that commands us to make all things new.

ALLA RENÉE BOZARTH, "Call,"
Womanpriest: A Personal Odyssey

Dream:

I am part of a royal family that is being held captive. We are held in a huge old Tibetan-type fortress or temple. Every attempt at escape, even the thought of escape, is met with wave after wave of vicious attack. Our attackers stand in a single row, a long, endless line of men built like body-builders, holding huge Neanderthal-like clubs. Each one steps up to take his turn beating us with every ounce of energy and strength he has until he falls off to the side in utter exhaustion. Then the next man steps forward to continue until he is spent.

The king, the head of the royal family and its only member that is not imprisoned, is speaking with a young, dark haired woman about the state of things. She is making a strong, clear case for liberating the prisoners. She and the King are unaffected by the imprisonment. Sitting in an open hall which is at a higher level, yet clearly visible to the prisoners, they are discussing strategies to accomplish releasing the prisoners. At the end of their conference, the young woman stands and sings a hauntingly beautiful and strong, poetic and clear song about her longing for the homeland.

A question is posed. It hangs in the air and seems to come from everywhere: "If the old order is destroyed, who will lead?" The answer, too, comes from everywhere. It fills the space.

She will.

———◆•◆———

The One Who Leads

The king seeks the counsel of The One Who Leads
And finds in her the seed of the future,
The way out.

She is possessed of quiet nobility,
Her lean, clear bones speak of an inner definition.
Her eyes, deep blue,

flash with the transparency of silver,
like crystal striking the blade of a sword.

I will marry this woman,
I will ask her to be in me.
To be my teacher,
my life partner within my own skin.
I will open my mind and heart to her wisdom;
   to the teaching of her being;
      to her solid strength;
         to her clear heart and fearless mind.

She is my soul in possession of herself.
Contained, at home in the body,
She walks the earth calmly,
   unafraid of the body or the world,
With full access to the powers of her own being
   and of all creation.

Rooted in the infinite, she has entered me.
Today is the seed, the conception,
   the beginning of a new way.

I had experienced dimensions of my soul before,
felt the movement of its fluid life.
But I had never met her.

The light from her eyes
   runs through my forehead,
a brilliant liquid,
   filling my body with her silent speaking:

All the wood does not have to be gathered in one night...
Only what can be held in your arms each day,
What is needed for the evening fire.

You only need what the heart can absorb.
Be at peace with that.
And confident of tomorrow.

———◆●◆———

In the center of the circle is The One Who Leads.

Who is she?

She stands tall, erect. Elevated by a quiet, regal dignity that radiates from an inner core, she draws herself up from that center into life, moving with a fluid, silent, timeless grace.

Her eyes, deep and bright crystalline blue, are lit with the diamond-white brilliance of a living fire. They flash with a startling, vivid clarity that makes me want to drink from them. I have seen these eyes before; they are familiar to me. They remind me of the spiritual eye that Yogananda spoke of, with its field of blue and a brilliant white star at its center.

Suddenly, I want to leap into these eyes. Seized by the irrepressible longing to follow them all the way back to their source, I spring upward and dive headlong into them. I am riding a ray of starlight, in another dimension altogether, swimming in blue, gem-like light that is alive, which breathes with a fluid purity that is breathing inside of me. I am losing myself, being washed away in the sweetness of this brilliance.

Her life is drawn from this diamond-white brilliance at the center and projects the sheer, ecstatic force of its rarified essence into all circumstances.

———◆●◆———

I am less and less able to function, battered by my thoughts and fears, assaulted by what I cannot handle. I am on the edge of crumbling at any given moment.

I need to lie down. To stop everything, but I can't. There is too much to do. Looking around at the physical chaos of my life – all of those things calling on me for completion when I have such diminished capacity – I pray for help, but feel none coming.

Everything in me, every cell, every hammered fiber of organ, muscle and bone, every nerve and molecule pounding through my adrenaline drenched veins – all that I am or ever hoped to be – is melting into one interminable, blood curdling, insistent scream to the universe for help.

———•◦•———

DREAM:

The Dalai Lama comes, materializing out of nothing beside me, in response to a prayer for healing. He asks me, "What is wrong?"

At first I have trouble remembering or putting it into words. Finally, I remember. *I am so afraid. I have so much fear*, I tell him. I kneel in front of him. He places his hands on my head, sending indescribably tender and soothing currents of delicate blue light and healing pulsing through my brain.

We walk through the house that I live in and he asks, "What is your path? Who is your teacher?" I start to say Ananda, but realize that doesn't quite fit. I finally remember, "Yogananda." He asks, "Why aren't there any pictures of him here? They should be all around you."

The scene shifts to a house where I am with a group of people. A baby is being held by a man and is wrapped too tightly. I unwrap her gently. She is marked up with indentations of the blanket and one eye is mashed shut. She is going to be fine, though, when she is handled more sensitively and mindfully.

I sing "Oh Beautiful, for Spacious Skies," and "Mine Eyes Have Seen the Glory of the Coming of the Lord." My voice is incredibly clear and sweet and fluid. It comes purely from the heart and has a melodic quality it has never had before, utterly unforced. I notice how different it is from the full operatic strength I have when I sing like my mother.

Later I am able to do things mindfully, more slowly.

————— ●•● —————

Dream: My House of Fear

I am inside a deteriorating ranch-style house that has a long wall of ceiling-high, all glass windows with a sliding door facing out to a narrow, faded blue, painted wooden deck. The area behind the deck is wooded. On the deck, two men are waiting to kill me if I step outside. One is my father and one my husband (though neither looks like my father or Stewart.) The father sits on the end of the deck from which there is no exit. The husband stands with a shotgun at the other end, blocking the stairway. They have an absolute intention to kill me if I step outside. They are resolute that I won't get away. But they aren't coming in after me.

Something is burning. At first I wonder if it is wood. Then I realize it is turning into metal, copper, in the process of burning. The burning is a purification process that makes the metal strong and solid.

Reflections on the Dream:

I have taken a stand to refuse the fear. To trust that it will work out.

NO! You will not keep me locked in this house of fear! The urgency of smashing the glass in my dream is intensifying with every passing nano-second. Vivid, compelling images of crackled glass swirl around me. Flashing, mesmerizing light runs like quicksilver along each cracking edge. I can't tell where I end and the light begins.

I am clutching a huge, heavy bat-like club with both fists and begin swinging. Raising it in a high arch, I slam it, with all my strength into the glass, again and again. Each impact lands with pounding, bodily impact. *The light, the light of the glass smashing is brilliant white, white-gold, flashing fire along thousands of glinting edges that leap out to me as the broken pieces fall in silent and slow, timeless, motion to the floor.*

This is so physical, so satisfying. My breathing gets heavier, thicker, more labored and full with each renewed blow. Time slows to a loud and weighted, distorting slur, like the needle left on a vinyl record after the phonograph has been turned off.

Dark, thick, viscous waves of energy heave up from my pelvis in slow, raw volcanic convulsions, bursting to violent intensity through my chest and shoulders. My body thickens with each rising, pressured wave. This is centuries-old, not-to-be denied power, rage at being repressed for millennia. Loosed from its prison of fear, it rises from my pelvis, shooting up through my belly and chest, and out through my head like a bursting dam. *My chest, my arms and legs hulk up to a huge and hairy, Neanderthal-like, coarse thickness with each mountain-heaving breath. My hair is long and thick, wildly black and matted. But my eyes are wilder, blue against wild, wide, leaping white. My teeth are gnarled, my nose a snout. Each step a strong, sure stride, lands with a leaden thud.*

I swing my roughly hewn, now solid copper club in sweeping arches, shattering everything in my path. I am growling in a low, animalistic, guttural roar. My resolve to kill them is every bit as great as theirs is to kill me. But when I step out onto the deck, they are gone.

I fall to the floor sobbing. It has been a long, dark night. Three years without a center or a point of balance, with just enough healing thrown in intermittently to keep me from going totally insane. I have been slammed into the core of fear that was beneath everything. Fear was my center. It overtook me, devouring every vestige of escape or healing, every resource I had ever found to use against it.

After three years of being swept away in the wild currents unleashed by the obstacle mantra, is it over? Is it finally over, this hellish night?

—●●—

OUR 23RD ANNIVERSARY

Early on in our marriage, everything fresh and new shut down, blanketed by the thick and dull numbness of habit. Whenever we left town, though, by the time we were 20 miles outside of the city limits, the invisible, deadening veil would magically lift. Without processing anything, we were just there, alive again, engaged, meeting each other, effortlessly talking about real things. Laughing, naturally sharing ourselves, our fears and concerns and hopes again.

It was deeper than that today. Driving through the backroads to Bagby Hot Springs for our anniversary, the plan was to relax. We had the windows down. I held my arm out to meet the cool and exuberant, revivifying mountain air rushing against the palm of my hand. With the greens of the towering forest rushing past us on both sides of the road, the space between us opened. We dropped down into honesty, to the truth of the bond between us, to the depth of our connection and how hard it has been; to all that has gone wrong with his father and my mother locked in battle in our marriage bed.

There were no recriminations. No blame. But there it was. When he said he would be OK without me, I realized that was what I had been waiting for, all these years... the ultimate permission to leave.

The finality of it had come clear during this week's marriage counseling session, our 5th. He can't change. It simply isn't in him to own up to any part of the responsibility for our core dynamic. As long as all of it is my fault, he'll work on things. The therapist saw it. She tried again and again to coax him, as gently as she could, in what she reflected back to him. He simply couldn't go there.

I couldn't deny the certainty of it any longer, or the inevitability of what it means. The decision registered with a reflexive, physical clunk in my abdomen.

I cannot live this way. I am not strong enough. I am not good enough or conscious enough to rise above it and love him anyway, at least on the surface. I would become my mother (not that I haven't already), raging until it destroyed us both. I cannot stay.

And so it was quietly settled.

Over. On our anniversary.

I will stay until Lisa leaves for college and move out the following week.

LEAVING FOR LITTLE ROCK TO VISIT MY FAMILY BEFORE MOVING OUT OF THE HOUSE

It is 4:30 a.m., still dark as we drive up to the terminal building. Stewart drops me at the curb. As I open the door, putting my foot down to the ground is like stepping out of a skin, outside of time itself.

This is the first step out of my old life. Away from my family and how they have eaten me. Everything disappears, falling away into dreamlike distance, as I step into nakedly open and hallowed, resonant interior space.

Movement is fluid, luxuriant, silken. I get my suitcase from the back seat, say goodbye to Stewart, then glide through the velvet darkness. The cold night air caresses my skin as I walk toward the brightly lit terminal. In the slowed attention of a moving prayer, I have become clear and heightened, transparent awareness, floating in a dark and living, fertile round.

This state of prayer that has so unexpectedly descended grows quieter. It deepens into steady state while I stand in the check-in line, walk to the gate, and sit, waiting for boarding. Everything is holy in this newly felt aloneness. Taking my seat on the plane, I luxuriate in the hope that no one will sit next to me while people move in a constant stream down the aisle to their seats.

Yogananda becomes a palpable presence in the seat to my left. I can almost see him sitting there, a hearty, robust transparency. So, you will be my traveling companion, I say to him silently. Waves of grace stream out from him, washing over me. I am broken open by their tenderness. He tells me that I will finally find peace. I put my hands over my eyes and cry softly. Somehow I know the other passengers don't see me. They are preoccupied.

Just as we are about to take off, someone sits down in the seat next to me after all. I avoid giving the slightest cue of readiness for conversation. Wrapping myself in silence, Yogananda is inside me and I stay inward, in prayer, for the entire flight.

Visiting my family in Arkansas

My family sucks on their racism like a nauseating old bone. The essence of it hangs in the air with the heavy thickness of a noxious soup that makes it hard for me to breathe. After a family dinner, two nephews stand with their backs leaning against the wall, facing the dining room table where the rest of us are sitting. The 17-year-old pronounces unchallenged by any adult but me that we should line up all gays and shoot them (his sister is gay, though he does not know that yet). Another sister's son, 22, stands next to him, smacking a balled cud of chewing tobacco. He holds a large, red plastic cup in his left hand, spitting brown-black, pungent slime into it with a regularity that makes me want to run to the toilet and throw-up. I can't bear to look at this ritualistic spitting and always turn my head casually in the opposite direction. But I can't avoid hearing it splatter noisily into the plastic cup.

He stands with one hip set cockily out to the side in his cowboy boots and a never-to-be-removed black cowboy hat. Tonight he is talking about slavery as a move forward to a better society than Africa offered blacks.

I have flown back into the 18th century. I want to scream, "Wait, there has been a mistake. You were supposed to fly me home, to the people I love, not into the diseased belly of institutionalized ignorance and cruelty."

I have the image of a late 19th century insane asylum, overgrown with menacing vegetation so dense that it is encircled with never-dispelled shadows. Its grimy, dark halls echo the silent screams of demoralized inmates who are terrorized, knowing they can never get out.

These attitudes are everywhere here, not just in my nephews. The other night I was out late, for coffee with my sister Susie, at Waffle House. It was after midnight. The lights were bright on the white, trimmed-in-70's-orange tabletops. There was a lively crowd, all white. Most of them were into the *I-can-be-more-folksy-than-you* bravado that only a witness to southern culture can fully appreciate the absurdity of, which I was doing.

There was an easy exchange of jokes between parties at other tables, a lot of that characteristically southern way of talking loudly enough, using large enough gestures and eye contact to draw those beyond your own circle into your audience. It was all well received and responded to, like neighbors at a party.

But when a black family of five walked in, silence dropped like an instant, deadly pall, suffocating the previously festive atmosphere. A sense of danger crackled through the air and on my skin. Glances were quick and averted, but everyone was looking. Hardly a breath was taken. Everyone was checking everyone else out in a state of hyper-attention, feeling to see where any trouble might erupt. Or if it was safe to breathe out again. This on both sides of the racial divide.

Everywhere I go, there is a palpable, growing evil presence here in the south. I don't remember this electrifying edge, the charge of it permeating the atmosphere before. (How could I not, though, having lived through the Civil Rights Movement here? Was I really that oblivious, that removed from the horror of it?) It feels ready to explode at any moment, at any movement of an invisible hair trigger.

No wonder blacks are so full of rage, I think, when my mother treats the young black woman waiting on us at MacDonald's like she is stupid and wrong for no reason whatever. I try to apologize with a kind look and overly solicitous praise. But I don't correct my mother, as I know I should. I am squirming to defend against realizing how, in my cowardice, I have participated in her cruelty by allowing it.

What must it be like, on the inside – in the tender vulnerabilities of your heart and spirit – to never know who will be the next to insult you, to meet you with open hostility, intense derision, unspoken fear, outright violence, or a gunshot? What must it be like to get out of your car with your family, looking forward to treating your children, only to walk into an all-white crowd that greets you as if you could be the Manson family? What does it do to those children? What does it do to their delicately developing sense of personhood? How can they not be immeasurably diminished and enraged? How could you not be outraged for yourself and for your children, if simply walking into a Waffle House holds the possibility of being met with such repressed fear or, worse, the potential for violence? How does anyone live with that daily burden of fear?

My family's dominant subject of conversation is typical of so many Southerners who do not have a life that is going anywhere. Incessantly recounted anecdotes about blacks getting this or that undeserved, unearned advantage or job, committing some heinous new act of violence at the Mall – the real center of all life in the South – or insulting so-and-so (you know, that pretty little blonde girl that is so sweet to everyone) at the High School. Ain't it awful? Everything is going to hell. You can see it and feel it everywhere. And it's all because of these damn blacks.

My protests are not nearly frequent or strong enough. I have been a gutless wonder. Their answer is always the same. "We're not prejudiced. You just don't live here. You don't know." Mostly, I sit like a skewered pig, roasting over a spit, frying. Dying inside.

I love these people. How can they have such huge areas of snarling darkness? And though I might expect it to, this darkness does not totally cancel out their goodness. It makes them incomprehensibly small and ugly in this area, but goodness still lives on in them. It even thrives in other arenas of their lives.

God this is hard.

———•••———

LEAVING LITTLE ROCK

As my plane pulls away, I look out of the small window at these two people that I love. Mother and Dad are standing in the terminal, barely visible through its huge panes of dark glass as we wave goodbye to each other. They are so small and vulnerable. I cannot heal their pain. I can only bless them, love them with the hugeness of heart with which they have loved me, in spite of their suffering.

This trip has been a completion. I no longer fear my mother's negativity and bitterness. I am, at last, free to embrace her in the fullness of her life. All of the pathology and wounding that gives her so much anguish.

All the love and strength she has passed to each of us. She lifted us from birth, through childhood, and delivered us into our own scarred adulthoods. This woman gave me the road map for my soul and paid dearly to do it. I love her. I will hold back nothing. She wants nothing but to love me and be loved in return. I give her that, completely and freely. With gratitude. With blessings. With the prayer that she will finally be released from all the pain that bears down on her.

SAYING GOODBYE

Stewart is hurt. He can only feel rejected, insulted by my clarity and lack of ambivalence about leaving. He pulls in, to himself, away from me, making the worst interpretations possible so he can defend himself against the pain. In the process, he closes off the openings that might emerge out of it.

Tonight, I went in to lie down and talk to him after he went to bed. He said all those things, that he had no one to talk to about it, that he is alone with it. And while I understand his pain, I cannot deny the clarity of my experience. I must do this. He will have choices to make... whether to close off or to open up in response to it.

I could only feel for him. I tried to press light into his heart with my hand as I stroked his chest, and asked, "What if I am right, that I cannot be clear about my love for you as long as it is entangled and constricted by your need for safety? I have wondered for a long time now if you use my love and our relationship as a first line of defense against all of your issues of trust and your own need to feel related to the world. How could I ever be free in that context?"

It was clearer than ever to me. This is something I am doing for both of us. It is forcing us to leave behind, to be stripped of the ways we have used each other to hide. We will be stronger, better people.

It may be painful, but it must be done. I will trust the truth of my experience. *You cannot talk me out of this because it hurts you. I hope you won't continue to misinterpret it in ways that make it easier for you to continue to hide.* But that is not my choice or responsibility.

I recognized the same depth and power of the love that flows between us that I felt this morning watching Mother and Dad from the plane window, and thought, maybe we will always be together, loving each other, in a new and better form that will emerge out of this. It was rich enough, complete enough, tender enough to last a lifetime. We made love.

I could feel his heart opening again, peeking out from behind the pain and fear, allowing itself to be comforted by the depth of what flows between us. We held on to each other with a fragile tenderness, reaching past what we don't understand and cannot rise above to the truth of our love for each other. And with the glow of love's softness still on our skin, I thought I could feel his gratitude, with mine, for this moment of finding our way back to each other as we said goodbye.

——•••——

An Evening alone

Tenderly crashing waves
   break on shores of the unseen,
      yet-always-longed-for.
Bathed in the half-light
  that lies between the worlds,
    echoes linger,
      waking every cell with quiet thunder.

I close the curtains to dance,
Moving in circles with angular, firmly planted steps,
My outstretched arms sweep up and round,
down and up and round again,
Gathering time, beginning to end,
  through hungry fingers.

Lightning runs,
  exploding wonder
    through legs and chest, throat and brain.
Offering the fire of my longings
  in cupped, extended hands,
I ride the ecstatic cusp
of the universes waiting to be born
  through this life,
    this body's heart and eyes,
      feet and back and bone.

———◆●◆———

Sunday afternoon in MaCleay Park

The late afternoon sun hovers in the tree tops, sending shafts of light that fall golden green on the ivy covered hills on the east side of the park. The trees on the hill opposite the open meadow are brown, bare skeletons, stripped to essential. But buds are there, if you look closely enough.

I, too, am stripped. Stripped raw and naked this winter. From the inside out. Have I finally found the bottom? It feels like I am resting there. Like the soggy brown leaves on the ground, I am wet and beaten in. But grass is coming up, a sweet and fresh, tender green, beneath the leaves. Birds chatter softly overhead as winter's sun shines with the thin clarity of grace, going down behind the forested hills.

I can rest here, in this place where there is nowhere else to go.

Today, it is enough to know that my fears are a part of me from which there is no escape. They will beat me mercilessly from the inside out whenever they want to. Today there is peace, even in that; nothing to be done.

Next week, I move to California, leaving a life that has shut down on every level. I would not be going if any shred of my life had been salvageable. My car will be crammed with the few possessions remaining to me. Old clothes. A pair of boots. A small green dresser. Two shelves of treasured and formative, luminous books. Boxes of old journals. A rocking chair. My painted globe, photos, candles for my altar. The tree of life we sculpted and painted together as a family.

I go broken and expectant. Leveled. Wondering if my lifelong yearning to be stripped of everything has finally been fulfilled. Or, God forbid, if there is more to come.

Only my immediate family knows I am not coming back. With no energy left for goodbyes, I am sneaking out of town, telling everyone else I am going for a two-month meditation retreat in the woods of the Sierra Nevada.

Today, the promise of green stirs below winter's stillness, beneath the brown and sodden leaves. It pushes tenderly, in faint currents of light, against the naked vulnerability I have become. In the quiet, hollowed-out space of an emptied life, I wait for spring.

———◆●◆———

Chapter VII

RETURN TO A SACRED WOOD

1994

> *Go your own way!*
> *Any other way is straying.*
>
> *The tiniest new particle is greater than all the old....*
> *Can you grasp in your heart*
> *what this tiny particle of the new means?*
> *It is able to change everything everywhere.*

Angel, *Talking with Angels: Budaliget, 1943*

SIXTEEN miles outside of Nevada City, California, in the foothills of the Sierra Nevada, between the canyons cut by three wending forks of the Yuba River, the spiritual community of Ananda Village[1] sits on 750 acres of pine, manzanita, and live-oak forested hills surrounding a central, boomerang-shaped valley.

I come to sit for hours at a small table on the patio outside the village market and deli. Staring out over the jewel-green meadow, my mind reaches like sensual fingers up into the surrounding hills, tracing the shadow-lined spires of pine as they strike against a deep blue sky.

I watch, listen, and feel the pulse of the life that flows through the village, stunned. *"This is my home now,"* I say over and over to myself, trying to let it sink in.

Looking up into the welcoming face of these hills is like stepping back in time – 150 years back, to rural Europe – to what a village used to be. A sense of quiet, of true proportion, sits like a presence in the midst of the green. Portions of two or three houses peek out from the trees, as if to remind you that 250 people do live here, even if you cannot imagine where they are hidden.

This land has a human scale. It is friendly. Accessible. Amenable to bicycling, to walking, as many do, and to quiet visits with a child or neighbor. It invites a deeper breath, a slower pace, a sense of wonder. The community life it shelters enhances and reflects the beauty of the land itself. Village life hums. It plays in the background, like a soft chord in a larger song that honors and celebrates the land.

The original, two-story frame farmhouse has been converted into a grocery-deli dubbed "Master's Market." This is the social heart of daily life in what villagers amusedly call "downtown Ananda." Cars curl toward it at well below the 18 MPH speed limit to keep the dust from the dirt road down. Drivers stop, step into the village mailroom (the size of a large tool shed, just large enough to house 260 mailboxes and a bulletin board), then

---

[1] Ananda Village is an intentional spiritual community of devotees of J. Donald Walters, also known as Kriyananda, and Paramhansa Yogananda, the first Hindu swami to live in the U.S. and author of *Autobiography of a Yogi.*

walk over to the village office or to the market to buy lunch, a snack, or a few groceries.

There is always someone, whether adult or child, to greet or visit along the way. Young mothers come with small children to meet their husbands or a friend at one of the picnic tables under the tree in front of the market. Children come and go on their bicycles after school. They chase each other, practice soccer kicks, or lie around in the field whispering secrets to each other. After 3 p.m., older kids gather at tables inside the deli to do homework. Today three early teenage boys trade advice on what girls like, and on how to get girls to let you kiss them, unaware that I am eavesdropping.

My home for the next year will be the Seclusion Retreat, a separate 67-acre, deeply wooded tract that is five miles away, off Jackass Flats Road. About 35 people – a few old-timers, a handful of staff, and 25 "monastic trainees" like myself who are new residents to the village – live at the Seclusion Retreat in small, rustic cabins that were cobbled together during the 60s and 70s. There is no electricity. We have running water and a central shower house, with one shower for men and one for women. Two flushing toilets are shared by all. Our cabins have outhouses. I am learning to hold it and walk fast up the hill in the morning.

In the center of the retreat property, two large and old, patched-together domes leak profusely and feel as if they might fall down at any minute. Together, they form the community dining room and kitchen. A new dome meditation temple, with tall windows looking out into the woods behind the altar, holds about 35-40 meditators sitting on its unfurnished, carpeted floor.

The schedule for our two-month "Monastic Training" (to introduce new village arrivals to village life) is a surprise. A wake-up bell, a gong, rings through the dark of the forest at 5:30 a.m. We meditate from 6:00-8:00 a.m., have breakfast, clean up, spend an hour and a half working on the property, then meet for class until noon, which is lunchtime. Afternoon class is from 1-3:30 p.m. Yoga postures are at 4:00, meditation from 5:00

to 6:30. Dinner is at 6:30. Most often, there is some sort of meeting or community activity after dinner at the Village until 9 p.m.

This is not going to remotely resemble the regenerative and leisurely walking-alone-in-the-woods I had fantasized.

———•••———

At the Seclusion Retreat

The soft, muffled splat-splat-splat of rain hitting the rooftop of my one-room cabin in these woods is comforting in its regularity and its rhythms, surrounded by the ebbs and flows of wind stirring the tall pines outside my window. There is a steady insistent roar within it all, a rushing force I want to surrender to and ride wherever it might take me. It is music, a symphony full of harmonies and counterpoints, the wild breath of heaven, calling with its roar of ecstasy. I almost see the wind, full of angels, sweeping through the cosmos on waves of joy. I am flying with them. They carry me up, up through the roar to the Great Mother of all the Worlds.

———•••———

This morning walking up the darkened forest path to the temple for 6:00 a.m. meditation, I was hobbling on the foot where I had picked a callous to a deep cut. I found the joy and beauty in the thick bed of pine needles and dried oak leaves crunching beneath my feet as I followed the quartz-rock lined path. Comforted by the reassuring, still presence of the trees around me and the deep black sky above me, there was even joy in the very fact that I was hobbling, in the pain shooting through my foot – derived as it was, from the absurd, ridiculously human and obnoxious habit of picking my callouses until they bleed, almost cripple me, and threaten me with blood poisoning.

———•••———

Sitting on the gently sloping hill under the large pine tree just outside my cabin door, the legs of my metal chair sink into the moist, porous earth that lies beneath the thick layer of dry, brown pine and oak leaf duff that covers the floor in these woods. The sun is shining through the pine, warming me. Three deer are rustling behind me, feeding on the mistletoe I had beaten down from oak trees for them yesterday. Restringing my prayer beads in preparation for the kriya meditation initiation ceremony tonight, each bead slips through the needle and glides easily down the corded thread.

With each bead, a prayer: Let the Divinity in life flow through me. Let every action, however small, be a prayer. Teach me how, give me the strength, to be faithful to what life asks in each moment. Let me learn to live and act simply, pouring as much love as I can generate into the smallest act. Let my self-offering be always deeper, more complete. Let me honor the Divine, serve its forward movement, its expansion. Let the Earth be healed. Let us all be healed, so that we might dance together in the beauty of who we really are in You.

——•••——

Rather than the hours of meditating, journaling, and walking in the woods I had anticipated, the monastic training program has been fourteen hours a day of class, cooking, clean-up, or homework sandwiched between meditations, with evening community meetings for dessert. There has been no time to go at my own pace, or to find the rhythm of my own syncopation in this new environment.

I have accumulated yet another torque of anxiety, a fear of letting down, rather than finding peace and healing. My soul aches from the busy-ness.

Seeking refuge outside on the knoll beside the meditation dome, the community cat is purring under my feet. The sun is sitting high in the budding tree tops. Everything is quiet except for the intermittent bird chatter and an occasional fly buzzing around me. Let me breathe in the pace of leaves lying on the ground and of light reflecting on puddles of water standing in the wood. One of my goals is to spend time outside, listening deeply enough to take the energy and peace and wisdom of these woods into my body and heart and mind. Help me to do that.

I have no place that I feel at home here at the Seclusion Retreat now that the Monastic Training program is over. The common dome is oppressively hot, with a mish-mash of drearily worn, sagging furniture and, inevitably, one self-absorbed trainee with no life of his own who latches on to me to drone on about the banalities of his existence. A stick would do, but he chooses me because I never have the courage to leave or send him away, even with kindness.

Outside, where I might get some relief in the beauty, the mosquitoes are nightmarishly intent. My own room has a bed, an uncomfortable chair, and an inadequate propane lamp that makes reading impossible. There is no place here where I can sink into my own skin, where I can let down into my own being.

But that is a metaphor for my whole life.

John

I have looked into his blue eyes, flashing with laughter and light and the present power of engagement, and been called awake.

He stands, 6 foot, 4 inches tall, exuding a solid and quiet, robust aliveness not unlike a huge, healthy old fir tree. We have been scheduled to cook the evening communal meal together again. As he washes and cuts carrots, then peels potatoes for soup at the vegetable sink in the old dome kitchen of the Seclusion Retreat, he reminds me of Paul Bunyan, larger-than-life, always in a plaid flannel shirt. His shoulders and chest look like they might burst from an overfull heart that is too large for even his god-like body. His mythically proportioned chest sits squarely over a trim waist, centered over straight, long legs and firmly planted feet, which seem rooted in the earth at some invisible, awesome depth.

"Leave that alone!" he calls out sharply to me, with a bit of nettle in his eye, when, for the second time in my nervousness (whenever I am around him, I am nervous), I prematurely turn off the water filling the large pot he has placed in the sink. He is playfully, truly, irritated with me.

Far, far back, past remembering, I know this man. He is so known, so deeply, always known to me. My heart, my whole body, sings of home whenever our cooking duties throw us together for 3 hours preparing dinner for 30. We tease and correct each other and argue like an old married couple. We have since the first afternoon we cooked together. I have felt the full, ranging generosity of his heart as he shrugs his shoulders back laughing, rolls his eyes up and then lowers his shaking head toward his chest in disbelieving amusement at things I say and do.

I am totally crushed out on him. I have let him in to my spirit, into my emotional body – though he does not know that and I dare not give him a clue. I am so embarrassed by my weight, falling in love is more a humiliation than a joy. I would rather die than let him know.

———•••———

This is a place I can feel at home: Under the trees, in the shade, watching squirrels and robins foraging among pine needles. Counting the brood of wild turkey chicks that have come grazing with three mother-hens while I am sitting here, lost in leaves set against blue sky. There are 18 chicks, though they move so quickly it has taken me 30 minutes to establish that.

I can enjoy whatever coolness comes on the breezes of a late, hot summer day and appreciate the elegant wisps of clouds that look like they are a form of Divine dance.

Here I can start to let down into myself, into the quality of beauty that has been so essential to the unfolding of my soul, that quality without which I am so bereft and restless. I could bring my meals here. I could spend hot afternoons writing or just falling into the rhythm of the leaves, into the patterns of light and shade, into the sounds of the high, distant wind rising and falling in the pines and rustling the oaks, as insects dive bomb the back of my head.

———•••———

The pine trees take on a mythic dimension at night. Their strong, dark silhouettes elongate, stretching into the silent depths of the night sky like an inviting bridge that narrows into the finely pointed heart of eternity. I love to stand beneath them under the stars, like a child among beneficent, protective giants. It is reassuring to be so small, dwarfed by their unnamable magnificence.

These are friends, ancient teachers I had forgotten. By some miracle of grace, I have found my way home to them. So I stand in the darkness of a quiet gravel road, honoring them, welcoming them back into my life, talking to them. Wrapped in their presence, echoes of distant universes rumble through my heart.

Tonight they remind me that I walk through a world of giants whose hugeness of spirit I cannot comprehend. Yet, it is possible for me to walk among them, as small as I am. Dwarfed, while at the same time sharing in the immensity of their being, I draw on their wisdom and nobility, their strength and magic, for the textures and colors, direction and energy of my own life.

Calling on a vastness that is beyond yet fully available to me for entrance to the infinite which is my true home, I pray to them, these trees and the giant spirits, the lifetimes and dimensions they represent, gathered around me: *Walk with me through this lifetime; make your presence felt and seen and heard. Share your secrets, your ways of knowing, the fullness of your being with me as I learn how to be fully human. Teach me how to let go of all that is within me that would impede, distort or misuse your gifts.*

———◆•◆———

This is the life I remember and longed for: a constantly opening stream revealing nuances of beauty and joy at every turn, where large and small universes co-exist in their completeness and heightening counterpoint, in their ability to satisfy and exhilarate and reveal the nature of things.

It's not that I ever lived in such a state of grace without the ravages of my inner torments hammering away at me. Hell has always had an active life inside me. But there have been glimpses that were deep enough, transcendent enough, to at least hold the darkness and pain in a mitigating context. They were intimations to the soul – a call of the soul – to another life.

Something in me grasped, was reminded, that this was the life I was promised. Part of me knew, having tasted Divinity in motion in life, that I could never be content with anything less than that, as much as is humanly possible, permeating every aspect of my life.

So I hold myself up to You now in the moonlight, asking, demanding that You make it so: every cell of my body formed within, born out of, and expressing the power and sweetness of Your life.

—◆•◆—

Chapter VIII

ENTERING THE RIVER NAKED

Summer, 1994

...she hears voices from under the Earth.... wind blows in her ears and trees whisper to her....the dead sing through her mouth and the cries of infants are clear to her.

SUSAN GRIFFIN
Woman and Nature: The Roaring Inside Her

WATER rushing over smooth, people-friendly rock at the Yuba River. My soul wants to let down, but can't quite find how. It's hot, even here next to the water, sitting in the shade beneath the old, covered wooden bridge. Even the water is warm, having travelled mile after mile over sun-soaked rock.

What did I want at the river? *A place to lie down in the cool of the water. A place to lose myself in beauty and the quiet monotony of gently falling water.*

What if I were to let life flow freely through me? Like water over rock, effortlessly? What if I welcomed life into my body like a lover, embracing the full range of its sensual awakenings as meditative mysteries, luxuriant gifts from God?

The cool, rich velvet flow of the river between my outstretched fingers and palms is sacramental, like something insistently calling me to dance and to communion. I walk over slippery rock, fully clothed, to sit on a large rock submerged in a deep, clear eddy and spread my arms carefully at the surface of the water, welcoming its teaching.

Let go, lie back, let me carry you away, it beckons.

I can't, I plead. My heart tightens. *There are so many other people here. This is too awkward.*

The river will have none of it. *Come... Come... Come to me*, she insists, whispering until I finally surrender and lie back.

I am floating in clear silk, praying to the angels of water: bring this water nature all the way into me.

———◆◆———

I wrap myself in moonlight and the night shadows of the woods each night now, luxuriating in them like thick layers of finely spun silk. I draw their beauty around my shoulders like a warm cloak and dive for the inner center, the source of the heat they give me. This is the time of my soul. I float in the rhythm of the crickets and get lost in the stars. Mother, I whisper, this is Your night. Take me where you will.

Do I have the courage to become my own lover? To treat myself with the tenderness and care I would want from another? To foster my own dynamism and self-expression that John has stirred in me as a possibility once longed for and then forgotten? Would I treat myself to the delicate sensual sacraments of exotic fresh scents for my own sense of being alive rather than for a romantic impression, a ploy of seduction, or the breaking tenderness of a lover's dance?

It is time to abandon all reliance on an external lover-friend. I will be my own lover, fostering my wild passion for life for its own sake, in all of its moods – not as a pleasure seeker, but as a seeker going to the source of the waters of a stream – taking time to appreciate the beauty, the small worlds that open up around each bend, each with its own fresh revelation of life and Divinity.

Within each pleasure I see the luminous face of God. I see and feel the Divine heart dancing. I hear it calling. My recent nights in pain with sciatica have taught me that sleep is not as important or necessary as I once thought it was to my functioning. So even when I am busy or in pain, I will take my nights beneath the moon. I will spend time diving into the heart of the beauty of the life that is available to me in these woods and serve it to my own soul as a lover's communion.

———•••———

Ceremony at Edward's Crossing on the Yuba River after reading *Women Who Run With the Wolves*:

Standing on the riverbank, I call inwardly to all the Mothers and Grandmothers who have gone before me. *You who came to me in dreams of long ago, I am your daughter, asking you to come again. Come with all of your power, all of your love.... With the great wild force of your hunger.... With the sweeping range of your wisdom.... As ancients who have experienced this world from within and watched it from afar, from the illumined heights of the beyond.*

Pour forth your connection, your passion, your commitment into this life of mine. Breathe the essence of your souls' fire into me. Impart all of your vigor, all of your magic. Come again as my invisible sisters on this path of Earth. Whisper your collective strengths and capacities for fulfilled expression into my mind and heart. Intercede for me with all the forces of heaven so my life can become pure life... a life roaring with the wild beauty of the Divine carried forward and released through your millennia of effort and longing. Be my partners in this undertaking, exploring and expressing my nature as woman, as I connect to all time, through my woman's body, to you and to the Mother of All Souls.

Gather here in my heart. My sense of connection to you has weakened. Help me to formulate a ritual capable of calling you back to me from the edges of the universe, in your highest nature, in the highest aspiration of your hearts as women, to teach me.

———•••———

ENTERING THE RIVER NAKED

I have entered the river naked,
  shed my fear, embarrassment, and shame,
    and all conventionality,
      along with my clothes,
        and left them neatly folded on the bank,
  as ceremonial offerings, on an altar of river-rock.

I have entered the river naked.
  I have drunk her wildness,
    welcomed the cool rush of her joy
      into the above and below,
        the inside and out,
          of every wakened cell.

I have entered the river naked,
  and there,
    dancing in the liquid, silk circles of her currents,
    swirling in the magic of her exhilaration,

I have sent my soul-call to the ancients,
    and gathered their whispering fire into my heart.

I will come again to the river,
  at dawn,
    to light a fire,
      and build another altar.

I will make offerings to the river,
  to the river of the generations,
    to women and all that women give birth to,
      to all that I seek to be connected to,
        past,
          present,
            future,
              eternal.

I will enter the river naked,
  offering my body and my dreams
    into the river of the generations,
      into the river of life,
        surrendering all that would keep me
          from what is trying to be born through me,
and be washed in the new.

Morning Light

The morning spreads its sweet gold
  over a broadleaf sea of forest oak,
Spinning white, angel-haired wonder through the pine.

Like the trees, I will spread my leaves
   in silent welcome,
     opening every cell
       to receive the warm, quiet rush
        of the new day.

——•••——

At Edward's Crossing

Walking home high on the path above the Yuba River, I have to stop. The opposite side of the canyon is alive, heaving rolling waves of deep summer green that flash with shards of golden light. The riverbank below is framed by random, inviting, small sandy beaches that lie between clusters of huge, smoothly worn river-rock.

Pulsating currents run in interlacing lines of clear light along the brown and grey, green and beige, rock mosaic of the shallow river bed. Bird calls pierce the surrounding hills, ringing in pure, crystalline echoes that linger in the heart long past all audible sound. An eagle glides in a slow and wide, majestic ellipse high over the edge of a distant canyon. A mother and her two early adolescent boys splash each other, then feed sandwiches to an intrepid, curious squirrel.

I wonder. *Didn't we come from the same womb, from the same, magnificent Divine hand as the river? Where along the way did we humans forget to expect this kind of densely-textured, irrepressibly wild, constantly streaming beauty in our lives?*

Isn't the river telling us, reminding us, calling us back to that from which we come? Don't river and forest, tree and wind, and all that the natural world contains sing to us, at thousands of levels, that we too are made of the free-flowing joy we see all around us?

——•••——

EMBRYO

Held head to foot
   in a delicate circle of light,
I have become a living seed,
   every cell a translucent embryo
drawing its sustenance and form
   from within a womb of golden-white.

—•◦•—

Reading *Women Who Run with the Wolves* and old journal entries has taken me back to the root of myself, where life bursts open at its deepest source, in raw, naked power, with all of its Cosmic hunger to express its essence newly – full, rushing Divinity, exploding its joy of being, into form.

I have traveled back, all the way back to that point of beginning, where the Divine enters life in the human body, enough to know that it is at that point I want to live. It is from that point that I want my life born. This is beyond theology or concept of God. It lies in the naked experience of Divinity rushing through my body, mind, and heart.

I will not be satisfied with any moment that is removed from that source of being and bliss, however unrealistic that may be. I stand for the right to live my life from that microcosmic point where new life enters me. I demand it of life and of myself.

And in those moments which are far removed from that place of beginning, the task is to return. To scour and dig in the truth. To surrender to it until I uncover once again the riotously ranging magic of my own soul.

Pour Your life into me, every instant of the instant. It is when I live in the mythic dimension, exploring its lush, numinous terrain, that You come bounding.

—•◦•—

A DISTANT FIRE

Late afternoon light breaks,
Spinning wonder through the pine.
Evening falls early in the grey, muted quiet
   and eerie haze of a distant fire.
But I hear your soft roaring
  high above the trees,
    from beyond the world,
As cricketsong and moon rise.

·

DRINKING MOONLIGHT

Driving home from work, I wonder how can I go to bed on a night like this, with the moon rising high and clear in its full, diamond-white brilliance, over the deep silence of the woods. Turning on to Jackass Flats Rd., cresting the steeply winding, narrow dirt road, I pass out of the shadows of the pine to the open flats. Moonlight strikes my chest with a gentle, piercing thud that has actual weight. It drives in as cleanly as a knife, cutting through my heart.

I drive slowly through the barren and dry, crystal-strewn, glowing-white flats, tracing the dark, intermittent figures of pine that accent the lighted edges of the distant eastern ridge. I am caught in the magic of moonlight hanging like a thin mist in the air.

Sitting on the oak knoll beside the temple late into the night, bathing in moonlight, I see a picture-clear image of my heart. It is cut, as if by a surgeon. A perfectly clean, straight incision runs its full length. Another, shorter incision runs the width, creating four cornered flaps which are drawn open, neatly folded, and pinned back. My heart has become a cup. One out of which I know I am to drink ... a wholly unthinkable thing, as natural as breathing.

I drink moonlight through my opened heart.

I taste moonlight.

Its inexpressibly fine, ecstatic milky mist washes through the exposed, hallowed chamber of every cell.

Pierced at the center, all substance and weight surrender. Hung spinning from the heart of startled pleasure, I am drawn upward in a spiraling rush of lifting light that swells to bursting and flares, like the sweetest of white fireworks whose life is inside me.

Dissolved... drifting... melting to sheerness... I am lost in a timeless bouquet of ecstasy, drunk on eternity's finest wine.

—●●—

Pranayama[1]...
   When we experience our own breath
     as God's breath,
     full of light,
and know that it has always been so.

I will trust this
  as the point from which my life will unfold,
     surrendering all I am and do
       into this quiet miracle of the body
        ...the breath...
where body meets soul,
  the life and beauty of God
  in its own breast.

—●●—

---

[1] From Sanskrit *Prana* (vital force, vital air) + *Yama* (restraint, controlled). *Pranayama* are ancient, controlled yogic breathing practices through which the body is reinvigorated and purified, and the mind calmed, by the concentrated, Divinely charged life force inherent in the breath. The breath is central to most Hindu meditation practices because, by relaxing deeply and attentively into the awareness of the breath, the mind quiets and eventually stills. Ongoing, deepening practice makes direct experience of the Divine possible.

Chapter IX

RE-ENTERING THE BODY
OF THE MOTHER

Fall, 1994

Our bodies form a freedom fleet,
our dolphin grace is power.

We learn and teach and as we go
each woman sings~ each woman's hands
are water wings.

ALLA RENÉE BOZARTH, "Water Woman,"
Womanpriest: A Personal Odyssey

FALLING in slow motion, the body and mind are settling into surrender to these walks in the woods. There is a long, unfolding rhythm that the mind cannot rush. It flows in thinly lit threads of consciousness emerging out of the shadows and the subtle night light of the deep wood. I am coming home to my body, to my life, in this forest. It is a life I have missed and longed for, and half-remembered. I am taking my place in the configuration of the creatures of the wood, in the community of its life.

Tonight I looked up at the trees, asking, *What will you open to me 20 years from now? If we can sustain this intimacy for that long, how far into the heart of things will you take me?* Wrapped in their presence, with their love soaking palpably through the skin of my back, I felt so welcomed, so secure.

I knew this love came from more than the trees and the moonlight, though. This is the love of all life that has ever been: every tree, every blade of grass, every fish and bird, every animal sacrificed to a predator, every human life, however uplifted or degraded. It was all there, part of a loving stream of sacrifice made so that I – so that each of us – might someday make this return.

It is undeniably personal to have our lives supported this way, by all of the life that has preceded us.

...If only we could grasp the magnitude with which we are loved.

——•••——

The flow of life's unfolding cannot be forced. It presents itself from within generous expanses of quiet. Given enough space and time, our attention, which is taken up with the fevered preoccupations of a grosser world, sinks into the deep, silent springs out of which life emerges. There, the new sprouts from hidden, fertile fields of the unknown. Its vulnerable, finely spun impulses come in half-lit images and muted, effervescent stirrings which linger in the heart like distant stars whose light must be gathered in the eye by prolonged exposure if they are to be seen at all.

Let me live in these nether regions, in the uncharted territories between the worlds, where the never-before-seen, the yet-to-be-felt, and longing-to-be-heard enter into existence. Let me be silent witness to that sublime instant of incarnation when the Divine becomes flesh.

I will be forager and huntress for the waiting, fragile treasure of the new. I will be midwife and priestess, tending to the needs of new life as it sprouts, with the wriggling vitality of semen and the tender vulnerability of the newly fertilized egg as it searches for the place in the womb in which to root itself: the place that will give it the warmest welcome, the richest nourishment, the strongest foothold from which to push itself out into the world.

———◆●◆———

If I tell the truth, I do not know why I come out every night to walk in the woods.

Tonight my mind runs ahead of the beauty all around me, looking for something to hang itself on, something it can put its arms around and name. But this is unnamable stuff. To walk in the woods with moonlight drenching every leaf, amid a noisy sea of cricket rhythms and the high whispering of trees, is to be mystified by levels and nuances of beauty too numerous for the mind to absorb.

They break upon my body, my mind and heart with a steady constancy here, coming in feather light intimations of other realms that softly brush at the outer edges of one another and of me, pushing me into new territories. These woods are giving me a stream of breathless glimpses into other realities. As I stand bewildered before the moonlight-dusted sheen glowing on a stand of saplings, or am caught in the dimension-blended mysteries of the thickly arcing body of an ancient oak whose arms sweep up with the joy and magnetic grace of a goddess, I am receiving initiation. The woods are speaking, drawing me back, into the original, forgotten language.

Often I stand with my arms around the massive trunk of a Great-She-Mother Oak, with my heart and all of its longings pressed into her, praying. I feel her take my prayers up through the great rainbow arcing curve of her trunk and send them gently soaring through her branches, out into the bowl of the night sky, to the farthest reaches of the universe. Sometimes she will take me all the way into herself and I know she is teaching me the language of her being and it is becoming a part of me. So I let myself farther down, into the currents of her silent speaking, absorbing through my body what my mind cannot comprehend.

———•●•———

MORNING OFFERING

I will let the sun soak into my body.
I will let its love run through me.
I will let the feathered rustling of leaves
  brush through me,
    inside and out,
      awakening me, body and soul,
with its sound of rushing waters.

I will let the Earth and sky caress the subtle, interlacing rivulets of new life that are stirring inside me: a thousand indecipherable, interwoven planes of existence dancing, coming to life in ecstatic harmonies.

There is too much that is emerging to have any hope of grasping it. I can only surrender to its rushes. Let it rise up and wash over me. It is as if a thousand-petaled lotus is blooming inside my body. The light-fingered touch of each petal delicately opens, brushing the surface of the within with breathless tenderness. In a symphony of backwashing currents of light and suffused joy, they send a multi-hued radiance flushing through my skin and spirit.

———•●•———

REFLECTIONS ON THE SCENE WHERE BUDDHA IS TEMPTED BY THE FIVE DAUGHTERS OF THE DEMON IN THE FILM, *The Little Buddha*

Have I gotten off track by allowing God to come to me through the physical, through exploring the wilds of my own feminine nature within nature?

I have left conventional interpretations of the spiritual path and its teachings behind in order to mine what feels like a deeper part of my instinctual nature. I have tried to understand it, but in the final analysis it comes down to surrendering to the deepest impulses of the heart, to that which most expands me, to following that thread wherever it leads.

I have thought of it as a dance with the Cosmic Mother Herself... that I am learning how to dance with my body in her body of the universe.

It is as if there is some primal, elemental thing about being a woman I have to explore. Because life has come to and through me, as a woman, primarily in the body. Women open to life through the body. We literally receive it into ourselves, welcoming the other through our pelvis. We feel new life taking root in our flesh. We wonder at its swelling and kicking, stretching and hiccupping against our ribs. We nourish its growing new life with each breath, with every bite we take, and bring it into the world with our genitals, our blood and guts and hope bursting. We nurse it at our breasts in awe, pick it up to comfort it when and however often it is hurt, and cradle it when it is frightened. We receive the imprint of its preciousness, the face of its tender need, upon our hearts in millions of times and ways until we watch it walk out the door of late adolescence hurling obscenities at us. We gladly – *OK, not always gladly* – offer up all previous concepts of our personal needs and limitations to the import, weight and sting of what is required to lift that child up, secure its well-being, and firmly plant it in its future.

So love has been very physical to me as a woman. It has been a body thing. And my body wants to come along on this journey home to God. It wants to play, like an irrepressible puppy, with the God that comes to me in the body of the world.

Nature is the body of a God that has become my Mother. She is a dancing, feminine God, a birthing God. And I want all of me out there, meeting and greeting Her, giving birth to Her in the body She has given to me.

Yet fear and insecurity strike. What if I am wrong in this? As I open to the wildness of my body and heart, as I let it burst unrestrained from my experience of nature, might I be traveling into some forbidden territory that will take me out of the field of grace and leave me wandering in darkness again?

Where are the mystics and mystical teachings that support this road I feel I must take? Do I dare rely on *Women Who Run with the Wolves* and Joseph Campbell's hero's journey in the absence of actual mystics?

But how could ten weeks of bliss, ten weeks of the absence of fear and torment, be wrong? I have never experienced peace or sustained joy like this before.

Isn't that the best test for truth that I have available to me?

———•••———

WRESTLING WITH ANGELS

I get furious at conventional interpretations of the religious life that leave us confined in narrow parameters of self-expression, and caught in limited concepts of the God-becoming-Goddess I experience as all-inclusive. Narrowness cuts us off from the endless avenues to the sacred. Infinitely worse, though, it cuts us off from the essence and nature of Divinity itself.

But conventionality is inside me, not outside. I have to stand for myself to myself.

This is the terror I felt when I left the Catholic Church, the fear of being cast out by God forever. It is the fear of committing an unforgivable sin. The Divine has always been there, an undeniable presence, whatever mistakes or transgressions I have made, with its endless outpourings of grace. If I go too far, I will sense it and make the correction.

I am stepping outside the terms of conventional understanding, even of my own. Yes, there is natural vulnerability in that. But in giving my heart to the Divine, I have always been resolute and clear in declaring *only the Divine need apply!* I have to trust that my best instincts for what it takes to be true to my own nature come from grace and the legitimate impulses of my soul until I experience otherwise.

———•••———

HOUSESITTING AT SATYA'S, ON THE EASTERN RIDGE OF THE SECLUSION RETREAT

A fading, deep burnished glow lay above the broad, flat horizon of the opposite ridge as I opened my eyes from the deck this morning. *I never want to sleep inside again, I thought. To go to sleep in the open air, beneath the stars, flanked from behind by the dark, full-bodied silhouette of a row of pine trees while facing an open expanse of rolling, forested hills and valleys is too much richness.*

But there is something deeper than this beauty involved in my persistent longings to sleep outside. It is a longing to be returned to the body of the Mother in a complete and physical way... a need to surrender my body back into hers, into the living womb of her flesh.

It is a prayer for return, with my mind silenced by sleep, that she would wrap me in her subtle, flowing, living energies head to foot, above and below, inside and out. Then I could breathe her starlight through every pore, soak it in, farther in, until it becomes a part of me – even in those stubbornly hidden, unknown places I cannot reach to heal for myself.

I have this belief, an assumption, that if I am outside long enough, if I open myself completely enough, the outside will come inside, and I will never have to feel separate again.

That was my prayer last night when I went to bed. The Milky Way was glowing, active and intense with light. I wondered if it might be the scattered light of my Cosmic Mother's dancing. I asked her to come in, all the way in, to my aching for home that never goes away. Then I drifted off to sleep, occasionally waking like an infant at the breast, to drink in more of the sweet clarity and vivid closeness of her body strung through the jeweled sky above me.

So I stood on the deck singing this morning as the sun's gold lit the edges of the clouds hovering close to the horizon. *"When I awake, I will see Your face,"* ...this is your face. *"When I awake I will see Your light,"* ...this is the light of your body! Put its life inside me.

It was so intimate, this singing. She was there in the hills and in the sun and I knew I was singing into her heart, and she was there receiving my song. I sat down, shaking.

A cluster of clouds near the breaking sun looked like the profile of an angel, greeting the sun with its arms extended and its hands cupped in joyful self-offering. Standing again, I put my arms out, with my hands cupped open around the rising circle of the sun. I was calling the sun, drawing its light through the open shaft of my arms, into my heart.

As the golden fullness of the sun lifted, the angel-cloud shifted. It was standing, full-face to the sun, with its arms opened high and wide to receive this celebration of light. I opened my arms, still singing. Looking straight into the golden-white burning of the sun, it was in my own body. It was in my chest, rising up through my head. And I knew that by some miracle, I am being brought home to God through the body of the world, and God's body is in me, singing its burning joy.

———•••———

With the membrane between me and the world melting away in golden brilliance, I know what it is to be a priestess. I recall how, the other night walking in the moonlight along the gravel road to Jackass Flats, I had the feeling of the priestess in my body, how I could draw the energies and powers of the Earth up through my hands. Now, I understand that from the inside. The priestess has welcomed the natural world into her body so completely that its wisdom, rhythms and capacities flow freely through her. They have remade her body and mind, heart and soul in their nature. The priestess commands the natural world and its forces because out of love and reverence, she has surrendered herself into its body, and life has entered her as itself and she has lost herself in it.

I do not know by what mystery the sun has entered me with the golden white joy of its burning. I can only drink its unconsuming fire, and let it melt away the lines of mind. This communion sings with one body. It is in me as the body of my mother, and I am in it. My separateness has begun to dissolve, and life is dawning as a single-bodied sea of grace which

patiently erodes traditional concepts of you and me and other, and of how
the world works.

—•••—

Moon Song

You have set my soul free,
mended a heart that has been breaking
since the day it was born,
and sent it out to play,
   adventuring,
     in a world of magic.

You have lifted and comforted me
  in the soft white light of a tree's inner spine,
    and taken me inside its Oming
      to listen and feel the source of its rising.

You have sent the iridescent ecstasy
  of purer-than-white clouds
    spiraling through my quickened heart.

You have sat me high and alone at midnight,
  in an expanse of glowing, bone-white, quartz-rock hills,
  praying through the dark solid majesty of trees,
    singing my love to the moon.

  You have brought me staggering
   under the waning moon,
     drunk from the wonder of dancing
      with an old she-mother-oak,
  each movement mirroring the energy-form of her rising

until her joy came flying through my chest and arms,
   and out of my fingertips
    in a fan of light
      that would have given birth to leaves in her body.

You have called me to the river at dawn,
   burning bowl in hand,
    to sit naked on cold river rock,
wrapped in the warmth of a thick cotton shawl,
     to offer goddess-tree leaves and prayers into fire,
      and be baptized in icy river waters.

You have taught me to greet the day singing,
   in surrendered prayer-dance to the sun,
and to welcome its visitation
  as golden-fired joy
   burning wildly through my body.

Pounded from within by waves of grace,
   immersed in the ecstasy
    of a life newly born,
     broken open,
   and free to drink
     from an infinite, luminous sea
      of tender mysteries,

You have stood me up, singing,
  in a roaring fountain of joy
   that burns through me
    like an endless column of fire.

My Kingdom, My Kingdom

"Be in your sovereignty," my friend Susie said to me at work, sweeping her hands in front of my chest with an expansive gesture, "In the power and magnitude of your selfhood...."

Then driving home, the waning three-quarter Moon was rising high above the clustered spires of pine, breaking through thick streams of mist with golden intensity. She was establishing her domain across the expanse of sky and the mists running along the furrowed hills and valleys below.

But the space of the sky filled my body as well, and I knew that my sovereignty is akin to the Moon's. Akin to her nobility and all of the space she commands and contains. Akin to all that she turns to magic with her light. These things are in me now, in my body and heart in a real way. They are dimensional territories whose energies and life of fluid revelation have laid claim to me and become my own. These vast inner landscapes are opening into an ever-widening, deepening river of discovery and joy. And in the midst of this ecstatic flow, the priestess rises up in my body unsought, full of the self-contained majesty of the realms which have become her home.

You have given me a kingdom higher than the moon, as wide and deep, glittering and clear as the bowl of the sky on a cold mountain night, and made me sovereign over all that it contains.

You have given me a kingdom, a royal inheritance most know not of, but which we are all meant to own. And I am beginning to experience myself as one who is as full of elegance and grace as the Cosmos herself, as I lie beneath high and thin, soul-white clouds glowing in the deep stillness of early morning over dark, forested hills.

—◆•◆—

Forest Interlude

The steady, gurgling irregularity of a small forested creek bed makes its way through the pine, singing softly past each rock, large and small, and each browning, fallen leaf strewn in hapless perfection. The late afternoon sun filtering through the trees reveals a painted dance of light flowing along swirling rivulets of current.

It's all beautiful ...
    something to come home to,
        to come to rest in,
            to be taught by,
                to go inside of.

My eyes and heart trace each rock and leaf, each clump of moss and grass, each root and stump. But that is not enough. I ache to touch and be touched by all that is here, to smell it and feel it reaching into my bones.

I run my hands hungrily along each smooth curve, each cold and sharp, chipped edge of rock, drinking in each splotch of color, each black, grey, and green lichen-etched scar.

What hidden life, what burning lies buried in the center? I wonder at one deeply burnished, blood-rose heart of massive stone.

And in the midst of this revelation of beauty felt and found, a lonely aching pulses through my chest, like that for a lost beloved who has been away too long to bear. I crawl into the large, hollowed out circle and curl up, letting her hold me like an infant in the lap of its mother, as I let my body's longings sink down into her center.

———◦•◦———

We humans are meant to hold the beauty of the world in our hearts in a literal sense. To have the breath drawn out of us by the startlingly pure, sun-splashed, living luminescence of white clouds vibrating in a field of blue. To walk among the mottled orange and yellows of perfectly tipped, elegantly curled maple leaves lying randomly along a stone path until we are compelled to pick them up, slow and trembling, and press them deep into our chest with a prayer for union.

The Earth will write the book of life into our minds and our bodies if we let Her... if we cast aside the certainties of our everyday ways of knowing and being... if we look with open, inner eyes — the feeling eyes of the heart — at the light and color dripping from trees strung along the cliffs beside the roadway.

If we let nature speak to us in its language, the language of original being, we will learn the true language of our own being. We will discover how to draw the densely-layered, ever-opening beauty of each day up through our fingertips and palms and into our bodies as naturally as we draw breath. The river of life will run wildly through our arms and chest and brain in streams of ecstasy and prayer, washing away the old in our mind and heart.

Then our old life and its ways, and all of the old world and its sufferings, will be shattered by joy.

——◆•◆——

I had no idea on that clear, March morning in Portland years ago as I was going in to work, when I took five minutes to sit beneath the tall, newly leafing elms beside the library, of the power of the prayer that came to me. I asked the trees to come inside me, to become a part of me, to plant their being in my blood and bones and heart, to impregnate me with their essence.

It was a simple, spontaneous, honest prayer. It came unsought from a quiet moment that I just as easily might not have taken. And though the longing was real, I never believed that it was even remotely possible. Yet today, a thousand new worlds have been born out of that moment – a life more tender in its multifaceted, interactive openings than I could have dreamed.

What does it mean, that the magic of the universe can be born to us out of that kind of small impulse of the heart? How can we comprehend the importance to us and to the world that the opening to the new comes in vulnerable threads of light so small that they are likely to go completely unnoticed and unresponded to?

Has the wonder of the world we long for, the beauty of the life we ache for, been sprouting in tender shoots at our feet all along as we have run, unseeing, through our tense, hurried lives?

What running streams of the new, taking what unexpected twists and turns full of beauty and joy and pulsing light, could be born to and through us, if we listened for and attended to those quiet promptings of the soul which wait for us to make room in our lives for them?

———•●•———

WITNESS

I am swimming in currents too deep to name,
   flowing,
     being carried along by a Cosmic river
       the dimensions of which I cannot comprehend,
        like a tiny pine needle.
The swells that carry me
    come from sources and directions I have no intimation of,
      but it is a river of light
      and I am secure as I surrender
to the magnitude of the unknowable.

I am only a human being,
  a small thing,
    given the privilege
to find myself in this Cosmic sea,
freed to float on its mysteries,
    to feel and witness the body of its revelation
  in my own body,
    burning away my body,
       melting all that is inside me
       in longing for its light-filled life.

———•●•———

MORNING

An exuberant wind, blowing wildly with the new, greets me when I come out of the temple this morning after meditating. I run to Satya's house, screaming my joy. Getting the house cleaned for Mother and Dad's arrival and visit, I beat the bathroom rug so hard against a tree that I fall over, laughing. Standing in the driveway in the sun, I dance, calling out my gratitude to the sky for this beautiful day.

LATE EVENING

Mother gets irritated with Dad so often. I shut down reflexively in a quiet, distant civility born out of dread. Thinking ahead to spending an entire week together at this superficial level, something in me refuses. I pray for the capacity to take it to a higher level, to something genuine.

I tell Mother and Dad about my walks in the woods, and the stream of revelation that has come through it all. Magic happens. I am sharing the richness of my life with them and they are getting it. I read them some of my journals. Dad is visibly touched, opened, by these things he has not the slightest framework to understand. He gives me a new, tenderly endearing name, "Dances with Trees".

As they get ready for bed, I go out for my walk. The night is deep and moonless. The stars are clear, clear crystal, flaming with life. The air is cold, and I am praying into all of it – the stars and trees, the night itself.

I am here; I have missed you. Let this beauty give me its teaching.

Going down to the five huge pines that I have christened 'Master's Gate' because they stand like guardian spirits at the entrance to the Seclusion Retreat property, I lean against the one next to the gravel road that I associate with Yogananda. I feel the singular, upward direction of the tree's energy blessing me. It is as if Yogananda is there, holding me with my forehead pressed into his. His tender light is washing through me once again.

Walking home, I wonder. Is it possible to heal the cellular memories of the body, the damaged little girl who felt hated by her father, the one who lived in terror for so long? Is it possible to free her?

I invite the shrunken self she pulled herself so tightly into, that terrified, huddling little seed of a self, to come tonight to this new relationship with father: "See how he has come to revere you," I say to her. "How he loves, honors and respects the woman you have become. How he allows you to teach him, to open his heart and touch his soul with dimensions he never knew existed."

I wonder as I walk home under a dark sky full of vivid stars: *Will this new relationship with father open the space for the old pattern to end, that of being a rejected, devalued irritant to the men I love?*

On my way to and from work, the hunger for reunion breaks open when the ancient energy of the mountains pulses up through my body in a fountain of strength and longings, or as I catch all-too-short glimpses of gold scattered in a wild, exuberant trail along the creek bed beside the road.

Often while driving, I roll down the window to put my hand out to draw the cool, living freshness of the day up through my palm and into my chest. It's always with a prayer ... that the essence of the sky, of soul-white, pearlescent clouds, and the endlessly unfolding beauty of the world outside come inside. *Live inside me literally. Not sort of, really.*

I want all of it in me, alive, its wild essence singing, dancing, breaking me farther, farther open until I die from the joy of it. *Lay me waste to this beauty.* Let me become all of these things. Taste them. Be them. Let them be fully available, bursting into light, shattering the smallness of mind and heart, the preconceptions of who I am and what is available to me, and of the territories in which I am meant to range as a human being.

God... God... God. Life in all its manifestations. In me. Giving birth to all that is wider and deeper, more inclusive and joyful than anything I am capable of imagining. Singing me up a new body that has all of this beauty bursting open inside it.

HOUSESITTING AT JOHN'S CABIN WHILE HE IS ON A 10-DAY RETREAT

It seems like so long ago, I think as I drive home from work, too long, since I have been out inside the night. I am homesick. Will it take weeks to let myself far enough down into the night rhythms to have them inside me again? The almost-full moon is already high in the sky. Her light hangs in an inverted bowl of arching light that I am inside of and that hangs inside of me.

But it is so cold, Mother, I plead. *As much as I have been missing you, I don't think I have it in me to go out tonight.* I do, however, have to go to the outhouse.

Stepping outside, the moon welcomes me back into the field of her light, embracing me with the tender intimacy of a dear friend. The bowl of space in my heart grows as vast as the one her light makes in the sky. We are like sisters with twin domains, seeing and loving each other in their fullness.

What else is there to do? I bundle up in four layers of turtleneck, a sweater, John's borrowed flannel shirt and down coat, a wool hat, two scarves and am off.

It is quiet. I could walk all night, I think. With the exhaustion of the day suddenly gone, I let my body down into the stillness, stopping every few feet to absorb the deeply shadowed forms of trees contrasted against the glow of the night sky. They seem to sink through my skin and wrap themselves warmly around my heart, taking away all sense of cold.

Streaks of mist radiate out through a high circle around the moon. *Rain tomorrow,* I think. *This is probably the only night I'll have to be with you for a while.* I stop in an opening beside the road to stand in the delicate shower of her light. Prayers come in an easy, constant stream, but they are too deep, too full of wonder and gratitude, and I am too lost in them for words.

This is a perfect night to take the ashes back to the two goddess trees that gave me their leaves for my river ceremony, I realize as I am almost to the zendo. The ceremony won't be complete until its circle is complete. So

I turn back, laughing, pleased at having to go all the way back to retrieve my burning bowl full of ashes.

Coming back up the hill, I hold the bowl forward with both hands in ceremonial offering. I stop to hold it up to the moon and ask her to bless this impromptu ceremony of gratitude. At the She-Mother tree, I stand in front of her, bowing in greeting, crushed at the honor of the intimacy between us.

The inspiration for the ceremony comes of itself. I call the Divine above and the Divine below that come to us through all of life as it has been, the Father and Mother, all the gurus and saints, the ancestors, the mineral, plant, animal kingdoms, asking them to join me, to receive my prayers and to bless them.

I take a handful of ash and rub it into the bark of her thick trunk, praying: Thank you and all the spirits of these woods, for all you have given me, for this mythic life that now fills my body. *Thank you for the comfort and warmth you have extended to me as I have prayed and cried into you, night after night, and for the silent ways you have taught me. Thank you for the inspiration for the river ceremony, for the gift of your leaves. I took them to the river at sunrise and gave each one into the fire with a prayer of my heart. Hear those prayers still lingering, echoing and singing, in this ash that I am returning to you. Give them your blessing. Take them into your strong body, add your intention and powers of fulfillment to my own, carry them up, and send them out through your branches to the farthest reaches of the heavens.*

There is something earthy and basic and good about this rubbing. It cuts through me, releasing something primitive and instinctive that rushes in a torrent up through my body, into my heart and arms, and out through my palms as I press handful after handful of ash into bark. *Never let the promise of this magical, ever-opening life be lost to me,* I pray. *Keep it alive and authentic in me always. Make me worthy of it. Never let me dishonor it.*

The raw longings of my whole life are now rushing feverishly through my palms and fingertips. This rubbing of ash concentrated with prayer-essence is so physical, so deeply satisfying and cathartic. My whole body wants to pray through it. I begin rubbing ash as I go from body part to body part. Forehead and eyes. Nose and ears. Mouth and tongue and throat. *Let everything I think and feel and see be of this new life, its sacredness. Let everything I smell, everything I hear, every word I speak, everything I taste and eat awaken deeper, subtler levels of this communion in myself and others.*

Warmed by the increasing heat of the ceremony, I am actually hot. I take off my hat and scarves, my coat, sweater and shirt. Rubbing ash along the full length of my arms, over my breastbone, then the cool, smooth skin of my breasts and stomach, I pray: *Let everything I touch and do, all work in the world, all play, every motion, all that I love and give, be born of this beauty.* Through my socks and jeans, I rub ash to my feet and legs, thighs and pelvis: *Let every step I take move me farther into the heart of this forest life, into its mythic dimensions and teachings. Let every expression of love flow out of and honor the magnificence of my womanhood; let it impart the richness of the goddess life you have opened to me through this wild and magic wood.*

Walking clockwise around the tree singing, I lay a circle of ash around the base of her trunk. Then I stagger awkwardly in the now-risen wind getting my clothes back on. I laugh imagining how crazy this would look to anyone who might see me out here in the dark at 2 a.m., in this blistering cold wind, with no shirt on, rubbing ash all over my body. How could they possibly understand? How could they know how primally sacred this is? Then I walk down the hill to Mother-Ten-Trunks (the other leaf-giving tree at the zendo), feeling as if I have shed a skin, and found that long-lost part of myself that is wholly free.

—◆•◆—

Child of the Moon

The winds are sharp and cold as I get out of my car under the full moon, looking up at her for signs of the eclipse that is supposed to be in progress. She maintains her brilliant, round presence despite a sky full of storm clouds. The thin, beaded crust of refrozen snow crunches beneath my feet and glistens under her light as I walk up toward John's cabin, where I am still housesitting.

What a life you have given me, I marvel, looking up at the cabin and out over the wide range of snow covered hills stretching out below it.

Please, Mother, don't let yourself be covered by clouds tonight. I don't want to miss your eclipse. For me, stay with us tonight.

Inside, I snuggle with the cat, Yogi, while we eagerly warm ourselves to the crackling of a newly made fire. The small space lit by the fire and the narrow band of warmth it gives is an inviting cozy, little universe. But the full moon on the night of an eclipse exerts a stronger pull, so I bundle up and go out for a walk.

The wind has picked up. Its lashing bites to bone. Something in me shrinks to unwilling and makes a hasty retreat. Discouraged, I turn back up the stairs toward the kitchen door on the other side of the deck. I am silently scolding myself for not pushing through my resistance. Looking through the window, I spy the lid of the wood box just on the other side of the glass, next to the woodstove. *Ah! I'll curl up on the wood box! I'll pull up the chair with John's meditation pillows and blankets and use it as a footrest since the wood box isn't long enough to hold me.*

I lie for two hours, wrapped in the warmth of John's wool blanket, beneath the wooden frame of the window of his rustic cabin, with my eyes and heart trained on the moon. There is no visible evidence of the eclipse yet, despite the fact that we are now half-way through it. But that doesn't matter. I am having my time with the moon, curled up like a child on this wood box. The moon holds herself in the open, in a sky full of drifting clouds the whole time, as if in answer to my earlier plea. I talk and pray to her. But mostly I am just lying here, receiving her, in what feels like a child's body, with a child's open heart, surrendering to the hold she has over me.

———◆◆———

The great ocean of Your becoming roars through my body, with the tender wonder of a thousand suns and moons emitting their light into me. I sing Your thousand names *Kali, Shakti, Mary, Meera, Durga...* and You are all in me. You blow through me like a primal wind, with the immensity, joy and power of the feminine carrying time forward through eternity. This is my true lineage. This one flowing body of light, giving birth to itself in form, streams through all of life and into me as an incarnation of Herself.

This is the lineage of every woman. The whole of the past is in our female bodies, carrying the force of its treasured aspiration, the magnitude of its holy life, its secret rhythms of emergence and connection, forward into the future. In the mysteries of the womb, in the ova we offer into it each month, in the lives we live and what we bring forth, whether or not we ever have a child, we carry and transmit it.

Whether or not we realize the immensity of all in which we participate, even if we never gain personal access to it, we are the embodiment of the sacred feminine and its magnificence. Its essence passes through us. We are priestesses of life, the guardians of its sacred flame. We are the goddess of birth in her current incarnation.

How do we dive, through our sacred bodies into the rich soil of that, our own, deepest nature? In a culture born out of and circumscribed by the male psyche that fears, disregards, devalues and degrades our unpredictable impulses and ways of knowing, how will we recover that which is our true nature?

Have I stumbled on a universal path of re-initiation in these woods? Reconnecting to the body of the feminine in nature, entering her body, her rhythms and energies, letting our bodies down into hers, we learn the language of original beauty and being. Opening our heart and every cell to receive the revelation and imprint of her freely flowing, feminine nature, how can we not be restored to the grace of its life in us?

I suspect that the true nature of the feminine has been so deeply repressed and denied, mistrusted and distorted that our only access to it is through our own body's wisdom as it opens in mirrored reflection to the free-flowing feminine of the Earth around us.

<hr />

I go for my walk tonight alone in the rain that is really a mist, listening to the quiet, solid wetness of my footsteps along the road, trying to recover the absolute call of the heart that brought You last night.

When I go in to meditate, the temple is empty. It is just You and me. So I kneel close to the altar and bow, touching my forehead to the floor, feeling Your body of light in front of me. It is as if I am touching Your feet and speaking straight into Your heart: *Don't let this be wasted time.* – Break my heart open so that I can receive You. Eventually, my breath settles into light, quiet light, and the deep peace that comes from melting into nothing but the breath and the life of light that is within it. You come from above in fluid streams of peace that settle, slowly settle, into my chest, my heart and mind and breath. I sit, breathing them in, deeper and deeper in, until there is nothing but the light breathing me. This light is Your being, coming to me, growing into joy. Still light... still golden... still tender... still quiet joy... unspeakable stillness.

I slowly feel my way down the narrow, winter-still and darkened path, stumbling over rocks, turning into trees, making frequent, stinging acquaintance with overhanging branches as I try to find my way by the imperceptibly faint, often disappearing glow of the white quartz rock outlining the path. As I crawl into bed, I ask You to be with me in my sleep, to use this night to bring me further home than I can bring myself consciously. All night I feel You there in my dreams working inside me. I wake, aching for home, knowing I have been there. Walking out onto the deck, You are smiling brightly through a sun-splashed sea of green.

—•••—

Chapter X

PERSEPHONE'S SURRENDER

January, 1995

Pack nothing. Bring only
your determination to serve and
your willingness to be free.

Alla Renée Bozarth, "Passover Remembered,"
Womanpriest: A Personal Odyssey

DREAM:

I am in an open field with a young girl. A huge funnel cloud is rapidly approaching, heading directly for us. I am scrambling to find a ditch, some place in which we can take refuge. At the last minute, I find a ledge of earth, about four or five feet high. We jump over it and crouch down, pressing ourselves into the wall of the ledge as the tornado passes over us.

Volunteering for Mother Teresa has been my dream for almost 20 years now. Yet it looms in the foreground, only weeks away, as a death, an annihilation of life as I have known it. I have no idea why.

Still, it is as if the tornado from the other night's dream is in my torso, swirling fierce and black through my middle. Ripping away everything that is known. Tearing every aspect of my life away from its moorings. There is no escaping the sense that I am being gutted, that everything I have loved and expected is being torn away.

What does it mean? There is a column of fire running from my pelvis to my chest. Burning. Eating me away. It feels as if You have cast into the wild winds of that fire all the human comfort I have ever known and longed for. I am frozen, unable to surrender.

I can't stop the fire. I can't stop weeping. I turn to God half-heartedly. This is so unexpected. I am not ready for this.

I still want semblances of a normal life. And though I have tried to surrender it, my reawakened, lifelong vision for a lover has returned, craving a relationship with John, or someone else one day, who can see the depth of who I am. A lover who will share the magnitude of his being, and dance with me in the freed cosmic fire.

You are a jealous God, asking for everything. But if I manage the wherewithal to give it, will You be there for me? Will You come into all the holes in me, into all those spaces left by what I give up?

I dive into that place where I want only You... where I willingly release all longings for human love returned which so stubbornly and frequently resurrect themselves. I dive into the root of myself, drawing every ounce of my energy, strength and will into a wholehearted, full-bodied call. *Come.*

———•••———

At one level, I know there is nothing else in the whole world that I want this year other than to have You go with me on this journey to India. To have You beside me at every step. To have You inside to talk to. I offer up my strength and my weaknesses, begging for the capacity to surrender.

———•••———

Falling in love with John was not remotely about John. It was about letting my heart run. It was about gathering strength, bringing me to surrender what I most long for at a human level. Love, love returned from a man with an immensity of soul, a hugeness of heart, a dynamic capacity for engagement... a willingness to tell the truths that hurl my soul into the farthest realms of its potential life the way John has every time we have spoken. So I gather up those longings, the specific, implacable ones that draw my heart and mind and body out in reaching for him, and give them to You.

But You must give me Yourself. You must give me access to all the domains of the homeland. A life received as the body of grace coming to me with all the tenderness and intimacy I have wanted from a lover. That was the deepest, most central longing of my life. Unmet, it holds the greatest reservoir of my life's energy and aspiration. Falling in love with John has released that energy in a rushing, exuberant torrent of desire. So I know it is fitting that you ask it of me. I lay it at the altar, still grieving for its loss, with the foretaste of Your totality on my tongue... only because You have demanded it. It was the quality of love I most wanted and never had. You are seeding Yourself in my body, comforting and reassuring me.

I will go to India alone, with You inside me.

———•••———

Why this morning, Mother? I only walked out on the deck to sing good morning to You. What triggered the deep longings for home? Was it the quiet stillness of the hills, the dull grey of the low-lying clouds, the absence of the sun on the leaves that I missed? Your beauty was all around me, yet I couldn't feel a part of it. I felt separate, cut off from Your body, once again.

Singing brought You back to me. *Oh, my Mother, You have always loved me. Oh, my Mother, I have always loved You.* Your nearness made the separation that comes and goes unbearable. I was calling out to You, crying yet again... those deep, primal, aching tears that come with moans rising up from the pelvis in convulsive, reverse peristaltic waves, heaving something up from the bottom of me.

It wasn't the 20 billion years of separation I was feeling today – just the separation of these recent days as unbearably deep, having felt You so near in recent weeks. The words of the chant would float back in ... *"Oh, my Mother, I have always loved You,"* ... *When will the separation end?* ... *"Oh, my Mother, I will always love You,"* ... *O.K., I'll give up everything. I'll let go.*

I was offering my tears and my loneliness into Your heart which had come closer now, and which was above my head, in front of my forehead. I remembered that You are all I have ever wanted. If only I could re-enter Your heart as a womb, I prayed, I will give up everything.

I offer my body, my life into Yours with each in-breath. I draw Your love down to the depths of my body with each out-breath. I rest in Your body of light between the in and out breaths. I remember the spark of light that I could almost visibly see in my mother's love for me as a child. It is that same spark I see in anything beautiful – a pure and living, leaping and joyous, diamond-white light. You have been coming to me in that spark all my life, drawing me back to Yourself through it. This is what I want, of all things in all the worlds: to merge into that light, to be in the presence of it, to breathe that light in until there is nothing but its life and I know it is all that I am.

This is the one prayer of my heart, the one John said I would need to find, the one Jack Kornfield talks about in *A Path With Heart*. It is the meditation that will bring me home. Singing into this light that is You and Your love for us, all other realities melt away, into its one sweetness.

———•••———

I can't bear to go inside the temple to meditate yet this morning, so I go to the gravel knoll just east of it, to sit in the wooden chair beneath the large, now-bare live-oak which stands at its center. The sky is grey, but the sun is up, glowing brilliant white through the clouds. Drifts of fog lay between the dark ridges of the horizon and the nearby hills. Three young deer are feeding just below the circular edge of the knoll and stand rigid, staring watchfully as I sit down. They resume feeding as I avert my eyes and go inward. My anxiety of recent weeks has melted away.

I am part of all this.

———•••———

The quiet beauty of a grey winter morning in woods newly soaked by rains soaks into me as I watch a young, red-headed woodpecker going from branch to branch on the smaller live-oaks circling the knoll. Aware that India is only weeks away, I pray to be able to remember the quiet beauty of these fog banks and ridges, trees and deer, and the peace that is in them, when I am aching in the harsh, city-squalor of Calcutta, volunteering for Mother Teresa. For now, I breathe it all in, savoring the timeless space and comfort it gives me, grateful for being part of it once again.

Pausing at the temple door, I bow to this morning and to the forest life which has welcomed me back into the body of the Mother with a completeness I was lost without. The fog is lifting. Perhaps my separation was not twenty billion years deep after all. Perhaps it was simply the unbearable loneliness of a lifetime which was felt as forever. The Divine home I have craved so relentlessly was here all the time – shot through, ringing and singing in the living body of the world around me. *Hear, O Child of Light, the Lord our God, the Lord is One!* The life I thought of as abandonment and separation from the Divine home was its lap, the living body of Your Oneness breathing and holding me all along.

The pure, encompassing body of Your love reaches out to me and to us all in one unending, multifaceted, brilliant and consummate act of a Mother's tenderness. This is home: twenty billion years of painstakingly wrought beauty, each manifestation of which is an entrance into the endless array of Your delicately distilled care. You touch me every instant of my life, resonating in every molecule of Your sacred body of the world. Every touch of wind and sun and rain, every mountain, river or desert, every cloud or bird, each blade of grass, every tree in the city or the forest, every hopeful or aching human heart, and yes, every struggle and pain, is Your awakening kiss.

I didn't know.

Inside, I am alone. I bow face down on the carpet, with my arms extended straight out above me toward the altar. I am diving into You, receiving You.

Thank You, I whisper.

I lie like a child, crying, with the silent depth of Your love pressing gently into me. *You are my beloved.* You are the always comforting love of my life who has taken me in Your arms and heart forever in the very life You have given me. You hold me, asking for all the pain and loneliness I have been so afraid of surrendering. You never left me. You have given Your love in a lasting, forever way that I can always return to and drink from in the body of the world. My tears are of relief.

This lifetime of loneliness, of never feeling loved or given to, is ending.

—◆●◆—

Chapter XI

FIRE IN THE MORNING

Dove that ventured outside,   flying far from the dovecote:
housed and protected again,   one with the day, the night,
knows what serenity is,   for she has felt her wings
pass through all distance and fear   in the course of her wanderings.

The doves that remained at home,   never exposed to loss,
innocent and secure,   cannot know tenderness;
only the won-back heart   can ever be satisfied: free,
through all it has given up,   to rejoice in its mastery.

Being arches itself   over the vast abyss
Ah the ball that we dared,   that we hurled into infinite space,
Doesn't it fill our hands   differently with its return:
Heavier by the weight   of where it has been.

RAINER MARIA RILKE, "Dove that ventured outside"
Ahead of All Parting: Selected Poetry and Prose of Rainer Maria Rilke

I

NIGHT PSALM

You have brought me down.
Stripped me,
hammered me against the walls of mind and heart
until they shattered like glass,
and I fell,
cut, spinning, naked and alone,
through hole after opening hole
in the dark floor of eternity.

I love You
and the darkness
You have brought me through.
It is sweet, nourishing wine that I dive into,
and never hope to come out of,
now that I have stopped screaming.

I have fallen to the soft bottom.
It was a terrifying fall,
and I an infant,
but there is rest now
in nothingness
that holds the tender promise
of everything.

II

OF DEAD POETS AND LOVERS

Rereading Rilke, I fell in love again last night. I finally met a man whose range of soul, whose god-like hunger, fierce intelligence, and encompassing vision could see into, honor and celebrate the measure of the cup I have learned to drink from.

I can let go at another, deeper level now. I can tell the truth. John was merely the awakener, the trumpet call to the sleeping memory of my wanting. Besides not being one whit attracted to me, he was not looking for, did not trust, actively feared, and would never have given consent to being touched by the power of the fully released feminine in any woman. That was not what his life was about.

I could not let go because he embodied, more than any man I had ever met, at least the capacity for full engagement. His life energy is equal to it, if he ever someday were to make the leap into that life lived out with a woman.

Maybe the great love of my life had to be unrequited. With it unreturned, I was driven to the exploding cosmic root of my woman's need for love. With no opportunity to get stuck on love's object, all need, all desire were inflamed for their own sake. There was only the burning, the vast range of my wanting life, nakedly experienced in the pain of its denial. With no avenue for dissipation, with no focus or feeling stolen by the mundane, there was only the intensely clarified, heightening essence, the rarified, crystalline experience of meaning distilled out of and away from what the heart had set itself upon.

My heart, my soul, were after something infinitely larger that could only be attained by allowing the heart to run, unimpeded, whatever the cost. Until my wanting grew as large as the world itself, it could not be offered, as the world lost, into fire.

Will all I ever have be a dead poet? Has the mettle of my womanhood been distilled in these fires of wanting only to return and be offered again?

Might love appear one day, step out of the distance to run with me and, if it does, would I be ready for fulfillment?

Is the fulfillment of love, at a human level, even possible? Or will desire itself someday disappear, emptied and outgrown, lost in the love of burning?

III

FIRE IN THE MORNING

All meditation melts into this: there is fire in the breath. And having found it there, the only prayer is offering, offering, offering yourself into its sweet flames.

Life boils down, at last, to a simplicity. To the clear and certain knowing that you must give whatever is asked, whatever is taken, however painful and far from what you have imagined. You pray with fear and trembling, with the peeled knowing of what brought you here still fresh as opened flesh, for God to take away everything but this burning.

This is your communion now, to offer the tongue of all your longing, all desire, its burning life alive, in flames inside you, into a more encompassing, sweeter fire.

Desire is not to be repressed, or feared, but felt... the wildness of its life inwardly allowed, seen and tasted, until its deepest meaning in the heart's imagination is grasped. Only then can the cost of its loss, felt in the heart, in body and mind as searing heat, be offered into a holier, eternal and ascendant flame whose ecstatic life is both lamp and high altar.

IV

DYING TO FIRE

And she found, etched in her own heart, this inscription: *Seek, with all the relentlessness of the unimagined deep, the fullness of what you most love.*

But know also that there are times in every life when nothing is equal to the power of loss confronted. Times when your only hope will be to allow the ravaging heat, to stand still in the dead center of a fiery wind that is searing across the plane of your life, reducing the world you have known and loved to an ash-thin layer of blackened rubble.

The only effective recourse available to human beings at such times is self-offering. We offer all that we are into the storms of flame that have overtaken us. There, holding on to nothing, we surrender all of our knowing into this hot and rushing, beating breath of God. Releasing all that we are into the formless liberation of unknowing, we come quivering, stripped like a young sapling twig to moist, virginal whiteness. Offering our newly exposed and delicately fragrant tenderness as both fuel and frankincense on the flaming altar of a God whose loving, savage hand we failed to recognize, we give up. We finally surrender to the possibility that all our rights may be wrong, or at least gripped by a distorting essence; that all our wrongs may be right and, if welcomed as the living hand of revelation which everything surely is, might become an entrance to a new universe altogether.

For God help us and those around us if we resist the burning up of what life is sweeping away. For the God of the life we seek doesn't come only as light and grace, beauty and joy. Sometimes She comes as pure annihilation.

And if we find the courage to name the pain, to witness its fearsome life, to keenly observe the hysterical, thrashing death of care denied what it insists upon, the flames leap higher and hotter still, until, as we continue to offer ourselves and the pain of the world we are losing into them, everything becomes white heat. Dying to fire, we are purified burning, a molten miracle, ready to be recast in the healing hands and heart of the unknowable new we have surrendered to.

For the lighted thread at our feet by which we find our way is the streaming remnant of the hidden flame of our own heart. And the insistent heat of all that it will ultimately burn away is a lifeline leading us to precious and waiting, unseen fruit.

ACKNOWLEDGEMENTS

THERE are so many people–many more than I can name–whose light, being, heart and work have lifted me along the way, making my life and this book, with its 24 years of gestation, possible. I am grateful to every person who has been there as a beacon of inspiration.

To my daughters Julie and Lisa, and my granddaughter Aria: you have loved me so well, so constantly, deeply and tenderly. Your presence, feedback, clarity and proddings spur me on. Surrounding me in an ever-present circle of the Feminine, you give me the precious, safe base from which to move farther out into the world. Thank you for being who you are so authentically and courageously, for lifting me and calling me to account in the invaluable ways you do.

First and foremost beyond family is Sister Jacques (who later reclaimed her given name, Sister Ann Hardcastle). She walked into our first Senior English class in her nun's habit with the nobility, carriage, and command of a royal... with her keenly intelligent, fully embodied presence and self at play. Setting her books down on her desk, she met each of us eye to eye, silently and intently gathering our attention as we gave our names. Then she began at the beginning: vividly retracing the evolution of the Cosmos, through the birth our solar system and the formation of the Earth. She took us from the emergence of life as a single cell organism in the oceans, to its crawling onto land, through human evolution to hunter gatherer societies and the foundation of agriculture, before arriving at written language and literature. She was calling us awake. (How many classes of uniformed 17-year-old girls have you seen, utterly mesmerized, literally on the edge of their seats, in English class?) The whole sweep of time was present, dancing on my skin, alive with remembering that, somehow, I had been there, a part of it all!

Sister Jacques became a lifeline, the seed image of the kind of woman I wanted to become when, at 19, I decided to forever close the door on suicide as an option.

I also offer profound homage to Emelia and Harry Rathbun, and the leaders, classes, and ceremonies of Creative Initiative Foundation. Creative Initiative played a central role in firmly establishing me in the life of my soul. And to Teilhard de Chardin, Carl Jung, Joseph Campbell, Paramahansa Yogananda, and Baba Shuddhananda Brahmarchari: You have made endless contributions to my ability to find my way "through a glass darkly". (Baba, your presence, grace and guidance has been primary and precious, along with your constant prodding to write and publish my own work.)

To the great authors who have given me, and almost every woman I know, the foundational works on the Goddess and the Divine Feminine: you and your work have been critical to the lives of countless women, to my personal path, and to the richness I have been privileged to find. Special mentions go to M. Esther Harding (*The Way of All Women*); Jean Shinoda Bolen, M.D. (*Goddesses in Everywoman*); Merlin Stone (*When God Was a Woman*); Susan Griffin (*Woman and Nature*); Clarissa Pincola Estes, PhD. (*Women Who Run With the Wolves*). For the celebratory, intimate relationship with nature they have shared with us all and have modeled: Annie Dillard (*Pilgrim at Tinker Creek*) and Mary Oliver.

On a more personal note, a special thank you to Darci Nielson, for inviting me to bring something to read at your childrens' "Publishing Party" in June, 2017. What a catalyst that proved to be! Going through the manuscript again, after putting it away in despair of ever finding a way to resolve its structural problems, was just the prompt I needed—at just the right time—to take yet another stab at stripping it down to essence.

To my dear readers, Faye Powell, Leonora Perron, Ellen Davidson, and Kathleen Brigidina: I cannot thank you enough for your enthusiasm, invaluable feedback, and encouragement. They came at a vulnerable time when I might have put the manuscript back into storage and consigned it, yet again, to oblivion. Leonora, you are a beloved friend and mentor, and have been a mid-wife to my soul from the early 70s.

To Clare Dubois, TreeSisters, and its billion trees campaign, for the hope you have given rebirth to in me, by embodying the possibility–more powerfully than I have ever found elsewhere–of turning human consciousness back to a reverential relationship with nature, our source being, through the fully released Feminine.

And to the Earth, our precious Mother, from whom we derive and upon whom we depend for every aspect of our existence, my deepest bow… to the living being that you are, for the beauty and abundance with which you nurture us and call us home. May we learn, and quickly, to honor, emulate, and reciprocate your giving essence.

BIBLIOGRAPHY

Bozarth, Alla Renée. *Womanpriest: A Personal Odyssey* (Revised Edition). San Diego: Luramedia, 1988.

Bozarth, Alla; Barkley, Julia; and Hawthorne, Terri. *Stars in Your Bones: Emerging Signposts on Our Spiritual Journeys.* St. Cloud, MN: North Star Press of St. Cloud, 1990.

Campbell, Joseph. *The Hero with a Thousand Faces.* Princeton: Princeton University Press, 1973.

de Chardin, Pierre Teilhard. *Hymn of the Universe.* New York, Harper & Row Publishers, 1965.

Estes, Clarissa Pinkola, PhD. *Women Who Run with the Wolves.* New York: Ballantine Books, 1992.

Griffin, Susan. *Woman and Nature: The Roaring Inside Her.* New York: Harper & Row, 1978.

Harner, Michael J. *The Way of the Shaman.* New York: Harper & Row, 1980.

Kornfield, Jack. *A Path with Heart: A Guide Through the Perils and Promises of Spiritual Life.* New York: Bantam Books, 1993.

Mallasz, Gitta. *Talking with Angels: Budaliget, 1943.* Einsiedeln: Daimon Verlag, 1988.

Rilke, Rainer Maria; Mitchell, Stephen. *Ahead of All Parting: Selected Poetry and Prose of Rainer Maria Rilke.* New York: Random House, 1995.

Taylor, Dena; Sumrall, Amber Coverdale. *Women of the 14th Moon: Writings on Menopause:* Toronto: Crossing Press, 1991.

Yogananda, Swami Paramhansa. *Autobiography of a Yogi.* Los Angeles: Self-Realization Fellowship, 1974.

———◆•◆———

Seventy percent (70%) of all net sales proceeds from *Entering the River Naked: Field Notes from the Feminine Wild* are contributed to aid in raising funds for the charity TreeSisters, registered UK Charity No, 1149961.

TreeSisters is dedicated to reforesting the tropics and fostering nature-based feminine leadership globally to foster a shift in human consciousness to that of a restorer species.

For more information, visit: `www.treesisters.org`

———◆•◆———

CPSIA information can be obtained
at www.ICGtesting.com
Printed in the USA
LVHW081748131118
596976LV00030B/922/P

PELOPONNESE

ATHENS

Authors:
Anne Midgette,
Wolfgang Josing

An Up-to-date travel guide
with 45 color photos
and 13 maps

NELLES

Dear Reader: Being up-to-date is the main goal of the Nelles series. Our correspondents help keep us abreast of the latest developments in the travel scene, while our cartographers see to it that maps are also kept completely current. However, as the travel world is constantly changing, we cannot guarantee that all the information contained in our books is always valid. Should you come across a discrepancy, please contact us at: Nelles Verlag, Schleissheimer Str. 371 b, 80935 Munich, Germany, tel. (089) 3571940, fax. (089) 35719430, e-mail: Nelles.Verlag@t-online.de

Note: Distances and measurements, including temperatures, used in this guide are metric. For conversion information, please see the *Guidelines* section of this book.

LEGEND

★★ ★★	Main Attraction *(on map)* *(in text)*	
★ ★	Worth Seeing *(on map)* *(in text)*	
❽	Orientation Number in Text and on Map	
▪	Public or Significant Building	
▪	Hotel	
▪	Market	
✝ ♦	Church	
☪	Mosque	

Korfos *(Town)* / **Olympia** *(Sight)* — Places Highlighted in Yellow Appear in Text

◀ ◀ Int'l, Nat'l Airport

Olympos ▲ **2917** — Mountain (altitude in meters)

\ 13 / — Distance in Kilometers

☀ Beach

🌳 National Park

ℹ Tourist Information

∴ Ancient site

▬▬▬ National Border

═══ Expressway

─── Throughway

▬▬▬ Principal Highway

▭▭▭ Main Road

──── Provincial Road

──── Secondary Road

⛴ Ferry

$$$ Luxury Hotel Category

$$ Moderate Hotel Category

$ Budget Hotel Category

(for price information see "Accomodation" in Guidelines section)

PELOPONNESE – ATHENS

© Nelles Verlag GmbH, D-80935 München
All rights reserved
First Edition 2000

ISBN 3-88618-473-0 (Nelles Travel Pack)
ISBN 3-88618-750-0 (Nelles Pocket)
Printed in Slovenia

Publisher:	Günter Nelles	**Photo Editor:**	Kirsten Bärmann-Thümmel
Managing Editor:	Berthold Schwarz	**Cartography:**	Nelles Verlag GmbH
English Edition		**Lithos:**	Priegnitz, Munich
Editor:	Chase Stewart	**Printed By:**	Gorenjski Tisk

- S05 -

2

TABLE OF CONTENTS

GUIDELINES

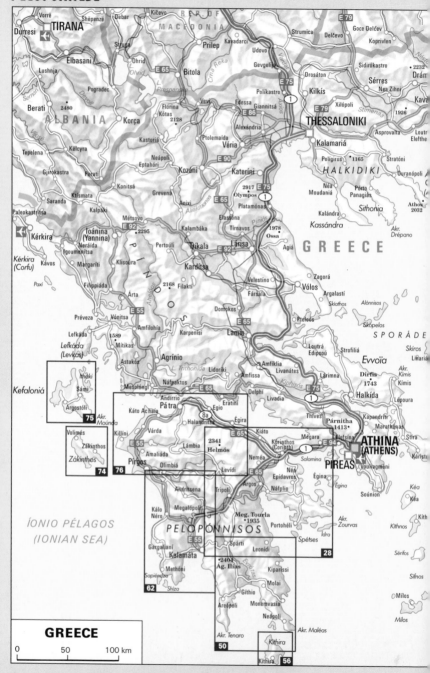

Note on Transliteration: The transliteration of place-names on the maps may vary from the spelling of the names in the text.

Paleolithic Period (30,000 B.C.)
Oldest traces of settlements in the Peloponnese.

Neolithic Period (6000-2500 B.C.)
Settlement centers include Tiryns, Lerna, Corinth and Nemea in the Peloponnese, and the Acropolis in Athens.

Minoan Period (2500-1450 B.C.)
The first advanced civilization in Europe blossoms on the island of Crete; the rest of the Greek Islands as well as the coasts are also influenced by the Minoans.
2000 B.C. The Ionians migrate to the Peloponnese and Attica. In the Peloponnese the Ionians are soon supplanted by the Achaeans.

Mycenaean Period (1580-1150 B.C.)
The first Achaean city-states originate in the Peloponnese, lead by Mycenae and Tiryns. Powerful kings also rule the Acropolis in Athens.

"The Dark Ages" (1150-900 B.C.)
The Dorians destroy the Achaean cities. Athens and Attica remain unaffected by the Doric migrations and continue to grow due to an influx of Ionian refugees.
Circa 950 B.C. Unification of Attica and creation of 12 districts (*demen*).

Geometric Period (900-700 B.C.)
So named because of the preponderance of geometric patterns that decorate pottery during this period.
776 B.C. First reference to the winners of the Olympic Games.
740-720 B.C. First Messenian War, during which Sparta conquers all of Messenia.

Archaic Period (700-500 B.C.)
Creation of the Greek city-state (*poleis*) and founding of numerous Greek colonies in the Mediterranean and Black Sea.

Persian War (490-479 B.C.)
Advancing Persian troops are soundly defeated by the Athenians in battles taking place at sea and on land.

Classical Period (479-338 B.C.)
As an insturment of the Delian League, democratic Athens becomes the hegemonic power in the Aegean. At the same time, aristocratic Sparta concentrates on strengthening its positions of power in the Peloponnese. Theater, philosophy and art flourish during this period.
431-404 B.C. *Peloponnesian War* between Athens and Sparta, and their respective allies. In the end Sparta is victorious, but all of the Greek city-states are greatly weakened.

The Calf-Bearer – an Archaic sculpture from the Acropolis in Athens.

Hellenic Period (338-147 B.C.)
338 B.C. In the *Battle of Chaeronea* the Macedonian King Philip II conquers all of the Greek mainland. After he is assassinated, his son Alexander (the Great) ascends the throne and soon sets out to conquer Asia and Egypt.
323 B.C. After Alexander's death, his generals begin an internal power-struggle for control and divide the empire amongst themselves. Attica and the Peloponnese remain Macedonian.

Roman Supremacy (146 B.C.-A.D. 394)
A.D. 50 St. Paul the Apostle travels to Athens and Corinth as a missionary.
A.D. 393 The final Olympics are held in Olympia.

Byzantine Period (395-1453)
395 Division of the Roman Empire into the Western and Eastern (Byzantine) Empires; Greece is now an insignificant province in the Byzantine Empire.
476 The Western Empire falls. The Byzantine emperor sees himself as the rightful successor.

Memorial to the Struggle for Liberation, near Kalávrita, the Peloponnese.

800 By crowning the Frankish king Charlemagne as ruler of the Roman Empire, Pope Leo III sets himself in clear opposition to the patriarchs and emperor of Constantinople/Byzantium, and lays the groundwork for the Schism of 1054.
1205 After conquering Constantinople, the Christian Crusaders (Knights of the Cross) storm the Peloponnese. Attica also falls under Frankish control. Venice erects secure military fortifications along the Greek coast.

1262 The Byzantine reconquest begins.
1430 Definitive end of Frankish rule in the Peloponnese, which is again under Byzantine control.
1446-60 The Turks conquer the Peloponnese; a few Venetian fortifications remain until 1540.

Ottoman Empire (1453-1827)
1453 The Turks conquer Constantinople; all of Greece, except Crete and the Ionian Islands, become part of the Ottoman Empire.
1456-58 The Turks take control of Athens.
1684-1715 The Venetians retain control of parts of the Peleponnese.
1821-27 Greek War of Independence.
1827 Russia, Great Britain and France intervene on the side of Greece (Treaty of London) and achieve victory against the Turkish-Egyptian fleet in the Battle of Navarino.

Since the Founding of Modern Greece in 1828
1828 Náfplio becomes the capital of Greece.
1832 The son of Bavaria's King Ludwig I, Prince Otto, is crowned King of Greece.
1834 Athens becomes the capital of Greece.
1863 King Otto I is forced to abdicate, an English-Danish dynasty governs Athens.
1874-76 Excavations in Mycenae.
1893 Corinth Canal opens.
1917 Greece enters WWI in support of the Allies.
1922/23 Greek attempts to conquer portions of Asia Minor are thwarted by Atatürk. During the resulting population exchange over 1.5 million Greeks are forced to leave Turkey, and more than half a million Moslems are forced to leave Greece.
1940-49 During WWII Greece is occupied by Germany and Italy. The civil war that follows, however, results in more deaths than the World War.
1967-74 Military dictatorship.
1974 Abolition of the Greek monarchy.
1981 Greece enters the European Union.
1996 Kostas Simítis, a member of the PASOK (Panhellenic Socialist Union) party, is elected to the post of Prime Minister.
1999 Inflation rate sinks to two percent, bringing Greece closer to its goal of joining the European Union's single currency.
2004 Athens is slated to host the modern era's XXVIII Olympic Summer Games.

ATHENS
Ancient and Modern Capital

Athens

**ACROPOLIS / AGORÁ / PLÁKA
MONASTIRÁKI
OMÓNIA SQUARE
SINDÁGMA SQUARE
VASSÍLISSIS SOFIÁS BOULEVARD
PIRAEUS**

Crowded and bustling, dirty and gritty, modern yet ancient, Athens is, for many travelers, something of an acquired taste. The transportation hub for all of Greece, it's a logical stopover for anyone flying in from abroad: here, you can recover from jet lag and visit the incomparable Acropolis before journeying on to the island paradise of your dreams. But there's no denying that returning to hot, sweaty Athens in the height of summer after a week or two on an island beach is like being doused abruptly with dirty water.

Still, Athens is a taste worth acquiring. A city which has seen many stages of historic evolution at wide intervals, it displays the layers of its past as clearly as the rings of a tree, open to the eyes of anyone who cares to look. Tiny gems of Byzantine churches stand matter-of-factly at the center of busy squares, parting the stream of car and pedestrian traffic as indifferently as a rock in a river; classical columns rear up from the dark coolness of cypress groves as if oblivious to the gray concrete of the roads and buildings around them. Many parts of the city bear witness to the years of the mid-19th cen-

tury, when a foreign king and his administration sought to create as rapidly as possible a capital that was worthy of the city's classical past and capable of holding its own with the other capitals of Europe: an ambitious transformation of a town that, in 1834, when the capital of the new country of independent Greece was transferred here from Nauplia, numbered all of 4,000 residents and about 300 houses. Other building booms followed: in 1923, when the city was hit with an influx of Greek refugees from Asia Minor, and in the years following World War II.

This juxtaposition of antiquity and youth is what gives Athens its unique character: on the one hand, it seeks to present the façade of calm serenity indicated by the gorgeous ruins on the Acropolis, still towering over the town; on the other hand, it has a kind of adolescent quality understandable in a city that has only existed, in its present incarnation, for some 150 years.

THE **ACROPOLIS

Nearly every town in ancient Greece had its own acropolis, a local hill supporting a "high city" of temples and shrines to the gods. But Athens' **Acropolis ❶** is so outstanding, and has preserved so much of its former glory, that it has become for

Previous Pages: Farm woman. In Athens' market hall. Left: The Minoan frescoes from Thíra are among the most beautiful items on exhibit in the National Archeological Museum.

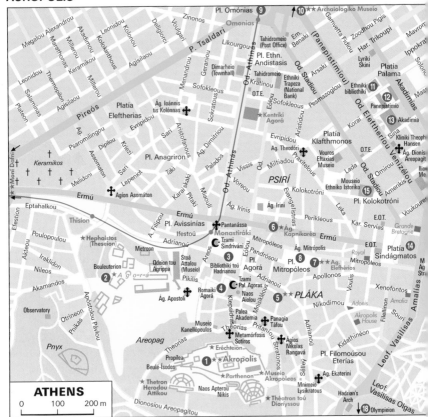

ATHENS

0   100   200 m

many visitors *the* Acropolis, the only one worthy of the name. In spite of the 17th-century Venetian shell that reduced the Parthenon, until then intact, to a noble ruin – the Turks were using the building to store ammunition at the time – and in spite of the arguably misguided ongoing course of renovations that are to return the buildings to their former splendor, the Acropolis of Athens remains perhaps the best place in Greece in which to appreciate what the classical world was all about.

The Acropolis, of course, didn't always have marble temples: in the 5th century B.C., many of the devotional structures were made of wood. These early structures fell victim to the Persian onslaught. Persia's growing might be-

came a concrete threat in 490 B.C., when King Darius led a huge force against Greece, only to be improbably defeated by the army of the much smaller city-state of Athens in a long battle on the plain of Marathon. Ten years later, Persia's King Xerxes led a punitive expedition against the upstart Athenians; this time, his forces overran the city of Athens and burned the Acropolis, but were ultimately defeated at Salamis (Salamína) by the already ascendant Athenian navy.

Scoring such decisive victories against what had seemed an invincible Eastern host gave the city of Athens a new self-confidence and pride with which it expressed both materially, in a navy which soon dominated the whole Aegean, and artisti-

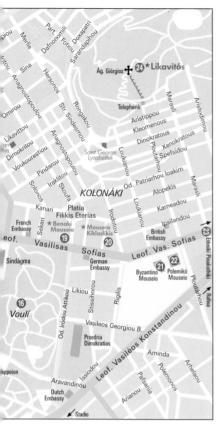

outbreak of the Peloponnesian War. On the left is the airy **Temple of Athena Nike**, built in 420 B.C. to commemorate the city's victory (*nike*) over the Persians (although the present edifice is a reconstruction). Thanks in part to the temple's fine vantage point – on a clear day (before the smog gets too heavy) you can see to Piraeus and the Saronic Gulf – there were sacred structures on this site long before the days of Pericles. Here, legend has it, King Aegeus watched for the return of his son Theseus from Crete, whither he had voyaged to free the city of Athens from its obligation to send 14 youths and maidens each year to feed the dreaded Minotaur. Theseus had arranged with his father to raise a white sail if he were victorious; but he forgot, distracted by his adventure with the princess Ariadne, and Aegeus, seeing a ship returning under blood-red sail, threw himself over the cliff in despair (though Cape Suninon might also have been the location).

A central legend of the Acropolis is that of Athens' patron goddess Athena; the story goes that she and Poseidon vied on this very hill to see who had more to offer Athens' citizens. Poseidon created a spring with a mighty blow of his trident; but Athena presented an olive tree, which was even more useful, providing people with food and oil, shade and wood, and the city therefore took on both her and her name. Athena was a virgin, or *parthenos*, and her main temple, which became known as the ***Parthenon**, remains one of the masterworks of world architecture. Forty-six Doric columns are arranged on a slightly curved base, and the columns themselves are slightly curved and slightly angled, all to create the illusion of perfect straightness. The Parthenon's sculptures were another of its glories. One recurring theme was the triumph of civilized man over the raw forces of nature and barbarism, a reflection of Athens' sense of supremacy after having defeated the Persians and brought the Greek

cally, in the temples which the city now erected on its Acropolis in thanks to the gods who had given them victory. Under its elected general, Pericles, Athens reflected its golden age in the buildings and sculptures of some of ancient Greece's greatest artists, notably Phidias.

The Acropolis was a sacred site, used in the context of rituals and religious festivals, especially the Panathenaic Festival, which began in 566 B.C. Festival processions snaked along the Panathenaic Way through the city and **Beulé Gate** (so named for the archeologist who "discovered" it) and up to the massive **Propylaea**, the entrance gateway to the site, an architectural masterpiece which was never completely finished because of the seas under its control. This was reflected less in the pediments (now lost), which illustrated Athena's birth and her contest with Poseidon, than in the 92 metopes, depicting scenes from the mythological battles between gods and giants, Greeks and Amazons, and centaurs and Lapiths. The theme carried over into the magnificent Parthenon frieze, a continuous band running around the building showing a Panathenaic procession very like the ones that would have taken place here: some of the finest moments are details of horsemen reining in their steeds or handlers controlling sacrificial oxen. The works were designed and supervised by the master sculptor Phidias, who was also responsible for the centerpiece of the Acropolis, the votive statue of Athena, fashioned of ivory and gold, standing some 10 meters high. Regarded in contemporary society as one of Phidias' masterworks, the statue vanished at some point in the early Byzantine period, and is known to us today only through copies.

Many of the other Parthenon sculptures and reliefs are gone, as well. Much of what wasn't destroyed by that fateful Venetian shell went off to London with Lord Elgin around 1800, and is now displayed in the British Museum. In light of the damaging effects of Athens' trademark *nefos*, or smog, on the fragments that remain, Lord Elgin's move may actually have been in the best interests of conservation, however defensible or indefensible from an ethical standpoint.

The on-site statues are only copies of the originals; in the *Acropolis Museum, you can see a few blackened, weathered lumps of rock that used to be proud reliefs of horsemen and coaches (the museum also displays some marvelous archaic sculpture that predates the Acropolis' current buildings: 6th century B.C.). Lord Elgin also removed one of the

Right: View of the Acropolis and the Likavittós from the southwest.

graceful caryatids from the south porch of the *Erechthion, the last of the triumvirate of great Acropolis buildings, constructed from 420 to 406 B.C. on the traditional site of Athena's first olive tree; although part of this disparate building was actually dedicated to the loser of the contest, Poseidon.

Another important aspect of religious ritual was theater; the plays of Aeschylus, Sophocles, Euripides and Aristophanes were performed as part of festivals to the god Dionysus (the standard format was a trilogy of tragedies followed by a satyr-drama; Aeschylus' *Orestaia* is the only complete trilogy to have survived). The marble elements of today's *Theater of Dionysus** were built in the 4th century B.C. to replace earlier structures of wood; the theater held 17,000 people, who were so captivated by the spectacle that some pregnant women miscarried out of sheer terror when Aeschylus' Furies made their entrance. More striking today, however, is the Roman Theater or *Odeion of Herodes Atticus**, a semicircular amphitheater with a masonry backdrop; dating from A.D. 161 and originally roofed over, it now hosts performances of the annual Athens Festival.

Athens was also a seat of government; the city council met on the nearby hill of the **Areopagus**, where, in A.D. 51, Saint Paul first preached to the Athenians. Farther to the west lay the **Pnyx**, where the combined citizenry of Athens assembled after the city's democratic process had been established and a minimum quota of 5,000 people – not counting, of course, women, children or slaves – was required to transact the business of government.

THE *AGORÁ AND **PLÁKA

Since its earliest history, Athens' bustling center has been located at the foot of the Acropolis. The city's ancient market- and meeting-place was the **Agorá ❷**; while the Acropolis' buildings repre-

sented the city's glory, it was in the Agorá that the actual day-to-day business of city life and government was carried out. Located here was the **Buleuterion**, or council chamber (now only a foundation); the **Stoá Basileios**, or Stoa of Zeus, housing the law courts; and the administrative center of the **Tholos**, where the Council of Five Hundred convened starting in around 500 B.C. A *stoá*, incidentally, is a roofed colonnade, although nothing remains of the Poikile Stoá at which Zeno taught here, and which gave the name to "stoic" philosophy; Socrates was also active in the Agorá.

Nor is there much left of the **Gymnasium** which was built on the site of the **Odeion of Agrippa**, which was later used as the University of Athens until that institution was closed in the 6th century A.D. Still in place, however, is the restored **Stoá of Attalos** (built around 150 B.C.), a kind of early shopping mall with stores running the length of its two stories, now an **Agorá Museum** filled with objects found here since excavations be-

gan in the 1930s. Running through the middle of the Agorá up to the Acropolis was the paved **Panathenaic Way**. One hub of this was the **Sanctuary of the Ten Eponymous Heroes of Athens**: these were the figures who gave their names to the 10 tribes of Attica; public announcements were rather prosaically posted on their pedestals.

There were other religious monuments here, as well: the **Sanctuary of Twelve Gods**; the **Altar of Ares** and the **Temple of Ares**, and the so-called Theseion, or **★Temple of Hephaistos**, a splendid Doric construction rising in near-perfection above the rubble of the past, the best-preserved classical temple in all of Greece. On the east side of the Agorá stands the red-roofed Byzantine church of **Agioi Apostoli** ("Holy Apostles"), built in the 11th century.

East of the Ancient Agorá is testimony to the days of the Romans. The **Library of Hadrian ❸** was built for that emperor in A.D. 132 near the site of the **Roman Agorá ❹**, an extension of the ancient

Agorá dating from around the time of the birth of Christ, which has yet to be completely excavated. A Roman landmark is the **Tower of the Winds** (Naos Aiolou), built in 40 B.C. and named for the reliefs of the eight winds that adorn the outer walls of this octagonal structure.

This area represents the border between ancient and modern, however, for the district closest to Athens' number-one tourist attraction has developed into a busy tourist center. Narrow pedestrian streets and stairways lined with neoclassical façades define the neighborhood known as **Pláka** ❺. In the evening, brightly-lit souvenir stands spill vases and statuettes into the streets; eager waiters try to lure passers-by onto the illuminated terraces of their restaurants; bouzouki music throbs from the interiors of eateries and bars. It's crowded, yet everything is rather convivial and won-

Above and Right: Ancient Athens (Pláka) and the modern city (Café Neon on Omónia Square) – a wonderful contrast.

derful, like a small-town fair: tourism notwithstanding, the Pláka has managed to retain some of the air of a village, especially in the afternoon heat when its streets and steps are populated only with dusty tendrils of wisteria and mangy cats. When Athens became the capital of Greece in 1834, the Pláka was basically all that there was of the city, and its neoclassical façades bear witness to the early attempts of King Otto to dress it up in appropriate style. Before that, this was the heart of the Albanian quarter: the neighborhood's name, which signifies a slab or paving-stone in Greek, is Albanian for "old," as in "old quarter."

Anyone who still has energy for museums after the wealth of ancient sites can stop in at the **Museum of Greek Folk Art**; the **Museum of Greek Folk Music Instruments**; or the **Kanellopulos Museum**, originally a private collection of *objets* from antiquity through to the 19th century, housed in a mansion from the latter period. There's also the **Children's Museum** on Kidathinéon.

But Pláka's main attractions remain its atmospheric tavernas and its music – all a little too touristy, perhaps, and a little too crowded, but who really cares in the soft air of a summer night illuminated with strings of colored lights in the trees overhead?

MONASTIRÁKI AND OMÓNIA SQUARE

After the last Turks left Athens in 1833, King Otto was able to construct the core of what remains today the heart of modern Athens. Helping him in this endeavor was an architect from home, Leo von Klenze, who tightened up the plans of a Greek-German architectural partnership, Schaubert and Kleanthes, outlining the grand squares (*platía*), boulevards (*leoforos*) and public buildings of the business center of today's city.

As its tourist paths combine ancient and modern, Athens' newer sections blend East and West. The spirit of the East is alive in the **Monastiráki** quarter,

the bazaar of the city during Ottoman rule, still crowded with little shops purveying all manner of wares to tourists. Strewn through here are some of Athens' finest Byzantine churches: ★**Kapnikaréa** ❻, on Ermú Street, an 11th- to 13th-century church to the Presentation of the Virgin, or the beautiful ★★**Ágios Elefthérios** (Little Mitrópolis) ❼, a 12th-century church built of fragments of ancient marble, now standing in the shadow of the flashier, but perhaps more shallow, 19th-century edifice of the **Ágios Mitrópolis** ❽, Athens' main cathedral.

The main north-south axis from Monastiráki to central **Omónia Square** ❾ is the **Boulevard Athínas**, the city's main drag, which runs past the ★**Central Market** (Kentrikí Agorá) and **City Hall**. "Unity Square" hardly projects the image of harmony that one might expect from the central spot of Athens, although there's a certain internationalism present in the foreign workers who crowd the kafeníon tables of this run-down, dirty district of anonymous office blocks.

From here, the parallel avenues of September 3 and October 28 run north through a district of boutiques (passing Athens' signature department store, **Minion**, which bears more than a touch of East Bloc character in its cheerless chambers) and fast-food stands toward one of Athens' greatest treasures, the ****National Archeological Museum ⑩**.

Gathered in this neoclassical building, behind its rectangle of dusty lawn, is the cream of archeology from all of Greece. Every visitor is resigned from the outset to the fact that it's impossible to do justice to the riches here in a single day, and yet every visitor is compelled to try. People who are heading for the Greek Islands may want to focus on relics from the islands, such as the frescoes from Minoan-Age Santorin, preserved Pompeii-like in a volcanic explosion around 1500 B.C. But even these will find it impossible to

Above: Garlic seller in front of the market hall.
Right: The impressive Corinthian columns of the Olympieion (Temple of Olympian Zeus).

bypass the golden mask of Agamemnon, found at Mycenae, or the magnificent bronze Striding God of Artemesion, whose authority is in no way diminished by the fact that scholars have not been able to agree on whether he is Poseidon in the act of hurling a trident or Zeus throwing a thunderbolt.

SINDÁGMA SQUARE AND VASSÍLISSIS SOFÍAS BOULEVARD

The hypotenuse of the triangle of modern Athens are the diagonal avenues of Panepistimíu and Akadimías, which lead down to Sindágma Square. On Panepistemíu, also called Eleftheríu Venizélou, are three public buildings constructed to show off the majesty of the new Greek state after independence: the **National Library ⑪**, the largest in the country; the **University ⑫**, with its frescoes of classical themes; and, most blatantly neoclassical of all, the temple-like **Academy of Athens ⑬**. All three buildings were designed by the Hansen brothers, two Danish expatriate architects, between 1839 and 1884.

Sindágma Square ⑭ is another focal point of modern Athens. For visitors, it's even more important than Omónia Square: near here are the main offices of the tourist authority, **EOT**; private buses depart from here for some out-of-town destinations; leading off the south end of the square is Filellínon Street, lined with travel agencies of all descriptions; and the range of eating and dining facilities runs the gamut from McDonald's on one side to the stately and very expensive Hotel Grande Bretagne on the other.

By the end of the year 2000, the city's extensive new subway line may even be completed, so that a subway stop will replace the large construction site which occupied the center of the square through much of the 1990s.

Dominating the square's eastern side is the **Parliament Building** (Sindágma),

Athens

built as King Otto and Queen Amalie's palace around 1840. Before this stands the **Tomb of the Unknown Soldier**, where visitors congregate to watch the changing of the guard of skirted *evzones* every hour on the hour in summer. The original seat of Parliament, just north of Sindágma Square on Stadíu Street, now houses the city's **Historical Museum** ⓯, devoted to Greece from the fall of the Byzantine Empire to the present day.

Extending around the current Sindágma building are the sprawling **National Gardens** (Voulí) ⓰, the city's main public park, complete with botanical gardens and a small zoo. Adjacent to the south is the park of the **Záppeion** ⓱, a congress and exhibition hall also built by one of the Hansens in the 19th century.

South of the Záppeion are the 13 remaining stately Corinthian columns of the **★Olympieion** (Temple of Olympian Zeus) ⓲, begun in 515 B.C. and not completed until A.D. 131. Thankful to the Emperor Hadrian for finally completing this lengthy project, the Athenians

erected the nearby **Arch of Hadrian** soon thereafter.

At the northeast of Sindágma Square broad **Vassílissis Sofías** begins; a boulevard of embassies, hotels and museums. The **★Benáki Museum** ⓳ houses what was originally a private collection of Byzantine and Islamic art and artifacts. Further down the street are the fruits of another private collector's activities, of particular interest to anyone heading for the islands: the **★Goulandrís Museum of Cycladic Art** ⓴. Originally from the island of Ándros, which they have also generously endowed with museums, the Goulandrís family made their fortune in shipping, something that enabled Nikolaus P. Goulandrís to build up one of the leading collections of Cycladic art in the world. Signature displays here are the white marble figurines, which in their simplicity and elegance of abstracted form presage Picasso by some four millennia.

The **Byzantine Museum** ㉑, on the same street, is essential to anyone's un-

derstanding of how the forms of classical Greek art evolved into the icons and gold mosaics of the Byzantine world, which dazzled Europe for centuries but today seem unfamiliar and impenetrable to many Western eyes. Yet from the stylization of classical funerary stelae, depicting the deceased in a few regular poses, it was but a short step to the stylization that governs the Byzantine icon. Some of the objects show the early church taking over and adapting "pagan" themes – Apollo morphing into Christ – as well as pagan sites: the Acropolis temples were used as sites of Christian worship. Next door, incongruously, is the **War Museum** ㉒, with weapons from the Stone Age to World War II.

Further along, on Vasiléos Konstandínos near where that street runs into Vassílissis Sofías, is the **National Gallery** ㉓. Born, like so many other Athens

Above: The Pantocrator Mosaic in the Dafní Monastery in the western part of the city is worth a detour.

museums, from private collections, it mainly documents the course of Greek art of the last few centuries, including early works by El Greco (who was born on Crete) and "The Greek Rider" by Delacroix, up to contemporary Greek artists.

To unwind from museum-going, head for a café in the exclusive residential district of **Kolonáki** behind the Benáki Museum. This is one of Athens' trendiest and most upscale neighborhoods, home to ambassadors and international businessmen, and with a fine array of boutiques for window-shoppers and serious purchasers alike. It nestles under *★Likavitós Hill* ㉔, which, legend has it, was a rock that Athena absent-mindedly dropped on the city on her way to attend to other business. When the Turks departed, the hill's steep slopes were barren, but a reforestation program begun in the 1880s left it blanketed in pines and cypresses. Anyone daunted by the steep footpaths can take the funicular, which departs from the corner of Aristípou and Plutárhou, up to the top, where in addition to stunning views

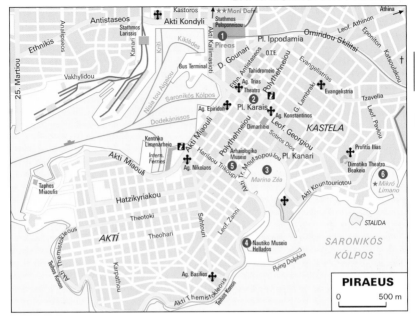

there's a restaurant, the church of Ágios Giórgios, and an open-air theater.

DAFNÍ MONASTERY

For those with a little extra time on their hands while in Athens, a visit to **★★Dafní Monastery**, 10 kilometers west of the city center, is recommended. The monastery's 5th-century church is world renowned for its wonderful Byzantine mosaics from the 11th century.

PIRAEUS (PIREAS)

Anyone traveling to the Greek Islands by ferry in summer knows Piraeus as a hot, crowded, confusing headache of a place, mobbed with cars and resounding with the stentorian horns of departing ferries. But Piraeus also includes exclusive residential districts, yacht harbors, tavernas, beaches and a couple of noteworthy museums; and knowing where these are can transform a stopover in Piraeus from a necessary evil to a pleasant adventure.

Piraeus has been Athens' harbor since the needs of this maritime power outgrew the capacity of Phaleron, the old port, in the 5th century B.C.; the Athenian general Pericles was responsible for the construction of the "Long Walls" that linked the port to the town. Later known as Porto Leone because of the lions that guarded the entrances to each of its three harbors, the town was built after plans by Hippodamos of Mílos, and his original plans were used again for the street layout of the modern city in 1834.

The **metro station ➊** is a short walk from the main ferry basin, where boats depart for the Saronic Gulf islands, the Cyclades, the Northeast Aegean Islands, the Dodecanese and Crete. In general, the atmosphere around here is one of utter chaos, so that it seems incredible that foreign visitors are ever able to find their way to the boats they want. On Sunday mornings there's diversion, albeit only augmenting the hustle and bustle, in the **flea market**, one of the largest in Attica, held in the streets around the Metro sta-

i

tion. Duck into the new large church of **Agías Paraskeví**, across the street from the harbor, for a moment of quiet.

Cutting over on Dimokratias or one of the parallel streets, you come to a still busy, but less touristy part of the city. Locals convene in the numerous coffee shops around the open square in front of the **Municipal Theater ②**. One can also linger in the yachting-oriented establishments around Piraeus' second harbor, **Marina Zéa ③**. Not only for pleasure craft, Zéa is the departure point for Flying Dolphins to some destinations. Green squares and lawns frame the banks of pleasure craft; at the southern end of the marina, in a modern building, is the **Maritime Museum ④**, displaying more than 3,000 years of Greek naval history.

The finest museum in Piraeus, and one of the finest in Athens, is the **Archeological Museum ⑤** on Harilaou Trikoupi, with the ruins of a classical theater in its back yard. Among the sculptures here is a lion that may be a copy of one of the original guardians of the harbor (which the Venetians carted off); other objects were found at the bottom of the harbor, such as fragments of a Parthenon-like frieze that was bound for Italy when the ship it was on sank. Most impressive of all are four stunning bronze sculptures from the 4th century B.C. and earlier, including an archaic Apollo and a figure of Artemis who has retained her original, absolutely naturalistic eyes that seem to gaze back into your own. Three of these bronzes were discovered in a warehouse where they were hidden before the sack of the city in 86 B.C.

On the other side of **Kastela**, the area's most exclusive residential district, Piraeus' third harbor, ***Mikró Límano** ("Small Harbor") ⑥, is lined with a row of bars, cafés and fish tavernas. On the other side of Mikro Límano are the beaches of Piraeus, although the sight of ferries and freighters does little to recommend the purity of their water.

ATHENS (☎ 01)

i **EOT** has several offices in Athens. The head office is at 2 Amerikis, tel. 3223111; there are branches at the airport's Terminal East and the National Bank of Greece on Sindágma Square, tel. 3222545.

PLANE: Construction is underway on a modern new airport in Spáta, 23 km east of the city, scheduled to open in March 2001 (for information call 3698300 or go to www.athensairport-2001.gr on the Internet). Until then, flights still arrive at and depart from the old airport at Ellinikó, 10 km south of Athens. There are two terminals: **Terminal West** for Olympic Airways flights, and **Terminal East** for everyone else. If you're flying in on another airline and making an Olympic connection to the islands, you'll have to take the airport bus from one terminal to the other.

BUS: **Express Bus 91** connects Omónia Square (downtown Athens) with Terminal East; **Bus 90** runs to Terminal West. To get from downtown Athens to Piraeus, take **Bus 40**. There's also an Olympic Airways bus from Leofóros Singroú 100 to Terminal West every half-hour. Buses to **Rafína** depart from smaller Terminal C, at Egyptou Square, tel. 8210872. For further information on long-distance buses, see "Guidelines" (p. 86).

METRO: The new, expanded Metro is supposed to open in 2001. Until then, the city's sole **metro line** remains a direct, quick and cheap option from downtown Athens (Omónia Square or Monastiráki) to Piraeus (20 minutes). **Public transportation information**: Tel. 185 (daily 7 am to 9 pm).

TAXI: Taxis in Athens are an adventure in themselves. If you're trying to hail one on the street, you have to shout out your destination as it drives by (sometimes with other passengers in the car). If you fit on the driver's itinerary, he'll stop; otherwise, he'll drive on imperviously.

Keep in mind that the meter rates rise once you leave the taxi's operating area. You can tell where the taxi is from by looking at the license plate: A is Athens (town), Z is the airport. Taking an A-plate taxi from Sindágma Square to the airport will run you around 4,500 drachmas; a Z-plate taxi costs about 1,500. So try to hail a cab from the area you want to go to.

You can save some of the headache by calling a radio taxi, such as **Athina 1**, tel. 9217942; **Kosmos** (downtown & Piraeus: tel. 4200042; Glifáda/airport: tel. 9642900); **Protoporia**, tel. 2221623; or **Piraeus 1** (Piraeus and downtown), tel. 41823335.

LEFT LUGGAGE: At the airport, you can leave and pick up bags round the clock across the street from Terminal West (Olympic Airways terminal). Some of the hostels around the Plaka will let you leave luggage, such as **Festos**, at Filellinon 18, tel. 3232455.

◼ ☺☺☺ **The Grande Bretagne**, Sindágma Square, tel. 3230251, fax. 3228034. Athens's leading hotel, may make you yearn for the more lowbrow Greek friendliness. **St. George Lycavitos**, 2 Kleomonos (Kolonaki), tel. 7290711, fax. 7290439; attractive, nice views, pool. **Amalia**, 9 Xenofontos (corner of Amalia), tel. 3237301, fax. 3238792, e-mail: hotamal@netor.gr, website: http://www. greekhotel.com/amalia/. Modern, pleasant hotel across from the National Gardens, down from Sindágma Square.

☺☺ Apollonos, between Sindágma Square and Pláka, has a number of hotels; try **Omiros** at number 15 (tel. 3235486, fax. 3228059) or **Hermes** at number 19 (tel. 3235514, fax. 3232073), with an in-house travel agency. **Hotel Museum**, 16 Bouboulinas, tel. 3605611, is right behind the Archeology Museum. **Athenian Inn**, 22 Haritos (Kolonaki), tel. 7238097, fax. 7218756, was once patronized by Lawrence Durrell.

☺ There are some cheap hotels around the Pláka, but the **Hotel Royal**, Mitropoleos 44, tel. 3238596, has some high-ceilinged rooms with showers and a distant sense of (much-) faded elegance. Pretty **Pension Adonis**, Kodrou 3, tel. 3249397, and **Akropolis House**, Kodrou 6-8, tel. 3223244, are more up-market and higher priced.

❎ *EXPENSIVE:* **Gerofinikas**, Pindarou 10, Kolonaki, tel. 3636710, among Athens' finest. **Apotsos**, Panepistimiou 10 (Sindágma), tel. 3637046, long-time haunt of upscale Athenians.

MODERATE: **O Thespis**, Thespidos 18 (Pláka), tel. 3238242; pleasant outdoor dining with views of the surrounding countryside; quite good standard food. **Strophi**, Rovertou Galli 25 (Propyleon), tel. 9214130. A rooftop terrace with Acropolis view, decent food; but crowds of tourists lead to harried, peremptory service. **Ithaki**, Agías Filotheis 2 (Mitropoleos Square); a great location under the trees, near the cathedral. **Sokrates' Prison**, Mitsaion 20 (Makriyianni), tel. 9223434, perennially and deservedly popular.

BUDGET: **Peristeria**, Patroou 5, tel. 3234535, simple taverna, standard repertoire, no décor, very popular with Greeks.

🏛 **Acropolis Museum**, tel. 3236665. Open Mon 11 am to 2:30 pm, Tue-Sun 8:30 am to 2:30 pm, until 8 pm in summer. **Ancient Agora**, tel. 3210185. Open 8:30 am to 3 pm, closed Mon. **National Archeology Museum**, Tositsa 1/Patission 44, tel. 8217717. Open Mon 10:30 am to 5 pm, Tue-Sun 8:30 am to 3 pm, in summer until 8 pm. **Museum of Cycladic Art**, Neophitou Douka 4, tel. 7228321, fax. 7239382. Open 10 am to 4 pm, Sat until 3 pm, closed Tue and Sun. **Byzantine Museum**,

Vassílissis Sofiás 22, tel. 7231570. Open 8:30 am to 2:45 pm, closed Mon. **National Gallery/Alexander Soutsos Museum**, Vasiléos Konstantínu 50, tel. 7211010. Open 9 am to 3 pm, Sun 10 am to 2 pm, closed Mon. The marvelous **Benáki Museum**, Koumbari 1/Vassílissis Sofiás, tel. 3611617, is unfortunately closed for renovations at least until the summer of 2000.

🎭 The **Athens Festival** takes place in July, with outdoor performances in the amphitheater of Herodes Atticus. Festival Office: 4 Stadiou, tel. 3221459.

🧵 The **National Welfare Association** shops feature hand-made crafts, from icons to weaving to needlepoint pillow-cases. Ipatias 6 (corner Apollonos), tel. 3211761, or Vassílissis Sofiás 135, tel. 6460603. The **Benáki Museum** and the **Museum of Cycladic Art** both have large museum shops, with reproductions and a broad selection of books (the shop in the Benáki Museum is open despite the renovation work). **Compendium Bookshop**, Nikis 28 (Sindágma), tel. 3221248, is an English bookstore with magazines, a used book exchange, and lots of books about Greece.

➕ **Police**: 100. **Ambulance**: 166. **SOS Medecins** (24-hour medical service): 3310310. See "Guidelines" (p. 88) for more emergency numbers.

PIRAEUS (☎ 01)

📱 See above for information on public transportation. Taxis from downtown Athens will run you about 2,000 drachma. The metro stop is right across from the main harbor.

Some of the Flying Dolphins for the Saronic Islands and Sporades leave from Marina Zéa, on the other side of the Piraeus peninsula (about a 500-drachma taxi ride from the main port).

Express Bus 19 links Piraeus and the Ellenikó Airport (both terminals).

◼ ☺☺ **The Park Hotel**, Kolokotroni 103, tel. 4524611, fax. 4524615, "all mod cons" and an upscale air, on a central square not far from either port.

☺ **Noufara Hotel**, Iroon Politechniou 45, tel. 4115541, fax. 4134292. Clean, central, on the main north-south artery.

❎ **Dipylo**, Kodrou 3/Syndagmatos 34, tel. 4172105. Impressive, appealing selection of Greek dishes, prepared and served with both sophistication and comfort. Dinner only.

M **Archeological Museum**, Charilaou Trikoupi 31, tel. 4521598, open 8:30 am to 2:45 pm, closed Mon. **Maritime Museum**, Akti Themistokleous, tel. 4516822, open Tue-Fri 9 am to 2 pm, Sat 9 am to 1 pm, closed Sun & Mon.

THE ISLE OF PELOPS

CORINTH / EPIDAUROS

ARGOLIS / NÁFPLIO

TIRYNS / ARGOS / MYCENAE

ARCADIA

LACONIA / MISTRÁS / KÍTHIRA

MANI PENINSULA

MESSENIA

ÉLIS / OLYMPIA

ACHAEA

Peloponnese

THE PELOPONNESE

No other region of the Greek mainland has as varied a landscape as that of the Peloponnese. The peninsula measures almost 160 kilometers across at its widest point, is 190 kilometers long, and covers a land area of 21,440 square kilometers. The natural beauty and variety of the Peloponnesian landscape is enhanced by the legacy of ancient Greece, which left behind a wealth of ancient monuments and ruins that is unmatched anywhere else.

The peninsula is called the *Peloponnese* (Island of Pelops) after the mythical King Pelops, son of Tantalus, grandson of Zeus, and father of Atreus, the first king of Mycenae. As a Roman province it was known as *Achaea*. Its Byzantine name, *Morea*, was used from medieval until relatively recent times.

Today, the Peloponnese region is divided into seven districts: Corinth, Argolis, Arcadia, Laconia, Messenia, Élis and Achaea. The natural boundaries of these districts largely correspond with those of antiquity, however, the district of Corinth was once part of the ancient region of Achaea.

Left: The amphitheater in Epidauros is famous for its amazing acoustics. Whispers from the orchestra can be plainly heard at the back.

CORINTH

The district of Corinth includes the southern shore of the Gulf of Corinth from the city of Corinth to Dervéni, the Killíni mountain range, which reaches a height of 2,376 meters, and the Saronic Gulf coast as far eastwards as Néa Epídavros. Beyond the isthmus of Corinth, on the land bridge to Attica, the Geránia Mountains and the peninsula at their foot are also part of Corinth.

Highway 8 from Athens enters the Peloponnese across a narrow bridge high above the ****Corinth Canal ❶**. Huge parking lots, stalls selling *souvláki*, cafés and souvenir shops are evidence of the bridge's popularity as a scenic outlook. From the **bridge**, near the eastern end of the canal, you can look down into the channel that was carved 60 meters into the earth to link the Gulf of Corinth with the Saronic Gulf. Construction was completed in 1893. Just under 6.3 kilometers long, the canal is 8 meters deep and 23 meters wide.

The port and prefectural capital, **Corinth ❷** (*Kórinthos*) is near the eastern end of the canal. After an earthquake in 1858, the city was rebuilt at its present location, away from the site of ancient Corinth – only to be destroyed by another earthquake in 1923. Today, it is merely a

EASTERN PELOPONNESE

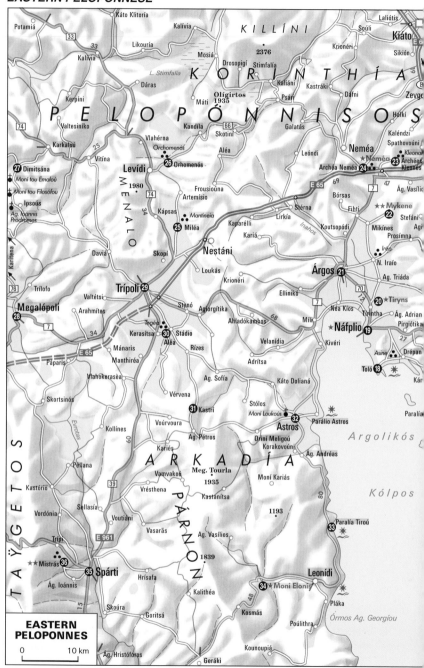

provincial city, without any features that are of great interest. From here, a road runs eastwards along the shore to the western entrance of the canal. To the right of the canal you can see two parallel grooves cut into the rock. These are the remains of the *diolkos*, or **slide way** from ancient times; tracks along which ships were hauled across the isthmus.

*ANCIENT CORINTH

*Ancient Corinth ③ lies eight kilometers west of the new city (signposted: *Ancient Korinthos*). Corinth saw its first great flowering under Doric settlers at the turn of the 8th century B.C. It reached its peak around 630-590 B.C., under the firm rule of Periander, one of the Seven Wise Men of antiquity. It was here, during this period, that the design of the Doric temple was perfected. The city was also renowned for the artistry of its pottery and bronze work. In 146 B.C., Corinth was destroyed by Mummius, and this set the seal on the Roman conquest of Greece.

Julius Caesar rebuilt the city in 44 B.C., and under Augustus it became the capital of the Roman province of Achaea, and thus the most important city in all of Greece. In A.D. 51 and 52, St. Paul the Apostle visited Corinth and preached against the luxurious life of its citizens, who at the time may have numbered as many as 300,000.

Near the large parking lot in front of the excavations you can see the **Theater** (5th century B.C.) and opposite it, the **Odeion** (1st century A.D.). Some 500 meters to the north are the ruins of the **Asclepion**; and there is a small **museum** behind the western entrance to the site.

Next to the museum are the remains of a **colonnaded temple** dating from the time of the Roman Empire, and which was probably dedicated to Octavia. Walking down the left-hand side of the site, you will pass through an iron gate and

into the middle of the **western row of shops**. The Agorá is now directly in front of you. Along one edge once stood six small Roman **podium temples**; their ruins are all that you now see. In front of these, a circular base with the stumps of columns is all that is left of the **Monument to Babbius**.

If you turn left and make your way between the row of shops and the temples, you will come to the foundations of the **Temple of Hera**. Behind this is the **Well House of Glauca**.

Standing on a nearby rock pedestal is the **Temple of Apollo**. This austerely designed building (dating from around 540 B.C.) is one of the oldest remaining temples in Greece. It is an early example of the mature Doric style, and seven of the original 90 massive monolithic columns, as well as parts of the entablature, are still standing.

Above: The columns of the Temple of Apollo in ancient Corinth. Right: The Spring of Peirene at the edge of the Roman Forum.

In the Forum

From the temple floor you can look out over the whole Agorá, or, to be precise, the Roman **forum**. Descend a flight of steps through a **colonnade** to come to the **northwest row of shops**. A tall structure still intact up to its vaulted roof, it reveals the architecture of what was once a row of 15 trading houses. Crossing the wide central square of the market, you pass the base of an altar and arrive at the **Bema** or the Agorá's speakers' platform. The Bema is flanked on either side by the **central shops** which line the lower forum.

The upper forum is bordered, for 165 meters of its length, by the colonnade of the **South Stoa** and the administrative buildings behind it. All 71 Doric front columns and 34 Ionic central pillars of the stoa are preserved, complete or in part. The most impressive administrative building in the upper forum is the oval **Bouleuterion** (city hall); the lower parts of its walls and its benches have been preserved.

You can now cross the massive base of a **circular monument** and descend to the central square. The **starting lines** for the stadium race can be seen in front of the long **Julian Basilica** (1st century A.D.). On a raised terrace, walk to the left around the basin of the Fountain of Peirene, which is shaped like a clover leaf, and you reach the **Propylaea**. To the left of the gate, the marble **Façade of the Captives** forms the front of a two-story **court basilica** along the well-preserved pavement of **Lechaion Street**, which leads to the harbor on the Gulf of Corinth.

The courtyard of the **Spring of Peirene** is entered through a Doric archway. This place was very well known in ancient times, and was associated with the legend of Peirene who, mourning the death of her son, wept so copiously that she ultimately turned into a fountain. The two-story curved building with apses dates, in its present form, from the late 2nd century A.D. It was founded by Herodes Atticus. The spring water fills three deep basins by the cliff behind it. Balustrades, with small Ionic columns on top, divide the openings in the rock above the basins into six chambers. Their walls are painted (1st century A.D.). Along Lechaion Street towards the exit, to the right of the colonnaded courtyard, you will find the **Sanctuary of Apollo**, followed by **latrines** with their seats still in place, and the Roman **Baths of Eurycles**.

Acrocorinth

From the village of **Paleá Kórinthos** a small road near the archeological site leads three kilometers up to the acropolis of **Acrocorinth ❹** (576 meters). As you drive up, you can see the small Frankish fortress of **Pendeskoúfi** (from the French: *Mont Escovée*) on a hill to the right. From the parking lot, a footpath leads through three tiered gates to the 2.5-kilometer-long encircling walls of Acrocorinth. The walls, towers and gates of the fortress reflect a mixture of Byzantine, Frankish, Venetian and Turkish styles, built on ancient foundations. The right-hand tower at the **upper gate**, built into the main wall, dates mainly from the Hellenic period. The view from the surrounding walls gives the best impression of the **ramparts**, with their casements and battlements. Most of the buildings within the ramparts have been destroyed. A wide path up from the main gate passes a few wells and a dilapidated 16th-century **mosque**. It ends at the steep cliff by the south wall, on the ridge between the twin peaks of Acrocorinth.

In front of some ruined Turkish barracks, 400 meters to the left, narrow steps lead down to the gloomy cavern of the **Upper Spring of Peirene**. A Hellenistic decorated pediment stands on columns in front of the basin.

Loutráki and Heraion

An avenue lined with eucalyptus trees leads from the western end of the Corinth

Peloponnese

isthmus, across a submersible pontoon bridge, and to the sophisticated seaside and health resort of **Loutráki** ❺ (eight kilometers from Corinth). Its hot springs have been used since ancient times and are famous for curing liver problems and arthritis (there are baths at the end of the main street, and in many hotels). To the west, the promenade beside the long crescent of sand is the finest in Greece.

Leaving the town, the road climbs up to **Perahóra** ❻ (10 kilometers). The road on the left leads down to the almost circular **Lake Vouliagméni** (25 kilometers). It is separated from the sea by a narrow land bridge through which a small canal has been cut. The ruins of ancient *Pera Chora* are scattered along a sandy track that leads up to a flat-topped hill. The track ends at a lighthouse on the high cliffs of **Cape Iréo** ❼, located 28 kilometers from Corinth.

Above: The path to the fortifications of Acrocorinth. Right: A familiar picture all over Greece – a shoemaker in his workshop.

In a small cove at the foot of the cliffs, on six terraces above a narrow strip of beach, are the remains of the ***Heraion** of Pera Chora, the shrine of Hera Limenia. On the highest terrace you can see the foundations of a temple dating from the 8th century B.C.; beneath it, there is a beautifully preserved well dating from the Hellenic period. There are also ruins of a stoa and two other temples in a square right beside the sea.

Isthmia and Kenchreai

To drive along the coast of the Saronic Gulf, head from Corinth towards the canal, turning right towards the eastern end of the canal before crossing the bridge. Next to the mouth of the canal is the village of **Kirás Vrísi**, on the site of ancient **Isthmia** ❽ (eight kilometers from Corinth). As the home of the Isthmian Games (*Isthmien*), established no later than 582 B.C. and held every two years, Isthmia was one of the four great centers of Panhellenic competition, along with Oympia,

Delphi and Nemea. The **museum** in the center of the village displays rather confusing plans and views of the hilly archeological site. Among the displays of small sculptures, vases, jewelry, weapons and coins, a few objects stand out: large, delicately colored glass pictures, including a rare wooden door, a harbor view on the back wall of the gallery, and the winch from an ancient block and tackle.

Behind the museum in the center of the shrine are the ruins of the **Temple of Apollo** (5th century B.C.). The walls of the Byzantine **canal fortress** (6th century) are very impressive. The **stadium** is situated opposite it, on the right.

The coast road leading south actually reaches the sea for the first time below the modern village of **Kehriés** ❾ (10 kilometers). The bay was the site of **Kenchreai**, Corinth's ancient port in the Saronic Gulf; through the waves, you can see the half-submerged foundations of ancient warehouses and an early Byzantine basilica. Further on, the charms of the welcoming seaside resorts of **Loutró Elénis** (15 kilometers) and **Almirí** (14 kilometers) are diminished by the proximity of nearby refineries and shipyards.

Highway 70 climbs through foothills of the central mountains into Argolis, and on to ancient Epidauros.

EPIDAUROS

Typical of new settlements that were built during the Middle Ages, the town of **Néa Epídavros** (New Epidauros) is defensively perched on a hill overlooking the sea and its beaches. In 1821, the village hosted the first Greek National Assembly.

It is the coastal resort of **Paléa Epídavros** ❿ (Ancient Epidauros) that gave its name to the nearby Shrine of Asclepius of Epidauros. During the summer the town is a lively resort, with ferries to Égina and Piraeus. It is on the southernmost of the two small peninsulas

facing the beautiful bay that you find the ancient settlement of Epidauros.

From Paléa Epídavros, Highway 70 heads west through hilly country towards Ligourió. Just before the village, a smaller road leads to the parking lot for the ****Shrine of Asclepius of Epidauros** (13 kilometers).

The cult of the healing god Asclepius, which originated in Thessaly, ousted an earlier cult of Apollo in this remote valley in the Archaic period. From Epidauros, the worship of Asclepius spread throughout Hellas. Both the shrine and its priest-physicians reached the height of their fame in the 4th and 3rd centuries B.C. A sophisticated health resort with hospitals, sanatoria and hotels, it was also a center of worship. The sick were not only offered medical treatment according to the current rules of orthodox medicine, but also "magic" rituals of discourse and exorcism – early forms of psychotherapy!

The main attraction at Epidauros is the **theater**, the most beautifully preserved in Greece (4th/3rd century B.C.). Built into

a steep hillside and overlooking a green landscape, its shell-shaped auditorium (*cavea*) rises 55 tiers and is divided into two blocks. The theater can seat up to 14,000 people, and still serves as a venue for summer festival performances of classical Greek tragedies. The paths on both sides (*parodoi*) to the circular orchestra, in front of the stage, pass through side gates. The theater is especially famous for its amazing acoustics; whispers from the orchestra can be clearly heard in the furthest rows.

In the Shrine of Asclepius

Beyond the rear façade of the museum, you'll come upon the raised foundations of the **Katagogion**, which was a hostel for visitors to the health resort. Adjacent to it on the left are some baths, and in the center are the ruins of a Roman **odeion** inside an older **gymnasium**. Beyond the

Above: The Tholos, or domed tomb, at the Shrine of Asclepius of Epidauros.

rows of trees on the western edge of the site, on a lower level to the left, is the **stadium**. The pathway beside the trees leads to the L-shaped enclosure of the **Temple of Asclepius**. Next to it stands the **Tholos** (ca. 360-320 B.C.), the most important building on the site. Its circular base (22 meters in diameter) with concentric ambulatories has been preserved. The rotunda, like its sister building in Olympia, was designed by Polyclitus. Behind the Tholos and the temple stood two **stoas**, used as rest halls for the temple's healing sleep. The small **museum** gives a clear idea of the original appearance of the site, with reconstructions of the Tholos and Temple of Asclepius, as well as some beautifully worked Corinthian capitals.

THE COASTS OF ARGOLIS

Heading south from the sanctuary in Epidauros, you can follow the entire curve of the Argolis coast. The road forks off to the left near **Trahiá** (17 kilometers from Epidauros), and just beyond **Ano**

Fanári it drops sharply down to the sea. Beyond **Psífta** (turnoff after 51 kilometers), follow a dead-end road out to the peninsula of **Méthana**. Crossing a dry lake bed, then driving over a narrow causeway, you reach the peninsula itself, which is in fact an extinct volcano 743 meters high. Pools reeking of sulfur and fitted out with bathhouses, just before the main town of **Méthana** ⑪ (13 kilometers from the turnoff; also a ferry port for Égina and Piraeus), quickly attest to its volcanic origins.

Continuing south along the mainland road for another three kilometers, a fork to the right leads the short distance to the village of **Trízina** ⑫ (*Damalá*), the site of ancient **Troizen** – mythical birthplace of the hero Theseus. In Frankish times it was a bishopric, and it was in the modern village that the "Constitution of Troizen" was passed by the Third Greek National Assembly in 1827. On the ruined site below the isolated **acropolis hill**, with its Frankish **tower**, are the remains of a number of **temples**, as well as the ruins of the **bishop's church** and **palace** and Byzantine **chapels**.

Excursion to Póros

The main road continues along the coast to **Galatás** (63 kilometers from Epidauros), a village surrounded by citrus plantations. Across a calm strait that is only about 300 meters wide is the island of **Póros**, which you can reach by ferry. **Póros** ⑬, the island's pretty capital, built on a hammer-shaped peninsula below the island's hills, is a popular vacation spot among Athenians. Moored off the first **arsenal** of the Greek Navy (1830; now the Naval Academy) is the historic cruiser *Avérof*, which saw action in the Balkan Wars of 1912/13.

Four kilometers east of the capital is the **Zoodóhos Pigí** monastery of the Virgin Mary with its richly decorated *templon*, which is well worth visiting.

Temple of Apollo ruins can also be seen on a hilltop in the north of the island.

Southern Beaches

Beyond Galatas, the road goes through hilly country round the eastern tip of the Argolis Peninsula, at some distance from the sea, and swings towards the south coast. Between **Pigadiá** (100 kilometers from Epidauros) and **Thermisía** (105 kilometers), the shore is lined with beaches, and you can see the islands of Hydra and Dokós. Because it is so close to Athens, the entire southern coast, as far as Portoheli, is a popular holiday area and is becoming increasingly built up with vacation homes.

The most attractive resort in the area is **Ermióni** ⑭, at least in the old town center. It stands on a headland covered with pine woods, between two bays crossed by colorful fishing boats. There are large hotel complexes in the vicinity. Ermioni is the ferry port for the island of Hydra.

Excursion to *Hydra

The people of the rocky island of *Hydra ⑮ (Modern Greek: *Idra*) have always been seafarers. It is to the sea that they owe their past wealth and their more recent reputation for tourism.

Hydra, the island's only settlement and town of the same name, is laid out like tiers in a theater, hidden from view from the open sea, around a safe natural harbor. During the late Ottoman period it was the main port of the Greek merchant fleet. Ships from Hydra also formed the main contingent of the Greek fleet in the War of Independence.

The **captains' houses** above the harbor, built by Italian architects in the 18th century, attest to the prosperity of bygone seafarers and shipowners. They make this one of the loveliest places in Greece.

In earlier years, Hydra attracted mainly artists (like Mykonos, in the Cyclades).

Peloponnese

Many of their houses have now changed hands and been turned into luxurious vacation homes; even the tourists on Hydra tend to be rather wealthy. A number of the island's post-Byzantine **monasteries** can be reached on foot or by boat. The 18th-century **Church of St. Mary**, on the harbor in Hydra, is worth a look.

Even the green, traffic-free island of **Spétses 🔞**, with its beautiful beaches (Anárgiri, Paraskeví), made its money through shipping and shipbuilding; but the defining feature in its identity was the role it played in helping to launch the fight for independence – it was the first naval fleet to fly the Greek flag after the outbreak of the rebellion on the Peloponnese in 1821.

One heoine is the island's own "lady admiral" Laskarina Bubulína, who won a number of battles for the Greek side, and whose bones are preserved in the island's

Museum of Local History and Culture in the town of Spétses.

Hills and Lagoons

From Ermióni, the coast road leads to **Kósta** (133 kilometers from Epidauros) on the southern cape of the Argolis Peninsula (ferries to the island of Spétses). Heading north of Kósta, you'll pass through the resort of **Portohéli 🔞** (ferries to the Saronic Islands and Piraeus). This overdeveloped town at the southwestern corner of the Argolis holiday coast lies in a deep cove and has a yacht marina. From here, the road turns away from the sea and runs through the high hills behind **Kranídi** and **Dídima**, 148 and 164 kilometers from Epidauros respectively.

In **Neohóri** you can turn left and head, via **Karnezéïka**, back to the sea. The Argolis west coast is not particularly attractive here, with marshy lagoons and grey beaches. Just past **Drépano** the beaches become much more inviting. Within sight of the tall hotels of the ex-

Above: Since cars are banned on Hydra, donkeys serve as baggage carriers. Right: Playing backgammon in one of Náfplio's lanes.

pansive resort of **Tólo** ⓲ (219 kilometers) you'll reach a small headland with well-preserved walls from the Hellenistic period; the ruins of ancient **Asine**. The coastal excursion from Epidauros (232 kilometers) ends in Náfplio.

ARGOLIS

The Argolis Peninsula is home to Greece's richest cultural heritage. The most highly developed region in Hellas during the Dorian period, it also flourished during the Classical age. Some of Greece's most impressive archeological sites are clustered here – Mycenae, Tiryns and Epidauros. Argolis is a small peninsula in the northeast corner of the Peloponnese; its capital is Náfplio.

*NÁFPLIO

With its neoclassical design, ***Náfplio** ⓳ (*Nauplia*) is the most beautiful town on the Greek mainland. Towering over the enclosed site are the hill of Acro-

nauplia (85 meters) and the rocky bluff of Palamídi (230 meters).

The site, in its protected position, was already occupied in the Mycenaean period. After the 7th century B.C., *Nauplia* was the harbor of Argos. It was abandoned in Roman times and resettled under Byzantium. From 1246 to 1387, the town was ruled by the Franks. Under Venetian occupation *Napoli di Levante*, as it was known, was, until 1540, one of the main fortresses in the Peloponnese. From 1828 to 1834, the city was the first capital of modern Greece. The architecture of the town reflects its turbulent history. Dominating from above is the menacing Venetian fortress of **Palamídi** (1711-14). The picturesque fort of **Its Kalé** (from the Turkish *Üç Kale*, "Three Castles," after its Byzantine, Frankish and Venetian fortifications) is perched above the city on **Acronauplia**. Nestled below these is the town itself, laid out on the Venetian plan, and filled with neoclassical buildings. The small island fortress of **Boúrdzi** (15th century) protects the harbor. In the

summer, it is one of the most cosmopolitan vacation spots in the Peloponnese.

In the Streets of the Old Town

The checkerboard of narrow streets in the historic town center, which runs parallel to the commercial wharf, is bordered by Od. Bouboulínas. At its heart is the elegant **Pl. Sindágmatos**, where a handsome Venetian administrative building (1713) now houses the **Municipal Museum**; opposite this, a **mosque** at the other end of the square is now a movie theater. From here, Od. Vasiléos Konstandínou leads to the palm-lined **Pl. Navárhon**. A neoclassical building on the right was the first **high school** in modern Greece (1833); the building opposite was the **royal residence** of King Otto, who first set foot on Greek soil in Náfplio after arriving from Bavaria in 1833.

Above: The island fortress of Boúrdzi in Náfplio's harbor. Right: The Greek salad – prepared fresh in every Taverna

Above **Pl. Sindágmatos**, the streets of the Old Town climb to the Acronauplia. On the corner of the first narrow street above the main square (**Od. Staïkoú Staïkopoúlou** – with many tavernas), immediately next to the museum, is the **Vouleftikó**. This former mosque was the seat of the Greek Parliament from 1827 to 1834. The parallel street, Od. Kapodistríou, leads left to the church of **Ágios Spirídonas**. Count Ioannis Kapodistrias, Regent of Greece, was shot outside the church door on September 27, 1831, by the Mavromihális brothers, Maniot separatists. The bullet holes in the wall have been preserved under glass.

A series of short climbs lead to the citadel of **Acronauplia**; there is even an elevator to take guests up to the state-owned Hotel Xenía, which is rather out of place on the citadel. The foundations of the long, narrow fortress date from the 4th century B.C., but the main structure is Venetian (around 1400). The entrance from the east leads through a Roman gate and a frescoed Byzantine gatehouse.

The fortress of **Palamídi** is reached by a steep footpath; you can see the covered stairway which zigzags up to the citadel from a distance. An easier way up is to drive from the crossroads at the edge of the Old Town along Leof. 25 Martíou up to the gate; about four kilometers. A number of staggered gates form the entrance to the fortress itself. The extensive building is a plain, military-style structure with a fine view across the gulf to Argos. The road to Palamídi continues on towards the beautiful sandy bay of **Karathóna** (eight kilometers).

*TIRYNS

The road from Náfplio to Argos passes first through ***Tiryns** ⑳ (4.5 kilometers from Náfplio). The massive walls of the fortress and palace of Mycenae rise from the Argolis plain on a hillock right beside the road. The site has been occupied since the 3rd century B.C. The present citadel was inhabited from the 16th to the 11th centuries B.C., and its fortifications are

the most important of any to have survived from the Mycenaean period.

The entrance leads through an **outer gate** that is flanked by towers, and swings to the left through a **central gate** that is the same size as the famous Lion Gate in Mycenae, it then passes through the narrow part of an outer ward and through the **inner gate** into a courtyard. Six **chambers** are built into the **east bastion** on the left-hand side. These chamber structures are a unique feature of the architecture of this citadel. On the right, a path goes through the **propylaea** to the **inner forecourt**. Its **south bastion**, on the left, bounds a covered, tunnel-like **gallery** that measures 20 meters long and has chambers in front of it.

Another gate on the right separates the inner forecourt from the palace area. This begins with a **colonnaded court**, where you can see the circular base of a **sacrificial altar**. You enter the palace itself at the top end of the colonnade, through a suite of rooms consisting of the **entrance hall**, **vestibule** and **great hall** (*megaron*).

Its center is occupied by the circle of the **sacred hearth** (*hestia*) on a painted floor. The base of the **throne** can be seen on the right-hand wall of the hall. Private rooms adjoin the throne room and below, on the left, is the monolithic floor slab of a **bathhouse** (12 square meters). From a **tower** on the west side of the adjacent courtyard, a **secret staircase** leads down to a narrow **gate** in the wall (the area is blocked off because of the risk of collapse).

ARGOS AND **MYCENAE

Argos ㉑ (just 12 kilometers from Náfplio), the town under the cone-shaped hill of Lárisa, has given its name to Argolis. Another ancient Mycenaean settlement, Argos is one of the oldest continuously-occupied towns in Europe. It has always been the agricultural center of the Argolis plain, one of the few large fertile coastal plains in Greece.

Right: The Lion Gate – entrance to the acropolis of Mycenae.

The **Bazaar Quarter** around the main square is very lively. There is a good **museum** on the square which displays finds from the ancient city (now almost entirely built over) and the surrounding area. On the right side of the road leading out of the city towards Trípoli is the **theater** (4th century B.C.), cut into the rocky slopes of the hill of Lárisa. After passing the city limits along the road to Mycenae and Corinth, you can see the ruins of the first acropolis of Argos on the right, on the **Hill of Aspis**. On the opposite side, a road goes left up the **Hill of Lárisa** to the gate of the ruined Ottoman **castle** on its summit.

Citadel of the Homeric Heroes

In the village of **Fíchti** (22 kilometers from Náfplio), a road branches off to the right through the village of **Mikínes**, with its many tavernas, to **Mycenae ㉒** (26 kilometers). The road was laid out as an avenue of plane trees by the German archeologist Heinrich Schliemann, who

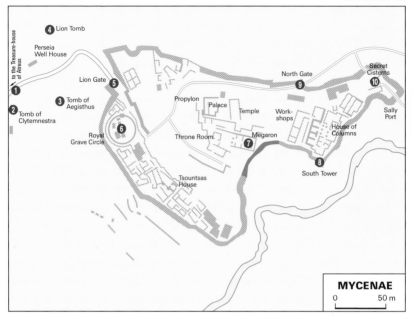

MYCENAE

0   50 m

started excavating in Mycenae in 1874. Mycenae, "hidden in the farthest corner of Argolis," as Homer tells us, has given its name to an entire prehistoric era. The place reached its cultural zenith in the late Mycenaean period (up to 1100 B.C.) with construction of the great vaulted tombs and the reliefs on the Lion Gate. In addition to the archeological evidence, Homer's epics also point to the central importance of Mycenae. The cause of its sudden disappearance and the eclipse of the great economic and political power of Mycenae remain a mystery.

The **Treasury of Atreus ❶** is on the left as you enter the citadel. It is the best-preserved and largest of the nine vaulted tombs that were discovered in Mycenae. Schliemann named it, borrowing the phrase from the writer Pausanias. Even assuming that Atreus was a real historical figure, the building could not have been his tomb; but since it dates from the period of the Trojan Wars (ca. 1300 B.C.), it may well be the tomb of King Agamemnon, who probably did exist. In any

case, there is no doubt that this impressive building was the tomb of a ruler.

The Treasury of Atreus has all of the features of a vaulted tomb (*tholos*) from the period. It is built into a hill into which a passageway (*dromos*) is cut; 36 meters long in this case. There is a monolithic lintel over the doorway (5.5 meters high): it measures 1.2 meters tall, 8.5 meters wide, 5 meters deep, and weighs 120 tons. The circular interior, 14.5 meters in diameter, is built of overlapping blocks of stone tapering towards the dome, which is 13.5 meters high. A larger dome was not built until 1,500 years later: the Pantheon in Rome. A doorway on the right leads to the spacious burial chamber.

Where Schliemann Struck Gold

Behind the entrance to the archeological site of the **acropolis** of Mycenae, on the right below the path, are two additional tomb vaults: the **Tomb of Clytemnestra ❷** and below it, the **Tomb of Aegisthus ❸**. Above the path on the left

is the ****Lion Tomb** ❹. The **Lion Gate** ❺ forms the citadel's entrance, which is guarded by fortifications. A heavy triangular slab in relief, nearly four meters high and three meters wide at the base, is set above the lintel. It shows two lions (now without heads) standing upright on either side of a column.

Immediately beyond the gate on the right, on a lower level, is the double row of vertical stone slabs from the **Royal Graves** ❻. Here Schliemann discovered six **shaft tombs** in a circular arrangement. They held 19 skeletons in a crouching position, as well as one of the most valuable discoveries in the history of archeology: jewelry, implements and gold death masks, including the one he called the "Mask of Agamemnon," now on display at the National Museum in Athens. However, Schliemann's descriptive name was wrong again – the site of the shaft graves (after 1850 B.C.) dates back to

well before Agamemnon could possibly have lived.

A path goes uphill towards the palace. A well-preserved **main staircase** leads through the **entrance hall** and **vestibule** to the **Megaron** ❼ (central hall) around the circular **Sacred Hearth**. Among the private rooms is a small **bathroom** on the north side. It is popularly supposed that this is where King Agamemnon was murdered by his wife Clytemnestra and her lover Aegisthus after he returned home from Troy. The **South Tower** ❽, at a height of nine meters, still stands, and the **North Gate** ❾ is still recognizable, as is the **Sally Port** on the narrow **Southeast Bastion**; opposite this, a hole in the wall opens to the north and onto a staircase that leads to the **Secret Cisterns** ❿.

To *Neméa

Highway 7 (to Argolis and Náfplio) and the new E65 expressway (to Arcadia and Trípoli) both pass the Shrine of Neméa.

Above: The entrance to the Teasury of Atreus in Mycenae.

From the expressway exit at **Ágios Vasílios** (26 kilometers from Corinth) or from the main road in the village itself, a minor road on the right leads to **Arhées Kleonés** ❷ (29 kilometers). Very little of ancient **Kleonai** now remains.

Outside the hamlet of **Arhéa Neméa** ❷, 33 kilometers from Corinth on a beautiful plateau, lies ancient *Neméa, the shrine of the Nemean Zeus. It was here, according to mythology, that Hercules strangled the Nemean lion. To commemorate his deed, the Nemean Games were founded. The ancient **stadium** has been beautifully restored and the athlete's entrance has been completely preserved

In the carefully-tended gardens of the site are the **baths** (3rd century B.C.). Only three columns remain of the **Temple of the Nemean Zeus**, built in the second half of the 4th century B.C. in the Doric style, with six rows of 13 pillars. Most of the column drums are still lying where they fell during an earthquake in the 4th century. The *adyton*, or secret chamber under the temple floor, can be seen through gaps in the foundations. Small finds (coins, vases, jewelry) are attractively displayed in the **museum**.

THE NORTHERN MOUNTAINS

You can use Neméa as the starting point from which to tour the northern mountains of Arcadia. Leave town on the E65 expressway towards **Nestáni**, then turn right towards **Skopí** and the **Plain of Mantineia**. In ancient times, this was the site of several battles, including one in the Peloponnesian Wars in 418 B.C., and another in 362 B.C. during the Theban invasion of the Peloponnese.

The few ruins of ancient **Mantineia** can be found on a lonely road not far from the village of **Miléa** ❷. Within the broad oval of the old city walls, little is left of the great Arcadian *polis* apart from the scanty remains of a **theater**. Its entrance, on the desolate plain, marks what has to

be the most unusual modern church in Greece: **Agía Fotiní** is a mixture of Classical and Byzantine elements, influenced by Japanese pagodas, and was built in 1972 by an engineer from Trípoli. It is supposedly an example of abiding piety.

The tiny village of **Orhomenós** ❷ lies on a nearby hill on the left-hand side of the road, at the end of a plain. Just in front of the church, on the right, a path runs though the fields about a kilometer and a half, and up to the walls of the ancient *polis* of **Orchomenos**. The ruins are spread out over a spacious site on terraced hills and include an overgrown **theater**, two **temples** and a **stoa**.

From below the acropolis of Orchomenos, you can take a side trip involving some eight kilometers of extra driving. Beyond the village of **Kandíla** there is a mountain pass about 1,300 meters above sea level, where Arcadia, Corinth and Argolis converge below the summit of **Mt. Olígirtos** (1,935 meters). This spot affords a fantastic view of the Arcadian mountains.

In the opposite direction, head towards **Levídi** and rejoin Highway 74. Winding up and down and around the northern end of the Menelá on Mountains (*Menalo*; 1,980 meters), this route passes through only a few semi-abandoned villages.

In **Karkaloú** (60 kilometers from Trípoli), a side road leads left across a narrow bridge over the Loúsios River to **Dimitsána** ❷. The village stands on a high, rocky bluff overlooking the Loúsios Valley. During the 18th and early 19th centuries, sleepy little Dimitsána was the spiritual center of the Greek nation in its struggle to overthrow the despotic rule of the Ottoman Turks. It was a bishopric and, for a time, the largest town in the Peloponnese when thousands fled from Ottoman oppression to the remote mountains of Arcadia.

Trade and industry flourished, and Dimitsána was famous for its goldsmiths and bell foundries. The forests provided

Peloponnese

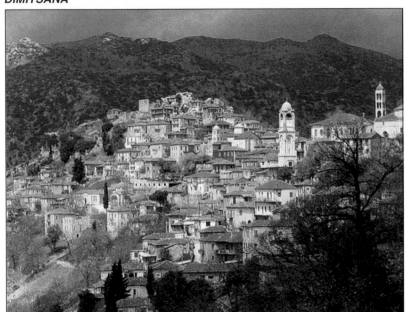

timber and the mountains offered pasture for sheep and goats. The rushing waters of the Loúsios drove powder mills – and without gunpowder from Dimitsána, the Greek revolutionaries would have stood no chance against the Turks.

Wealthy citizens founded what was then the largest library in the Peloponnese. A secret school was established in 1764; by 1834 it was awarding 300 scholarships annually to pupils from all over Greece. Archbishop Germanós of Pátras, who proclaimed the struggle for freedom in the Peloponnese in 1821, and the Patriarch of Constantinople, Gregórios IV, who was hanged by the Turks when the revolution broke out, both came from Dimitsána.

Despite its recent decline, Dimitsána has preserved much of its former appearance. Market-stall-like shops with wooden shutters line its narrow main street, and grand houses from more prosperous

Above: The mountain village of Dimitsána – home of the Greek independence movement.

days cling to the steep slopes. Just before a vantage-point above the **Loúsios Valley** at the end of the village, the last street on the right leads to the house where Patriarch Gregórios was born. The small **Museum of Religious Art** opened in the building in 1993. The books which remain from the historic **library** are kept in the old village school.

In the Valley of the Monasteries

After leaving the village of Dimitsána, turn to the right along a short road down to the floor of the Loúsios Valley, where a small **open-air museum** shows the traditional uses of water power. The narrow valley, with its three picturesque monasteries, is well worth a visit.

The first monastery you will come to, perched on a bastion of rock to your left, is the small convent of **Emaloú**, which houses some fine frescoes from the early 17th century.

Ágios Ioánnis Pródromos, a monastery that was founded in 1167 and where the monks painted icons, is closer to the valley floor.

Opposite, clinging high up on the rock face, is the ★**Moní tou Filosófou**, which was founded in A.D. 963. This monastery also ran a secret school during the period of Turkish rule. The Filosófou monastery can be reached by a side road to the right across the Loúsios Valley (15 kilometers from Dimitsána). Unpaved roads lead from the main road, just before Ipsoús, to the other two monasteries.

Ipsoús is one of the highest villages in the Peloponnese, at 1,050 meters above sea level. Beyond the village, a road with panoramic views descends to the gorges of the Alfiós, joining Highway 76 near **Karítena**. Nestling on a slope, Karítena is dominated by its 13th-century **fortress**. Highway 76 soon crosses the border into Élis, and follows the gorges of the Alfiós at great height and distance for over 70 kilometers, as far as the valley of Olympia.

Megalópoli ㉘, site of ancient Megalopolis, was founded as the capital of the united Arcadian *poleis* in the 4th century B.C. The modern town is dominated by the smokestacks of the surrounding lignite-fueled power stations. The only remains of the ancient city that are worth seeing are the neglected ruins of the **theater**, just before you enter the town; with 21,000 seats, it was once the largest in Greece. Highway 7 takes you over hill and dale back to Trípoli.

ARCADIA

Since the days of the Romans, the Arcadia portrayed by countless poets has been synonymous with pastoral idylls and the carefree life of a herdsman in the sunny fields. In reality, however, Arcadia is suitable for very little except goat-rearing. This central region of the Peloponnese is extremely harsh, rugged and lonely mountain country. Most of the Arcadian coast falls steeply to the sea below the eastern slopes of the Párnon Mountains. The capital of the Arcadia district is Trípoli.

The road climbs steeply from the coast of the Gulf of Argolis, to an altitude of nearly 1,000 meters, then descends from a ridge between Mt. Kteniás and Mt. Parthéni to the rugged plain of Trípoli. In the eastern part of the central Peloponnese, **Trípoli** ㉙ is the transportation center for the area. At an altitude of 650 meters, the town, founded by Albanians in the 14th century, has little more to offer than everyday market activity.

TO THE EAST COAST

The tour from Trípoli leads down to the coast of Arcadia. After driving nine kilometers along Highway 39 (Trípoli to Sparta), turn left in **Kerasítsa** and head toward **Aléa** ㉚, the village above ancient Tegéa. In the Archaic period, **Tegéa** was the most important city in the central Arcadian plain, until it fell under Spartan domination in the 6th century B.C. It was re-established by the Byzantines under the name *Níkli* and retained its importance as a Frankish barony until the late Middle Ages. The main building on the neglected site is the **Temple of Athena**, by Scopas of Paros, completed in 340 B.C. Built on the site of an earlier structure, this temple had Doric ambulatory columns (six rows of 14), and a double row of Corinthian pilasters in the inner cella, supporting the roof. The substructure and greying marble column sections are well preserved. Another notable feature is it's location: right in the middle of the village, surrounded by dilapidated houses of the Ottoman period. A small **museum** displays objects from the site.

Past the village church, a smaller road continues to **Episkopí Tegéas** (12 kilometers); site of the old cathedral of **Níkli**. The newer church on the same site houses a number of highly-prized Byzantine icons. It stands on the still visible retaining walls of the **theater** of Tegéa (2nd

Peloponnese

century B.C.). Excavations are in the process of uncovering the theater, a **stoa** (3rd century B.C.), the **agorá**, an early-Christian **basilica** (5th century), and the town of Níkli (7th-13th centuries).

Through Wild Kinouría

Pass through the gardens surrounding the church and turn right into the village of **Stádio**. Beyond the next hamlet, **Rízes**, there is a fork in the road (18 kilometers from Trípoli).

You can turn right (towards Kastrí) onto a narrow, winding road and drive up to the Párnon mountain range (1,935 meters). This is the where the mountainous region of **Kinouría**, which is almost totally uninhabited, begins. The center of this region is **Kastrí** ❸❶ (33 kilometers from Trípoli), also known as *Ágios Nikólaos*. From in front of the church in the middle of the village there is a wonderful

Above: The donkey – a practical solution for mountain transportation problems.

panorama of the wooded mountain peaks (up to 1,500 meters high) and deep ravines. Streams – dry in the summer – combine to form the Tános River. Kastrí and its surrounding hamlets come alive in the summer, when the many villagers who have moved to Athens return home for a couple of weeks. Even in the past, farmers, shepherds and woodcutters left the inhospitable mountains in winter to live in the olive groves along the coast.

Beyond **Ágios Pétros** (43 kilometers from Trípoli) the road swings eastwards, across rocky, scrub-covered uplands, and reaches the edge of the mountains above the coastal plain of Astros, beyond **Oriní Meligoú** (63 kilometers). From a height of about 800 meters you have a fabulous view over the gulf and all of Argolis.

The descent to **Astros** ❸❷ (77 kilometers) is short and quite steep. This small market town was the meeting place for the Second Greek National Assembly in 1823. The church at the nearby monastery of **Moní Loukoús** (four kilometers from Astros) dates from the 11th century.

A Frankish **fortress** sits on a hill above the seaside resort of **Parálio Astros** (82 kilometers from Trípoli).

From the Sea to the Párnon

Continuing to the south, the coast road passes through marshy alluvial land as far as **Ágios Andréas** (94 kilometers from Trípoli) and then runs along the steep, rocky mountains, directly above the sea. The coastline is divided by ridges of hills running down to the gulf; their silhouettes group in ever-new configurations, fading away in the distance in the haze rising from the sea. Beyond the resort of **Paralía Tiroú** ❸❸ (114 kilometers) is the short expanse, a few miles long, of the most attractive coastline in all of the Peloponnese. Here, the mountains slope gently towards the bays and the sea, clad in green and planted with cypresses, vines and fruit and olive trees.

The road leaves the coast through market gardens and fragrant orange groves just before **Leonídi** (132 kilometers), at the watershed of the Dafnón River. Leading out of Leonídi is the only road that crosses the **Párnon Mountains**. It climbs the Dafnón Valley high into the rugged, uninhabited mountains; as the road leaves the valley you can see the ***Elonís Monastery** ❸❹ (146 kilometers from Trípoli) high above you. The monastery dates from the 14th century and has recently been clumsily renovated. It is a water-shrine, standing by a cave with a spring in the rock.

Beyond the village of **Kosmás**, the road crosses the crest of the Párnon Mountains at a height of about 1,100 meters and enters Laconia. Beyond the Eurotas Valley are the mighty peaks of the Taygetus Mountains, which are covered with snow after late autumn, sometimes right into the early summer. Via **Geráki** (178 kilometers), you can either go north to **Sparta** ❸❺ (203 kilometers) or south to **Gíthio** (216 kilometers)

CORINTH

ANO TRIKALA (☎ 0743)
🛏 Ⓢ **Asteria**, tel. 91207.
CORINTH (☎ 0741)
🛏 ⓈⓈ **Acropolis**, tel. 26568. **Bellevue**, tel. 22068. Ⓢ **Akti**, tel. 23337. **Apollon**, tel. 25920.
🏛 ANCIENT CORINTH: **Museum**, Mon 11 am-7 pm, Tue-Fri 8 am-7 pm (Nov-April, weekdays thru 5 pm), Sat & Sun 8:30 am-3 pm. **Acrocorinth**, daily 6 am-10 pm.
🏖 Narrow, sandy beaches line the entire **Gulf of Corinth** (swimming areas: all coastal hamlets west of the Corinth-Kiáto area).
GALATAKI / ALMIRÍ (☎ 0741)
🛏 ⓈⓈ **Belle Helène**, tel. 33470.
ISTHMIA (☎ 0741)
🛏 ⓈⓈⓈ **King Saron**, tel. 37201.
🏛 **Museum**, daily 8:30 am-3 pm (parts of the archeologic site are open to the public.)
ISTHMOS KORINTHIAS (☎ 07412)
🛏 ⓈⓈ **Isthmia** (motel), tel. 23454.
KASTANIA (☎ 0747)
🛏 ⓈⓈ **Xenia**, tel. 61283.
KENCHREAI
🏛 Ancient Harbor, free access.
KIÁTO (☎ 0742)
🛏 ⓈⓈ **Triton**, tel. 23421.
KOKONI (☎ 0742)
🛏 ⓈⓈ **Karava's Village**, tel. 32091.
KORFOS (☎ 0741)
🛏 ⓈⓈ **Korfos**, tel. 95217.
LEHEO / CORINTH (☎ 0741)
🛏 ⓈⓈ **Corinthian Beach**, tel. 25666. **Ephira**, tel. 22434.
LIMNI VOULIAGMÉNIS / IRÉON (☎ 0741)
🛏 ⓈⓈ **Filoxenia**, tel. 43177.
LOUTRÁKI (☎ 0744)
🛏 ⓈⓈⓈ **Achillion**, tel. 42271. **Akti Loutraki**, tel. 22338. **Angelidis Palace**, tel. 22251. **Park**, tel. 26695. **Petit Palais**, tel. 22267. ⓈⓈ **Alexandros**, tel. 23524. **Beau Rivage**, tel. 22323. **Elpis**, tel. 28263. **Excelsior**, tel. 222354. **Grand Hotel**, tel. 22348. **Marrion**, tel. 42346. Ⓢ **Davarinos**, tel. 22233. **Segas**, tel. 22623. **Ekonomion**, tel. 22326. **Hermes**, tel. 22509. **Olympia**, tel. 22284.
🏖 Most popular swimming beach is **Loutráki**, a sandy beach that is about 2 km wide.
LOUTRÓ ELÉNIS (☎ 0741)
🛏 ⓈⓈ **Kanakakos**, tel. 33211. **Politis**, tel. 33249. **Sea View**, tel. 33551.
🏖 **Loutró Elénis**: Best beach on the Gulf of Argolis.

Peloponnese

NEMÉA (☎ 0746)

Ta Neméa, tel. 22763.

Shrine of Zeus and Museum, Tue-Sun 8:30 am -3 pm.

PALEOHÓRA

Heraion, free access.

Small, sandy beaches at Kap Iréo.

PALEO KALAMAKI (☎ 0741)

Kalamaki Beach, tel. 37652.

PEFKAKI / LOUTRÁKI (☎ 0744)

Holiday Angelopoulos, tel. 21662. Pefkaki, tel. 22426, on the edge of town, some rooms have ocean views.

SIKION

Sikion and Museum (anciet city ca. 30 km west of Corinth, south of Kiáto), Wed-Mon 8:30 am-3 pm. Parts of the archeological site are open to the public.

STIMFALIÁ (☎ 0795)

Stymphalia, tel. 22072.

TRIKALA (☎ 0743)

Ziria, tel. 91227.

XILOKASTRO (☎ 0743)

Arion, tel. 22230. Rallis, tel. 22 219. Hermes, tel. 22250.

ARGOLIS

ARGOS (☎ 0751)

Mycenae, tel. 68754. Palladion, tel. 67807. Theoxenia, tel. 67808.

Archeolocical Museum (Od. Vass. Olgas), Tue-Sun 8:30 am-3 pm. Theater and Ancient City, Tue-Sun 8:30 am-3 pm. Kastro (acropolis and fort on Mt. Lárisa), free access.

ASINE

Archeologic Site, free access.

DREPANO (☎ 0752)

Danti's Beach, tel. 92294.

EPIDAUROS (☎ 0753)

Apollon, tel. 41295. Xenia II, tel. 22003, only open June-Sept.

Shrine and Museum, April-May 14 and Sept-Oct, daily 8 am-7 pm; May 15-Aug, daily 8 am-8 pm; Nov-March, daily 8 am-2:30 pm.

ERMIÓNI (☎ 0754)

Hydra Beach (hotel & bungalows),Plepi, tel. 41080. Pórto Hydra, tel. 41112. Costa Perla, tel. 31112. Lena-Mary, tel. 31450. Akti, tel. 31241. Hermioni, tel. 21750. Olympion, tel. 31214.

BEACHES: The most beautiful, sandy beaches are around Ermioní.

GALATAS (☎ 0298)

Galatia, tel. 22227.

HONIKAS

Argive Heraion (Shrine of Hera, north of Náfplio, south of Mycenae), Mon-Sat 8:45 am-3 pm, So 9:30 am-2 pm.

HYDRA (☎ 0298)

Hydra Town: Bratsera Hotel, tel. 53971, refined elegance in a renovated factory. Ippokampos, tel. 53453, central location, old stone building with modern rooms. Hotel Sofia, tel. 52313, small, central location, a little noisy.

Several times daily: Ferry connections from Ermióni; also, ferry and hydrofoil connections to Piraeus and the other Saronic Gulf Islands.

KÓSTA (☎ 0754)

Cap d'or, tel. 51360. Lido, tel. 57393.

KRANIDI (☎ 0754)

Hermionida, tel. 21750.

LIGOURIO (☎ 0753)

Avaton, tel. 22059. Alkyon, tel. 22552. Koronis, tel. 22267.

MÉTHANA (☎ 0298)

Avra, tel. 92382.

MYCENEA (☎ 0751)

Agamemnon, tel. 76222. La Petite Planète, tel. 76240. Orea Eleni tou Menelaou, tel. 76225.

Hilltop Fortress, April 1-May 14 and Sept-Oct, daily 8 am-7 pm; May 15-Aug, daily 8 am-8 pm; Nov-March, daily 8 am-2:30 pm.

NÁFPLIO (☎ 0752)

Pl. Iatroú, tel. 24444.

Xenia's Palace, tel. 28981. Xenia's Palace Bungalows, tel. 28981. Amalia, Nea Tirintha, tel. 24401. Agamemnon, tel. 28021. Park (traditional), tel. 27428. Amphitryon, tel. 27366. Aspasia, tel. 61183. Acropole, tel. 27796.

Arch. Museum (Pl. Sindágmatos), Tue-Sun 8:30 am-3 pm; Ethnological Museum (Od. V. Alexándrou 1), Wed-Mon 9 am-2:30 pm; Acronauplia Fortress, free; Palamídi Fortress, daily 8:30 am-2:45 pm.

BEACHES: Náfplio has a small, groomed beach below the Acronauplia Fortress; the beach in Karathónas is about 8 km from the town center; next beach resort is the popular Toló.

NÉA EPIDAVROS (☎ 0753)

Avra, tel. 31294. Marilena, tel. 31279.

NÉA KIOS (☎ 0751)

Aktaeon, tel. 51477.

PALEÁ EPÍDAVROS (☎ 0753)

Christina, tel. 41451. Marialena, tel. 41090. Maronika, tel. 41391. Saronis, tel. 41514. Epidavria, tel. 41222.

BEACHES: Beaches near Paleá Epídavros are popular; just north is the resort of Kórfos.

PÓROS

📋 *EXCURSIONS:* Shuttle service between Galatás und Póros daily 6 am-midnight; in addition, ferries and hydrofoils connect Póros with Piraeus and the other Saronic Gulf Islands (Égina/Hydra/Spéstes) several times daily.

PORTOHÉLI (☎ 0754)

🛏 😊😊😊 **Hinitsa Beach**, tel. 51401. 😊😊 **Alcyon**, tel. 51161. **Giouli**, tel. 51217. **Pórto**, tel. 51410. **Touristiko Chorio Aghiou Aemilianou**, tel. 57518.

📋 Portohéli has beautiful beaches.

SALANDI (☎ 0754)

🛏 😊😊 **Salandi Beach**, tel. 71391.

SPÉTSES (☎ 0298)

🛏 😊😊😊 **Possidonion**, tel. 72206, Greece's first tourist hotel has flourished since 1914. **Kasteli**, tel. 72311, large, modern hotel and bungalow complex. 😊😊 **Villa Christina**, tel. 72147, nice guest house. **Akroyiali**, tel. 73695, on the beach.

🏛 **Ethnological Museum** in Spétses, including exhibits about the Greek War of Independence, Mon-Fri 8:45 am-3 pm, Sat & Sun 9:30 am-2:30 pm.

📋 *EXCURSIONS*: Several daily connections from Ermióni, Portohéli und Kósta; ferry and hydrofoil connections to Piraeus and the other Saronic Gulf Islands.

TOLÓ (☎ 0752)

🛏 😊😊 **Assini Beach**, tel. 59347. **Dolfin**, tel. 59192. **Knossos**, tel. 59174. **Solon**, tel. 59204. **Sophia**, tel. 59567. 😊 **Maria-Lena**, tel. 59342. **Tolo**, tel. 59248, family operated. **Tolo Inn**, tel. 59464.

⛺ **Camping Lido**, tel. 59396, near beach. **Kastraki**, tel. 59386, open May-Oct, good and expensive.

TIRYNS

🏛 **Tiryns Fortress**, Mon-Fri 8 am-7 pm (Nov-April only thru 5 pm), Sat & Sun 8:30 am-3 pm (only partially accessable because of risk of collapse).

TROIZEN

🏛 **Archeologic Site**, free access.

VIVARI (☎ 0752)

🛏 😊 **Areti**, tel. 92391. **Marina**, tel. 92248. **Vrahi**, tel. 92241.

ARCADIA

ÁGIOS PÉTROS / KINOURIA (☎ 0792)

🛏 😊 **Parnon**, tel. 31245.

ASTROS (☎ 0755)

🛏 😊 **Anthini**, tel. 22498.

DIMITSÁNA (☎ 0795)

🛏 😊😊 **Dimitsana**, tel. 31518.

IPSOUS / STEMNITSA (☎ 0795)

🛏 😊 **Trikolonion**, tel. 81297.

KASTRÍ / KINOURÍA (☎ 0792)

🛏 😊 **Parnon**, tel. 22247.

LEONÍDI (☎ 0757)

🛏 😊😊😊 **Kamaria**, tel. 22757. 😊😊 **Dyonissos**, tel. 22379. 😊 **Neon**, tel. 22383.

📋 *BEACHES:* Leonídi itself has fine pebble beaches. A number of sandy beaches, accessable from the coast road, are nearby.

LEVÍDI

🏛 **Ethnological Museum**, Tue-Sun 8 am-2 pm.

MAGOULIANA (☎ 0795)

🛏 😊😊😊 **Kosmopoulos**, tel. 82350.

MANTINEIA

🏛 **Archeologic Site**, free access.

MEGALÓPOLI (☎ 0791)

🛏 😊😊 **Leto**, tel. 22302. **Pan**, tel. 22270. 😊 **Achillion**, tel. 23276. **Arcadia**, tel. 22223.

🏛 **Archeological Site** and **Theater**, free access.

NÍKLI (PALEÁ EPISKOPÍ)

🏛 **Excavations** are in pasages, which are viewable, some parts are open to the public.

ORCHOMENÓS

🏛 **Archeologic Site**, free access.

PARALÍA ASTROS (☎ 0755)

🛏 😊😊 **Afroditi**, tel. 51596. **Paradissos Inn**, tel. 51186. 😊 **Crystal**, tel. 51313. **Chryssi Akti**, tel. 51294.

📋 *BEACHES:* Parálio Astros has the longest sandy beach in Arcadia.

PARALÍA TIROÚ (☎ 0757)

🛏 😊😊 **Apollon**, tel. 41393. **Blue Sea**, tel. 41369. **Kamvyssis**, tel. 41424. **Oceanis**, tel. 41244. 😊 **Arcadia**, tel. 41211. **Galini**, tel. 41210. **Tsakonia**, tel. 41322. **Tyros**, tel. 41235.

📋 Parália Tiroú has fine pebble beaches. A number of sandy beaches, accessable from the coast road, are nearby.

POULITHRA / KINOURÍA (☎ 0757)

🛏 😊 **Kentavros**, tel. 51214.

TEGÉA

🏛 **Temple of Athena**, free access. **Archeological Museum**, Tue-Sun 8:30 am-3 pm, closed Mondays.

TRÍPOLI (☎ 071)

ℹ️ Leof. Ethnikís Andistáseos 43, Tel. 239392.

🛏 😊😊 **Arcadia**, tel. 225551. **Artemis**, tel. 225221. **Galaxy**, tel. 225195.

😊 **Kynouria**, tel. 222463. **Menalon**, tel. 222450.

❌ **Garden Sosolis**, Pl. Areos, 100 meters away from the courthouse, delicious food and shaded tables in the garden.

VITINA (☎ 0795)

🛏 😊😊 **Villa Valos**, tel. 22210. **Xenia** (motel), tel. 22218.

Peloponnese

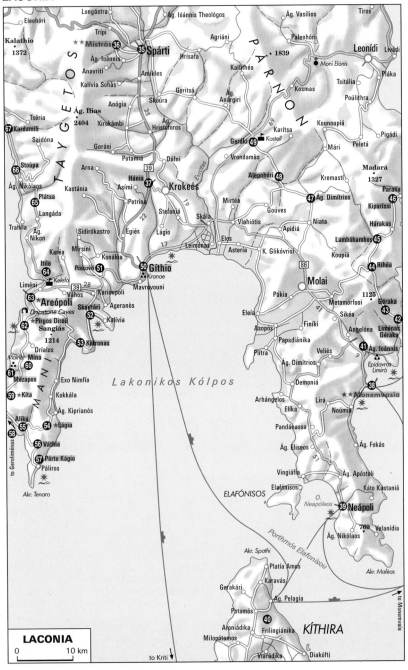

Longástra · Ág. Ioánnis Theológos · Ág. Vasílios · Tiros
Eleohóri · Trípi · Agriáni · Paleohóri · Leonídi · Liváxi
Kalathio 1372 · ★★ Mistrás 36 · 35 Spárti · Hrísafa · Kallithéa · · 1839 · Moni Elónis · Tsitália · Pláka
Ág. Ioánnis · Amikles · Kosmas · Poúlithra
Anavrití · Goritsá · Ág. Anárgiri
Kalívia Sohás · Skoúra · Kounoupiá · Pigádi
Tséria · Anógia · 25 · Karítsa · Mári · Peletá
67 Kardamíli · 2404 · Xirokámbi · Ág. Hristóforos · Geráki 49 Kastell · Madará 1327
Saidóna · Goráni · Vrondamás · Kremastí
66 Stoúpa · Potamiá · Dáfni · Alepohóri 48 · Paralía 46
Ág. Nikólaos · 39 · 47 Ág. Dimítrios · Kiparíssi
65 Plátsa · Kastánia · Hánia · Mirtéá · Goúves · Hárakas
Langáda · Asími · 37 Krokeés · Lambókambos 45
Trahíla · Ág. Nikon · Petrína · Stefaniá · Vlahiótis · Koupiá
Karéa · Sidirókastro · Egiés · Skála · Apidiá · Niata
Itilo 64 · Mírsini · Lágio · Leimónas · Elos · K. Glikóvrisí · 44 Rihéa
Liméni · Passavá 51 · Konákia · 50 Gíthio · Astería · 86 · Molai · 1125 · 43 Géraka 42
63 Areópoli · Váhos 39 · Karioúpoli · Kranae · Pákia · Metamórfosi · Liménas
Dripstone Caves · Skoutári · Ageranós · Mavrovouni · Eleía · Sikéa · Géraka
62 Pírgos Diroú · 52 · Kalívia · Asopós · Finíki · Angelóna · 41 Ág. Ioánnis
Sangiás 1214 · Papadiánika · Veliés · Epídavros Limirá
Dríalos · Mína · 53 Kótronas · Plítra · Demoniá · 38
Mainar · 60 · Exo Nimfío · Ág. Dimítrios · ★★ Monemvasía
61 Mézapos · Kokkála · Arhángelos · Lirá · Noúmia
59 ★Kíta · Ág. Kiprianós · Elíka · Ág. Fokás
Alika 65 · 54 ★Lágia · Pandánassa
58 · 56 Váthia · Ág. Elíseos
57 Pórto Kágio · Vingiáfia · Ág. Apóstoli
Páliros · Elafónisos · Káto Kastaniá
Akr. Tenaro · ELAFÓNISOS · O. Neapóleos · 39 Neápoli
Akr. Spathi · 769 Velanídia
Gerakári · Ág. Nikólaos
Platía Amos · Porthmós Elafonísou
Karavás
Potamós · Ág. Pelagía · KÍTHIRA
Afroniádika · 40
Milopótamos · Frilingiánika
Viarádika · Diakófti

Lakonikós Kólpos

LACONIA
0   10 km
to Kriti ▼ · to Monemvasia ▶
50

LACONIA

The district of Laconia encompasses the south-central part of the Peloponnese. It is bounded in the west by the Taygetus Mountains (2,407 meters), and in the east by the Párnon Mountains (1,935 meters). Between these two mountain ranges lies the valley of the Eurotas (*Evrótas*) River, where the region's population is concentrated. The prefecture also includes the Laconian Peninsula in the east, as well as the Inner Mani Peninsula in the west. Laconia's capital is Sparta (60 kilometers from both Trípoli in Arcadia, and Kalamáta in Messenia); its main port, Gíthio, is 51 kilometers south of Sparta, on the Gulf of Laconia.

Sparta

Today's **Sparta ㉟** (*Spárti*) shows little trace of the ancient city-state which ruled the Peloponnese and, for a time, all of Hellas. Thucydides' prediction, which he made 2,400 years ago, seems to have come true: If the city ever became deserted, he said, posterity would doubt that it had ever been powerful.

The town was inhabited until the 9th century under various Greek rulers, but the Slav invasions drove the population into the remote Mani region. Sparta was re-established during Byzantine times and given the name *Lacedaemonia*, but was eclipsed by the rise of Mystra in the 13th century. The city you see today was laid out in 1834 as a new market town.

Sparta is unexpectedly elegant. **Leof. Konstandínou Paleológou**, its central avenue, is lined with palm trees; colonnades surround the main square. The neoclassical **Town Hall** (1906), at the center of the square, is one of the finest of its kind in Greece. On the other side of the main street, Od. Evróta leads to the **Archeological Museum**, where finds from Sparta and the rest of Laconia are on display.

Leof. Konstandínou Paleológou leads up to the hill of the **acropolis**, which is only 20 meters high. Its walls were not built until the 3rd and 4th centuries. Entering through the south gate, you can see the **theater** (2nd century A.D.) on the left. Above it are the foundations of the **Temple of Athena** (6th century B.C.).

**MISTRÁS

The biggest attraction in Laconia is **Mistrás ㊱** (*Mystra*), the most important legacy of Byzantine medieval city architecture in Greece. The ruined city is on the road from Sparta to Kalamáta, above the modern village of Mistrás (eight kilometers from Sparta). Its ghostly buildings are impressively perched on a rocky outcrop at the foot of the Taygetus Mountains. A fort on top of the steep hill is known as *Mizíthra* and dominates the city – its name was corrupted to Mystra.

Byzantine Despots

The fort was built in 1248 by a Norman duke, William II de Villehardouin, as a defense against the Slavs. The population of *Lacedaemonia* then came to settle under its protective shadow. After the Byzantines reconquered it, Mistrás became the capital of the Peloponnese in 1263, and was the seat of the Despots, or imperial governors, of Morea.

The eight Despots of Morea, who ruled until the Peloponnese fell to the Ottomans, came from Constantinople's leading families: the Cantacouzenes and the Palaeologi. The Despot Constantine Dragatses succeeded to the throne as the last emperor of Byzantium. Courtly magnificence was combined in Mistrás with the last great intellectual and artistic aspirations of the Eastern Empire in the age of the Palaeologic Renaissance. After being destroyed several times, the city was finally abandoned in 1834, when Sparta was rebuilt. It fell into ruin until the early

Peloponnese

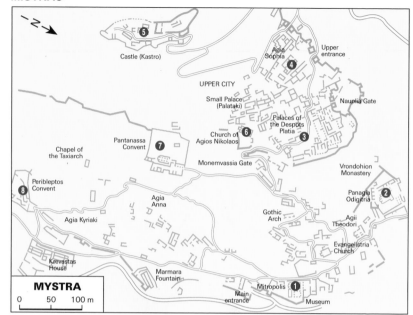

MYSTRA

0   50   100 m

Map labels: Castle (Kastro), Agia Sophia, Upper entrance, UPPER CITY, Small Palace (Palataki), Nauplia Gate, Palaces of the Despots Platia, Church of Agios Nikolaos, Pantanassa Convent, Chapel of the Taxiarch, Monemvassia Gate, Vrondohion Monastery, Peribleptos Convent, Panagia Odigitria, Agia Anna, Gothic Arch, Agii Theodori, Agia Kyriaki, Evangelistria Church, Krevastas House, Marmara Fountain, Mitropolis, Main entrance, Museum

1900s, when medieval archeologists were able to reawaken an appreciation of Mistrás' importance; it was here, during the fall of Byzantium, that the seeds of the future Greek nation were preserved.

The site is divided into three parts: the lower town, the upper town and the fortress. The entrances are right beside the road; after 7.5 kilometers, you come to the main gate of the lower town, and 15 kilometers further on is the upper gate, below the fortress on the summit.

In the Ruined City

On the right, next to the main gate, is the large complex of the **Mitrópolis ❶**, the cathedral of Mistrás (1270-1309). A cruciform domed building above a new gallery was added to the original three-aisled basilica in the 15th century. In addition to the central dome, it has four apses and corner rooms that are sur-

Right: The Pantanássa Church in the ruined Byzantine city of Mistrás.

mounted by domes. The interior of the cathedral was decorated in several phases, and by various hands, between 1270 and about 1325. A building in the north courtyard has been turned into a **museum**.

A path to the right leads off the road and through the lower town, towards the **Vrondohíon Monastery ❷** at the northern corner of the city wall. The city's two largest churches, Agii Theodóri and Panagía Odigítria, popularly known as *Afendikó*, are both maintained by the monastery. The **Church of St. Theodore** (1290-95) is an octagonal cruciform domed church – the last of its kind in Greece. The dome stands on an octagon of arches and from the outside, with its 16 tall windows, seems to weigh too heavily on the building. Remains of the frescoes and sculptures can also be seen.

The church of **Panagía Odigítria**, while it reverts to older styles of architecture, is actually the more recent building of the two (about 1310). This part of the Mitrópolis was much imitated later, but this was the original, organic structure – a

combination of the three-aisled basilica and cruciform church beneath five domes. Surrounding the building is a colonnade which is entirely appropriate to its superb position. The interior is painted with frescoes that have been beautifully restored, and is lined with multicolored marble.

Back on the main path, you will pass the **Evangelístria Chapel** (14th century). After climbing through the ruins of the lower town, you enter the upper town through the **Monemvasía Gate**. The path to the right ends at the **Platía**, the main square. At the end of its steep slope towards the valley are the two wings of the impressive **Palaces of the Despots ❸**. You can recognize the oldest part of the building, a *palas* dating from the Frankish period, by its windows with their pointed Gothic arches. It is easy to see where the adjoining buildings were added in stages; two of them by the Cantacouzenes and the third by the Palaeologi. The basement and ground floor of the central wing (after 1400) are occupied almost en-

tirely by the throne room of the Palaeologi; it is almost 400 square meters in area.

Behind the palaces, a path leads to the right to the **Nauplia Gate** and a bastion. Further up is the **Kastro Gate** (top entrance). Opposite, on a higher level, is the church of **Agía Sofía ❹** (ca. 1350-1365). Formerly the monastery church and palace chapel, this simple cruciform domed building is impressive because of its slender proportions. From here you can climb to a Frankish **fortress ❺**; its walls were mostly rebuilt during Ottoman times.

Walking down from the church, keep to the right and pass the **Palatáki** (small palace), a three-story patrician's house. Below is the church of **Ágios Nikólaos ❻**, dating from the Ottoman period. Turn right beyond the **Monemvasía Gate** and onto the broad terrace of the **Pantanássa Convent ❼**, which is still occupied. The **Pantanássa Church**, which stands on a small plateau, is also a combination of basilica and cruciform domed church. There are well-preserved frescoes from

the original period in the transepts and the upper gallery. The paintings in the crypt date from the 17th century.

Below the Pantanássa, the path leads right to the small **Perívleptos Monastery** ❽, which lies in the southeast corner of the city walls. A building that resembles a tower and the church with adjoining chapels are all that remain of the monastery.

St. Catherine's Chapel, a simple cruciform domed church (built after 1350), stands in a picturesque position in front of a cave shrine. Inside, its frescoes display a wealth of iconographic detail. Three cycles are interwoven: the Eucharist, church festivals and scenes from the Passion and the Life of Mary. The frescoes are masterpieces of late-Byzantine sacred art.

After it passes the residential buildings and a number of **chapels**, the path follows the town walls and leads back to the main gate.

Above: View from the upper town over the roofs of Monemvasía. Right: There's no room for cars in the narrow alleys of the town.

****MONEMVASÍA**
The Gibratar of Greece

Highway 39 (towards Gíthio) runs along the Eurotas Valley, beneath the high (up to 2,404 meters) Taygetus Mountains. Side roads lead to hillside villages which make good starting points for some tough mountain hikes. Just beyond **Hánia** ㊲ (25 kilometers from Sparta), turn left onto Highway 86, which follows the mountains along the Eurotas estuary and across low hills into the town of Monemvasía on Laconia's east coast (97 kilometers). This fortified Byzantine town, with Venetian and Ottoman additions, has been beautifully restored over the past 30 years and is now a top-class holiday resort.

**Monemvasía ㊳ stands in an inaccessible position on a spur of rock, 300 meters high, that juts into the sea. The "Gibraltar of Greece," it is surrounded by castellated walls on the seaward side and backed by the fortress rock. Beyond the only gateway through the city walls – too

narrow for cars – is the main street, **Drómos Iánni Rítsou**. It is named after the poet Iánnis Rítsos, who was from Monemvasía. The tiny streets are lined with souvenir shops and expensive cafés, and a small square overlooks the ramparts to the sea.

On this square stands the former cathedral of **Christós Elkoménos** (13th century), with a portal dating from 1697 when it was renovated. The church of **Ágios Pávlos** (9th century), on the landward side of the square, was renovated during the Turkish period.

Steps and zigzagging paths lead to the **upper town**. The view down over the small houses, built of warm, buff-colored limestone under red tiled roofs, reveals the harmonious design of the city. Gates and a covered walkway along the battlements lead into the ramparts of the upper town, which is in ruins apart from the massive church of **Agía Sophía** (about 1300), founded by Emperor Andronicus II (Palaeologus), which stands atop the steep cliff overlooking the sea.

KÍTHIRA

South of Monemvasía is the ferry harbor of **Néapolis** ❸❾, from which you can take a boat to Kíthira, a trip that takes about 45 minutes.

Southernmost of the Ionian Islands, to which it is linked historically rather than geographically, **Kíthira** ❹⓪, with its steep coast, has strong mythological ties to the goddess Aphrodite. It is here that she was borne ashore on her famous sea shell, brought to life from the foam created when Zeus castrated his father Cronus and threw his genitalia into the sea.

Near the north end of the island, the harbor of **Agía Pelagía** ❶ is where the ferries from the Peloponnese dock. There is a beach here, but Kapsáli, the harbor in Kíthira Town, is a more attractive destination to yachting tourists and backpackers alike.

Just south of Agía Pelagía, **Paleohóra** ❷ is the island's ghost town. In 1537, the Turkish Admiral Barbarossa invaded the island, slaughtering many of its inhabit-

KÍTHIRA

0   10 km

ants and allegedly carrying off 7,000 people. Mothers, it is said, threw their children off the hilltop to fall to their deaths rather than risk their enslavement at the hands of Barbarossa. Today, many of the local villagers believe the deserted town to be haunted.

Paléopolis 3 is on the southeast coast of the island. The Phoenicians came here for the murex shells they used to make the purple dye they traded throughout the Mediterranean, and they christened the island *Porphyroussa*, "Island of Shells." Remains of the settlement dating from this period are located on a lovely beach near Paléopolis. The Cretans, who colonized the area, were the first people in Greece to worship Aphrodite, but her temple here was later destroyed by early Christians; all that remains are a few foundation walls of the old acropolis. Just to the east there is a good beach, near the

Right: With their fortress of Kíthira, the Venetians were able to control the trade routes to Crete and Rhódos for many centuries.

fishing port of **Avlémonas**, that is guarded by the remains of a Venetian fortress.

On the southern shore is **Kíthira 4**, the island's main town and a pretty, blue-and-white place that is Cycladic in aspect and is dominated by the ruins of a Venetian **fortress** from 1503. The Venetians called the island *Cerigo* and "The Eye of Kriti;" it had strategic value because of its position at the entrance to the Aegean, on trade routes to Rhódos, Crete and even Athens (a position it maintained until the opening of the Corinth Canal). A few of the houses and chapels still date from Venetian times, including the castle's two churches, **Panagía** and **Pandokrátoras**, with their 16th-century frescoes. The small **Archeological Museum** displays a few of the island's finds.

The small port town of **Kapsáli** is frequented mainly by vacationers from Athens. A small lighthouse stands between two pebble beaches; in the summer, thanks to a few hotels and tavernas, this becomes the "tourist center" of the island. Opposite is an offshore islet known as **Avgó**, "The Egg," which is traditionally held to be Aphrodite's birthplace.

North of Kíthira is **Livádi**, where the British left an arched bridge as testimony to their presence on the island (1809-64). From here, a dirt road leads over to the beautiful monastery of **Moní Mirtidió 5**, which stands uninhbaited but still gorgeous with its striking bell tower, surrounded by gardens of flowers. It was named for a gilt relief of the Virgin and Child that continues to draw pilgrims, especially on August 15.

Milopótamos 6, another attractive village, is traversed by clear-running streams. To the north is the abandoned town of **Káto Hóra**, a Venetian settlement still encircled by 16th-century city walls; the gate is surmounted by the Lion of St. Mark. Some of the old houses are now being reclaimed and restored. On the coast, the beach near **Limniónas** offers

fine sand and good swimming. A little further to the north is the cave church of **Agía Sofía**, with stalagmites, stalactites and subterranean lakes; fragments of old frescoes and mosaics attest to its earlier use as a church.

THE UNDISCOVERED EAST

From Monemvasía, you can tour the almost undeveloped eastern side of the Laconian Peninsula. You'll need a bit of the pioneering spirit to tackle the rough gravel and sand tracks along the route, but the great beauty and variety of the scenery more than compensate for this. From Highway 86 (eight kilometers before Monemvasía), you can turn to the right towards **Ágios Ioánnis** ④. A flat-topped hill by the sea on a long stretch of sand near modern **Paleá Monemvasía** marks the site of the acropolis of the ancient Epidaurean colony known as **Epidaurus Limera**. A track through the hills, new in parts but only wide at the beginning, returns to the sea at **Liménas Géraka** ④

(26 kilometers from Monemvasía). This coastal fishing village is attractively situated at the end of a narrow, winding fjord which runs into a round, silted-up bay. As the road climbs through hilly country dotted with huge boulders to the village of **Géraka** ④, there is a view of the whole length of the fjord. A cul-de-sac to the right, just beyond the village, takes you to the **Evangelístria Monastery** (12 kilometer round trip), in a remote spot high above the cliffs.

Crossing a plateau, you come to the almost deserted **Rihéa** ④ (39 kilometers). Its stone houses, with their brightly-painted walls, present visitors with an ancient and unchanging village scene. The road is once again paved, but after the village (42 kilometers) you'll turn right onto a gravel track leading to **Lambókambos** ④ and its plateau, 50 kilometers from Monemvasía.

For an excursion to the sea, turn right in the village onto a dead-end road which climbs through a short, wild gorge (28 kilometer round trip) and continues to the

hamlet of **Hárakas**. Immediately beyond, the road emerges through a rocky gateway onto a high mountain crest; at a height of about 800 meters, the view of Mt. Hionovoúni's peaks (1,297 meters) is breathtaking. Below precipitous overhanging cliffs that drop steeply to the sea, the road clings to the mountain slope, which bombards it with showers of stones in windy weather. The descent down the mountain leads to **Kiparíssi** ㊻, and then onto a plateau above a beautiful bay and to the harbor at **Paralía**.

Continuing on the main route from Lambókambos, you drive across a dusty grey plateau. After turning right onto a narrow paved road (62 kilometers from Monemvasía), turn left and drive through wild mountain scenery to the village of **Ágios Dimítrios** ㊼. Once you are in the village, turn right and drive through

Above: Beautifully restored Váthia, with its tall towers, is the most beautiful village on the Mani Peninsula. Right: A hamlet above the coast of the Inner Mani.

Alepohóri ㊽ (79 kilometers) to reach Geráki, 89 kilometers from Monemvasía.

Two kilometers east of Geráki, on a hilltop, stands a Frankish **fortress** from 1254, the seat of one of the 12 baronies of the Frankish Duchy of Achaea. On a terraced slope below are the remains of the Byzantine settlement of **Geráki** ㊾ – Mistrás in miniature. Over a dozen chapels have been preserved among the ruined houses. The **fortress chapel**, a 13th-century basilica within the walls of the castle, is the best-preserved religious building on the site. Its altar bears the coat-of-arms of Jean de Nivelet, lord of the castle. The main roads from Sparta (37 kilometers), Leonídi (48 kilometers) and Gíthio (48 kilometers) converge in the village of Geráki, which was built upon a Mycenaean acropolis.

THE MANI PENINSULA

This almost inaccessible peninsula, the southeastern tip of the European mainland, has always managed to maintain its independence during the regular periods of foreign rule over Greece. It even enjoyed autonomous status in Roman times; and until the 9th century, when it became a refuge for the people of Laconia during the Slav and Albanian invasions, it remained pagan. The Mani was again autonomous under Ottoman rule, when the heads of the most powerful Maniot clans ruled the area as *beys* appointed by the Sultan.

The Maniots were renowned as violent warriors, feared as pirates, and were notorious for their clan feuds and vendettas which lasted for decades. The carefully cemented structure of Maniot clan rule was expressed in visible terms by the building of clan tower-houses.

At the Gates of the Underworld

The small port of **Gíthio** ⑤⓪ is where ferries leave for the island of Kíthira and western Crete, and is the starting point for a tour of the Mani Peninsula. On the little island of **Marathonísi** opposite – ancient **Kranae** – Paris is said to have married Helen after abducting her, before she fled to Troy. On the island, which is joined to the mainland by a causeway, the fortified house of the Grigorákis-Tzannetákis clan, built in 1829, has been converted into a **museum**.

Highway 39 crosses the Plain of Mavrovoúni and passes the Frankish mountain fortress of **Passavá** ⑤① (13th century). A dead-end road to the left (14 kilometers from Gíthio) leads to the village of **Skoutári** ⑤② and an extremely beautiful bay. To the south is the small resort of **Kótronas** ⑤③, at the head of a bay on the Laconian Gulf. Kótronas and a few other hamlets lie in the only fertile corner of the peninsula and from here you can see along its entire east coast.

***Lágia** ⑤④, with its fortified houses, is the finest village along the east coast – where there are almost no beaches. Beyond Lágia, the road turns west again.

Peloponnese

From **Alika** ⑤⑤, a dead-end road to the left runs for nine kilometers to **Váthia** ⑤⑥. Beautifully restored in 1988, Váthia is the prettiest tower village on the Mani Peninsula. In the months before the tourist season begins, this village of just 40 people is like a living museum.

Further south, beyond Váthia, the road leads to a neck of land high above the sandy bays of the two seas, the Laconian Gulf and the Messenian Gulf. A road on the left leads down to the bay of **Pórto Kágio** ⑤⑦, an overcrowded resort in the summer. Continuing straight ahead, a gravel track runs through barren country, past abandoned hamlets and towers, to the ruins of a church built on the massive foundations of a **Temple of Poseidon** (97 kilometers from Gíthio). From here, it is about a 30-minute walk along a footpath to the lighthouse at **Cape Tenaron**, the southernmost point on the Greek mainland. In ancient times, it was thought that this was where Heracles entered Hades to vanquish the three-headed Hell Hound, Cerberus.

West Coast of Inner Mani

After driving back through Váthia and Alika along the west coast of the Mani, the first place you will reach is **Geroliménas ㊽**, directly on the shore of the Messenian Gulf. After passing through Geroliménas, the road leaves the coast again. Countless hamlets and fine tower villages are huddled on the slopes below the Sangiás Mountains. **★Kíta ㊾** has retained much of its original appearance. Near **Mína ㉠**, a short detour to the left leads to the remarkably ugly resort of **Mézapos ㉡**, on the terraced shore of a deep inlet. On its slopes are the ruins of the fortress of **Maina** (13th century), which was the third of Laconia's principal fortresses under the Franks, along with Mistrás and Monemvasía. Just to the north of **★Pírgos Diroú ㉢** are the seaward-facing entrances to the **dripstone**

Above: Thriving on the Mani – a blossoming pomegranate tree. Right: An Ottoman watchtower near the fortress of Methóni.

caves of Dirós – the caves can only be reached by boat.

The market town of **★Areópoli ㉣** ("City of Ares" – the God of War), sitting high above the Messeniean Gulf, is the Mani's chief town.

North of Areópoli (28 kilometers via the direct route from Gíthio), an unbroken stretch of very beautiful coastline reaches as far as Kalamáta. Outside **Itilo ㉤**, a gorge, guarded by the Turkish fortress of **Kelefá**, separates Inner Mani from Outer Mani. The gorge runs into the bay of Liméni, which cuts deeply into sheer cliffs. Itilo was once the Maniot capital; there is the small **Mani Museum** in the village. Beyond Itilo, the road crosses into Messenia.

MESSENIA

The ancient region and modern prefecture of Messenia occupies the southwest corner of the Peloponnese. It includes the western slopes of the Taygetus mountain range on the Mani Peninsula, the peninsula of Messenia, and the adjacent highlands to the north, as far as the Nédas River. The capital of Messenia is Kalamáta (60 kilometers from Sparta and 90 kilometers from Trípoli).

The Coast of Outer Mani

The drive to Kalamáta from the south takes you from Outer Mani, below the crest of the Taygetus Mountains, along one of the most beautiful coastlines in Greece. As you enter Messenia, the village of Itilo, in Laconia, is followed by a string of small villages perched high above the sea. From **Langáda** (62 kilometers before Kalamáta) on through **Nomitsís** (59 kilometers) and **Plátsa ㉥**, you pass many Byzantine chapels along the road. The most popular stretch of coast for beach vacations is the six kilometers between **Stoúpa ㉦** and **Kardamíli ㉧**. Each resort has a medieval

fortress on an ancient acropolis. Surrounded by a lush wood, Kardamíli has a picturesque **island fortress** opposite.

Kalamáta ⑱ lies at the head of the Messenian Gulf and is the main port of Messenia. The town is divided in two, with a modern, lower town near the shore and the old center with a bazaar on the slopes below a Frankish **fortress** (1208). In the 13th century, Kalamáta was the residence of the Villehardouin family, the Norman Dukes of Achaea.

THE MESSENIAN PENINSULA

Passing through the run-down suburbs of Kalamáta on Highway 89, you come to **Messéne** ⑲. Beyond **Vélika** (17 kilometers), the circular route turns left around the Messenian Peninsula. **Néa Koróni** ⑳ marks the beginning of an attractive stretch of scenery: coastline and hillsides planted with vineyards, olive trees and cypresses. A dead-end street leads to the sea at ***Koróni** ㉑. This resort is beautifully located on the slopes of a spit of land

below a Venetian **fortress**. There are no roads to Cape Akrítas, the southernmost tip of Messenia, and the road crosses the interior of the peninsula westwards near **Harokopió** (58 kilometers).

*Methóni ㉒ is on a headland that juts into the sea, with a Venetian **maritime fortress** at its tip. Venice held Methóni from 1208 to 1500, and again from 1686 to 1715, and developed it into the principal Peloponnese fortified port along the shipping route between the Adriatic and the Levant coast. A bridge over the moat leads to the gate in the landward wall. Three more gates guard the way to the citadel. The zigzagging white limestone ramparts are decorated with the Lion of St. Mark in a number of places. The inner sea wall ends at a popular beach. Opposite, on a rocky island, stands an octagonal tower fort from the Ottoman period.

*PÍLOS AND SPHAKTERIA

The town of ***Pílos** ㉓ lies in the southern curve of the **Bay of Navarino** and

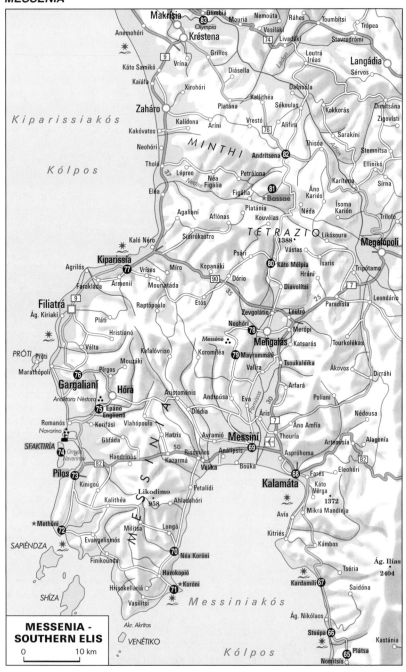

MESSENIA - SOUTHERN ELIS

0   10 km

was itself called *Navarino* in historical times. The bay is cut off from the open sea by the island of Sphakteria (*Sfaktiría*), a 4.5-kilometer-long rocky reef. The island and the bay were the scene of two famous battles: in 425 B.C., a force of Spartans was defeated on Sphakteria by the superior strength of the Athenians; and on October 20, 1827, the Ottoman-Egyptian fleet was defeated by an allied British, French and Russian naval contingent in the Battle of Navarino.

The small port of **Pílos** was built by the French in 1829. Arcades line the main square, **Platía tríon Navárhon** (Square of the Three Admirals), which faces the harbor. There is a monument to the three Allied admirals; Codrington from Britain, the Frenchman de Rigny, and the Russian commander, Von Heyden. The displays in the small **museum** recall the naval battle. A Turkish **fortress** (from 1572) stands above pine-trees on the hill of Ágios Nikólaos, at the southern entrance to the town.

Boat trips run to the uninhabited island of **Sphakteria ②**. On the island are several **memorials** to the freedom fighters; when the sea is calm, wrecked Turkish ships can be seen offshore.

At the highest point of the island (152 meters), in the northwest, are the remains of a Spartan **stronghold** dating from 425 B.C. On a headland to the mainland opposite, at the silted-up northern entrance to the bay, the Venetian **Palékastro Fortress** stands on ancient foundations above the harbor of Mycenaean Pílos.

In *Nestor's Palace

Driving north, the road climbs through fruit-growing areas to **Epáno Englianó ⑦**. *Nestor's Palace, on a hill outside the village, is recognizable from afar by its conspicuous modern roof. The roof protects the **New Palace** (ca. 1250 B.C.) of the Mycenaean royal citadel of **Pylos**. It was built in several stages and was most

likely the seat of Nestor, of Trojan War fame.

It is unique among Mycenaean palaces because it has no defensive walls at all. Its timber roof and upper story were lost in the fire which destroyed the palace around 1200 B.C. The lower stone walls survived the disaster and can give you a clear impression of how Mycenaean royal buildings must have looked. The site follows the standard Mycenaean palace design: official and private rooms flank the central axis of **gatehouse**, **inner courtyard**, **entrance hall**, **vestibule** and **throne room**. The circle of the **sacred hearth** in the middle measures four meters in diameter; the **throne** stood against the wall on the right.

Also on the site are the remains of an **older palace** (ca. 1280 B.C.) and a **burial vault**. A number of the finds from Nestor's Palace are on display at a **museum** in the nearby village of **Hóra** (69 kilometers).

The prosperous country town of **Gargalianí ⑦** lies to the north, high above a broad coastal plain as though on a balcony. The road descends to the flat shore, with many stretches of beach, and continues to **Kiparassía ⑦**. Above the small harbor stands a Byzantine/Frankish **fortress**. The district of Élis begins at the Nédas River.

MESSÉNE AND BASSAE

From Kalamáta, you can take a lovely tour combining the interior of Messenia with visits to the ancient city of Messéne and the Temple of Apollo in Bassae. Both places are among the great sights of the Peloponnese.

From Highway 7 (toward Megalópoli), leave the dreary plain of the Pámisos River near the village of **Tsoukaléïka** (24 kilometers from Kalamáta), turn left onto the side road to the large hill village of **Meligalás** (30 kilometers), and continue to **Neohóri ⑦**. The road leading left, off

the village square, climbs through hills that are covered with olive trees and enters Messéne (43 kilometers) through the Arcadian Gate in the city walls.

A City behind Walls and Towers

Messéne was founded in 369 B.C. by the Theban leader Epaminondas as a new capital for the Messenians and a stronghold against defeated Sparta. The city lies at a height of 420 meters, below the summit of the hill fortress of **Ithome** (798 meters). From the 8th to the 5th centuries B.C., this fortress was a refuge for the Messenians in three wars against Sparta.

The thick **walls** of Messéne, built of large blocks that are fitted together without mortar, are one of the best-preserved examples of antique Greek fortress architecture. The walls are over nine kilometers long and include 30 towers. At the

Above: A flight of steps in the Old Town of Pílos. Right: A protective canopy is stretched over the Temple of Bassae.

*Arcadian Gate two towers guard an outer gate. This leads across a circular forecourt (outer bailey) that is 19 meters in diameter with walls of stone blocks cut precisely to size, to the inner gate. The huge lintel over the inner gate spans the five-meter-wide road beneath.

From the small **museum** (sometimes closed) in the village of **Mavromáti** ❼❾, a path leads down to the site of the city. It passes the ruins of a **theater** and fragments of a **Temple of Artemis**, and enters a square surrounded by a colonnade, with the small **Temple of Asclepius** in the center. The well-preserved seats of an intimate **odeion** can be seen at the northeast corner of the square.

A gate on the eastern side of the square was the entrance to the **Bouleuterion** (city hall). Excavations have continued on the site at a deeper level since 1981, and a **stadium**, **stoa**, **palaestra** and the **Well House of Arsinoë** have been uncovered.

Temple beneath a Yellow Canopy

Return to Meligalás (50 kilometers from Kalamáta) and take the lane beyond the village that runs alongside the railroad tracks to the left. Near **Zevgolátio** (55 kilometers) it crosses Highway 9A and continues on through **Diavolítsi** to **Káto Mélpia** ❽⓿, where a good track leads off to the right. This climbs through wild country and past forlorn hamlets to the ***Temple of Apollo Epikourios** of **Bassae** ❽❶ (Vásses), 1,130 meters above sea level.

The position of the temple, high in totally remote mountain country, is unique in Greece. Sadly, the days are now gone when it presented a wonderful sight as it came into view from afar, crowning the mountain top and often wreathed in cloud. Since 1987 the temple has been hidden under a vast five-pointed canopy of heavy yellow plastic sheeting to prevent the damaged limestone from disinte-

grating. Under the canopy, the temple is held in a corset of struts.

Because the main parts of the building are intact, apart from the roof, the Temple of Apollo Epikourios of Bassae is the best surviving example of temple architecture from the Classical period, after the Hephaesteion in Athens. In its final form (425 B.C.) it was the work of Ictinus, the architect of the Parthenon in Athens. The six rows of 15 columns of the ambulatory are of the Doric order; the first four columns in the inner cella were Ionic. The last pair of columns in the row demonstrate the first Corinthian capitals in Hellas. Most of the columns, entablature and cella walls are preserved, but not the Corinthian capitals, the metopes from the *pronaos* (vestibule), the pediments and their sculptures, or the cella frieze, which is in the British Museum.

The usual route to and from Bassae passes through **Andrítsena** ⑫, a small hill town with pretty wooden houses that lies on the border with the district of Élis. It is here that you join Highway 76 (Meg-alópoli-Pírgos), which continues on towards Olympia.

ÉLIS

The district of Élis in the northwestern Peloponnese is dominated by broad, sometimes marshy salt flats. The widest is the great alluvial plain of the Piniós River, which thrusts westward into the Ionian Sea. The upper reaches of the Alfiós (ancient *Alpheios*) and its tributary, the Erímanthos, form the boundary of Élis' interior uplands to the east. The capital of the district is the unattractive town of **Pírgos**. The last vestiges of the Old Town were destroyed in a major earthquake in March 1993. At the heart of Élis, 17 kilometers from Pírgos, lie the ruins of Olympia.

OLYMPIA

The ****Sanctuary of Olympia** ⑬ (*Olimbía*) lies on the banks of the Alfiós and its tributary the Kladeos, under the

Above: Early vegetables under plastic covers near Killíni, Élis.

hill of Cronus. In antiquity, it was the greatest cult center for the worship of the Greek gods. Surrounding the temples of Zeus and Hera was the *Altis*, or Sacred Grove, decorated with thousands of statues and monuments. The grove was at the heart of a complex of buildings used for worship and ritual competition that developed over hundreds of years.

Olympia was a settlement and trading port in the Mycenaean period. Excavations have confirmed close links with Minoan Crete at a time when the Alfiós must have been navigable up to Olympia. A tree-cult in its luxuriant green valley may have been the seed for Olympia's development into a sanctuary, which was under the administration of the city of Élis from the Archaic period onward. The cult of Zeus and Hera superseded an earlier local cult of the hero Pelops, mythical King of Pisa, who was buried at Olympia. When the Olympic Games first began,

they were probably contests at the funerary celebrations of the Pelops cult.

The lists of champions of the Olympic Games, kept in Élis, go back to the year 776 B.C., though the games began even earlier. Dating from this period was a rather touching agreement among the Greek *poleis* to keep the "sacred truce" (*ekecheiria*) while the games took place. It was proclaimed throughout Hellas by Olympic heralds. The Olympiad – the period of four years between the Games – became the common measurement of time in all of the Hellenic states around the Mediterranean.

When the Games first started, the only event was the stadium race. A *stadion* was a measurement of length in Greece; at first, it was 200 paces (about 160 meters), then 600 Olympic feet (about 200 meters). Races were later supplemented by spear and discus throwing, long jump, wrestling, boxing, horse and chariot races, and the pentathlon.

The shrine employed a large bureaucracy of priests and officials appointed by

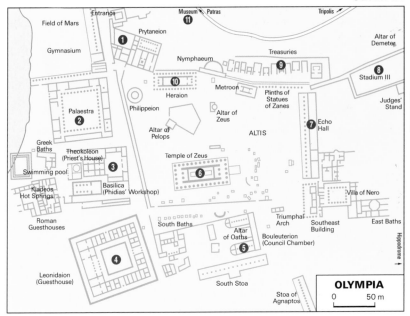

Peloponnese

Élis. Ten organizers (*hellanodikai*) were responsible for the Games; they were also from Élis. They selected the competitors, regulated their training, and acted as the judges. Some of the competitors even became national celebrities, much as they do today.

After being celebrated for more than 1,100 years, the Games were banned in A.D. 393 by Emperor Theodosius I. The buildings were plundered and burned, then they were completely destroyed in an earthquake in the 6th century, when floods covered Olympia with thick layers of mud. After 1875, excavations by the German Archeological Institute began to uncover the buried sanctuary.

A Tour of the Sanctuary

Beyond the entrance gate, the path to the right passes the remains of the entrance hall of the **Great Gymnasium** and, opposite, the **Prytaneion ❶** is where the priests and Olympic champions had their meals. Continue straight ahead,

along the wall enclosing the Altis; on the right, double colonnades of Doric columns surround the square inner courtyard of the **Palaestra ❷** (3rd century B.C.), a wrestling school. Adjoining it was the **Theokoleon ❸**, the house of the three high priests (350 B.C.). Set back beyond this are the towering walls of a Byzantine **basilica**, with two rows of columns and a marble choir screen. Excavations have shown that after 438 B.C., in its original form, this building was used as **Phidias' Workshop**. It was here that Phidias created the gold and ivory statue of Zeus which stood in the temple at Olympia. The foundations of the guesthouses and baths can be seen behind the workshop.

The large rectangular building next on the right is called the **Leonidaion ❹** after its founder, Leonidas of Naxos. It was built as a guesthouse for important visitors (4th century B.C.), and was later a residence for Roman officials. The façade and inner courtyard were surrounded by colonnades. Here at the edge of the site the level of mud from the Alfiós River re-

moved during the excavations can be clearly seen. Turn left below the south side of the Altis wall, between the **south stoa** raised on steps (4th century B.C.) and the **Bouleuterion ❺** (6th/5th century B.C.). An unusual feature found in the Bouleuterion (Council Chamber of the Olympic Senate) is its two parallel wings which end in apses. Between the wings stands the **Altar of Oaths**, where the competitors swore to abide by the rules of the Games.

In the Sacred Grove

The plinths of many statues surround the base of the **Temple of Zeus ❻**, which dominates the Altis. The massive column uprights, which have reimained stacked in sections on the ground since they collapsed almost 1,500 years ago, give a good idea of the former splendor of the

Above: Columns of the Temple of Hera in Olympia's Sacred Grove. Right: Olympia attracts visitors from all over the world.

building. The temple, one of the largest in Greece, was the work of Libo of Elis and was completed in the year 456 B.C. Even in its ruined state the temple dominates the area on its 2.5-meter-tall base, on which stands a three-tiered substructure. The Doric columns (six rows of 13) of stuccoed shell lime were 10.53 meters tall and measured 2.23 meters at the base.

A ramp from the east led into the entrance hall and the doorway to the cella. The inner chamber was about 29 meters long and was divided into three along its length. Two rows of low columns flanked the central aisle, supporting the visitors' galleries and two other rows of columns which formed the base for the timber roof structure. The 12-meter-tall ivory-and-gold statue of Zeus stood in the central aisle. The work of the sculptor Phidias, it depicted Zeus seated with the figure of Nike on one hand and an eagle scepter in the other. His face, hands and feet were of ivory and his garments of solid gold. The throne and pedestal were covered with reliefs and were sumptuously decorated.

The statue was one of the Seven Wonders of the ancient world. It was probably destroyed in a fire in Constantinople in A.D. 475.

The **triumphal arch** of Emperor Nero stood at the entrance to the **Altis**, at the southeast corner. The south front of the Altis was bounded by the **southeast building** (4th century B.C.), which was demolished in the 1st century A.D. in order to make way for **Nero's Villa**, and by the 98-meter-long **Echo Hall** . The hall was a stoa (ca. 350 B.C.) with a double row of columns in which voices threw back an echo seven times.

At the top of the Echo Hall, a tunnel leads into the **stadium** ❽, where you can see the **start and finish lines** for the runners at each end. The site has been restored to its original state. Only the judges' platform and seats of honor are, and were, built of stone. The rows of seats (for up to 40,000 spectators) were built on earthen ramparts.

To the right of the stadium gate are the **plinths** of the statues of Zeus called the *Zanes*. They were built with the money from fines paid by athletes who had cheated in the games. Adjoining these is the **Metroon** (3rd century B.C.), a small temple dedicated to the mother of the gods which was used by the cult of the emperors in Roman times. Above it, at the foot of the hill of Cronus, stood the **treasuries** ❾ of the Greek *poleis*, built in the 5th and 6th centuries B.C.

The adjacent broad, semicircular building was a well house, the **Nymphaeum** of Herodes Atticus (A.D. 160). It was built by Atticus as a memorial to his wife Regilla, priestess of Demeter. The Nymphaeum was the last great building to be erected in the sanctuary. In the niches of the curved wall, and on the ledge above, stood 20 marble statues of the families of Roman emperors and of Atticus. The Nymphaeum was at the end of a pipeline system that supplied water to Olympia.

A few of the columns of the Temple of Hera are still standing. Built a little before 600 B.C., the **Heraion** ❿ is the oldest temple in Olympia. It was converted from a wooden to a stone building in several stages up to Roman times. The varying quality of the masonry work indicates where the wooden columns were gradually replaced with stone columns over hundreds of years. A wall in the form of an irregular pentagon between the temples of Hera and Zeus is all that remains of the mythical tomb and the **Altar of Pelops**.

The circular building, whose fine foundations can be seen near the Heraion, not far from the entrance to the Altis, was the **Philippeion**. It was enclosed by a peristyle of 18 columns, while 12 columns inside the cella supported the roof. It was built by Philip II of Macedonia in 338 B.C., and displayed five gold and ivory statues representing Philip, his parents, his wife Olympia, and his son Alexander, who would come to be known as Alexander the Great.

Peloponnese

The Olympia *Museum

A short path leads to the ***Museum** ⑪ at the end of the large parking lot opposite the archeological site. The collection reflects the glory of Olympia over 1,000 years. A selection of the most important exhibits follows:

The **Entrance Hall** contains plinths from votive offerings and statues. The tour, in chronological order of the exhibits, begins on the left in **Gallery I** (Prehistoric to Geometric period): Cases 1 and 2: Clay pots and implements from the Early and Middle Helladic period (2800-1600 B.C.), the oldest finds on the site. Cases 3-7: Objects from the Mycenaean period (1600-1100 B.C.). Among the prize exhibits from the Geometric period (about 1050-700 B.C.) are small bronze **sculptures** and **votive vessels**. Case 8 shows

Above: One arch of the tunnel entrance to the stadium at Olympia has survived. Right: The Hermes of Praxiteles is the pride of the museum.

the development of human sculpture from the earliest **statues of the gods** of the 10th century (B1391 and B4245) to a figure of Hera (TC2285) from the 8th century B.C. Between cases 5 and 6 is one of the oldest **bronze vessels** (B1240), dating from the 9th century B.C. and in good condition. In the center of the gallery is a ***bronze horse** (B1741); a monumental cast figure from the transition to the Archaic period.

Gallery II (Geometric to Archaic periods): Case 3: Bronze human and animal statuettes that decorated the tops of votive vessels. Case 1: Bronze vessel decoration from the Orientalist phase around the turn of the 7th century B.C., including the earliest **griffin** (Br. 8767), around 700 B.C., and a cast **griffin** (B945) dating from about 630-623 B.C. The following cases display the best examples of the ancient weapons found at Olympia: In the trapezoidal case, a 6th century B.C. beaten bronze **shield device** (B110) about one meter in diameter, with a gorgon's head and three wings. In the case on the high platform: Back section of a suit of armor (M394) dating from about 650-625 B.C., with remarkable engravings of deities. In the wall case next to case 5: Female **griffin** suckling her young, a very lifelike representation from a Corinthian workshop dating from about 630-620 B.C. In the case on the tall pedestal in front: Winged female **demon figure** (B6500), a very rare beaten bronze three-dimensional sculpture from about 590-580 B.C., with inset eyes of bone. Beyond the wall case, up on the wall behind case 8: **Colossal head of a goddess** in limestone (1), probably from the cult statue of Hera in the Heraion, around 600 B.C. In the third wall case following, displays are the finest small sculptures found in the shrine; the statuettes of the **Marching Warrior** (B5000) and the **Old Man with a Stick** (B25). These are Laconian works from around 550 B.C.

Gallery III (Archaic period): Case 1: Female head in clay (T1), around 530-520 B.C. Other striking items in the gallery are the restored **pediment** from the Treasury of Megara, dating from about 520 B.C., which still has some of the pediment sculptures of the battle of the gods and giants. On the wall: Bronze **ram** (B3010), about 520 B.C., the only one to have survived from antiquity.

Gallery IV (Early and High Classical period): The outstanding terra-cotta group of ***Zeus with Ganymede** (T2), about 480-470 B.C., showing the god carrying the handsome Trojan prince off to Olympus. In the two cases on a high pedestal: **Helmet of Miltiades** (B2600), probably worn by the Athenian general during his victory over the Persians at the Battle of Marathon in 490 B.C., and dedicated by Miltiades to the temple, according to the inscription; the **bronze helmet** (B5100) is probably of Assyrian origin and is the only booty from the Persian Wars still in existence; and a superb Peloponnesian **terra-cotta statue of a warrior** (T3), around 480 B.C. Case 1:

Terra-cotta **head of a statue of Athena** (T6), a work in the Severe Style dating from about 490 B.C. In front, in the case on the high pedestal: Fine **bronze horse** (B1000), around 470 B.C. In case 3: Objects from Phidias' Workshop, including clay molds used for the gold castings of the garments on the statue of Zeus, and a small **wine jug**, in the base of which are etched, probably by Phidias himself, the words "I belong to Phidias."

In the **apse** of Gallery IV stands the ***Nike of Paionios**, by a sculptor from Mende in the Chalcidice; the oldest known sculpture of the goddess of victory. Standing over two meters tall, it was a votive offering from the Messenians and Naupactians, probably in 421 B.C. It stood on a tall triangular base at the southeast corner of the Temple of Zeus.

Central Gallery V: On both sides, in their original order, are the superb ***pedimental sculptures of the Temple of Zeus**. In a space that is 26.4 meters wide and 3.5 meters high at the center, the pediments showed the preparations for the

great chariot race between Pelops and Oenomaos (east pediment), and the battle of the Lapiths and Centaurs (west pediment). The spaces were filled with 42 monumental figures, large fragments of which have been preserved. Serene gestures and reflective faces characterize the work of the unknown artist from the mid-5th century B.C. as the zenith of the later Severe Style. The contrast in composition between the two pediments is striking. Tranquil vertical lines – and horizontal lines in the reclining figures in the spandrel – predominate in the figures on the east pediment; the crowd tensely awaits the contest. On the west pediment, the bodies are entwined in a breathless struggle; the center lines of the figures intersect many times in every dimension.

Zeus stands in the center of the **east pediment**. Pelops stands on his right (as you look up), and his beloved Hip-

Above: The west pediment of the Temple of Zeus shows the battle between the Lapiths and Centaurs.

podameia, daughter of Oenomaos, stands beside him. Oenomaos, the bearded king of Pisa, stands on the left with his wife Sterope; he will be beaten by Pelops in the chariot race and then killed. Servants crouch in front of the two four-horse chariots, spectators sit at the sides, and two figures lying in a corner are probably allegories of the Alfiós and Kladeos rivers.

The **west pediment** shows how the Centaurs – half man and half horse – wantonly tried to seize the Lapith women at the wedding of Perithoos, king of the Lapiths. In the center, the outstretched hand of Apollo indicates the will of the god: order and reason will overcome bestial chaos. On the right (as you look up), Theseus is about to strike a Centaur who is grasping a Lapith woman, while on the left Perithoos tries to rescue his wife Deidameia from the clutches of Eurythion, the king of the Centaurs. Other groups of fighters and prone Lapith women can be seen anxiously awaiting the outcome. Along the two narrow sides of the gallery are the **metopes from the Temple of Zeus**, which contain a powerfully moving depiction of the Twelve Labors of Heracles.

Gallery VI (Late Classical and Hellenic periods): Displays sculptures and fragments from buildings. **Side Gallery VIII** contains only the ***Hermes of Praxiteles** (330 B.C.). This 2.1-meter-tall statue is one of the great works of ancient sculpture. It was lifted almost intact, in 1877, from the ruins of the Temple of Hera, where the Roman traveler Pausanias saw it in the 2nd century A.D. and declared it to be the work of Praxiteles. The handsome male figure is shown naked and leaning casually against a tree trunk. On his supported arm he carries the newborn infant Dionysus, whom he will bring to the nymphs in Boetia for safekeeping.

Gallery IX (Roman period): Displays mainly statues, most of which come from the Nymphaeum of Herodes Atticus dating from the 2nd century A.D.

Gallery X (Olympic Games gallery): Displays objects from all periods that are directly connected with the Games.

In the village of **Olimbía**, which consists mainly of hotels, the small **Olympic Games Museum** displays a number of objects that commemorate the modern Games; from Athens in 1896 to today.

The Coast of Élis

Near **Pírgos** **❽❹** (17 kilometers from Olympia), you join Highway 9 (towards Pátras). A detour along a narrow side road to the west leads you to **Katákolo** **❽❺** on the coast (24 kilometer round trip). On a narrow spit of land approaching Katákolo (ferry port from the Adriatic to Crete and Turkey) the Frankish fortress of **Pondikókastro** stands over the acropolis of ancient *Pheia*.

Back on Highway 9 you can take a detour to the right (45 kilometers from Olympia) along a narrow road through the valley of the Piniós to ancient **Élis** **❽❻**

(10 kilometers each way). From the museum by the road a path leads to a Hellenistic **theater**. A road branches off from Highway 9 and heads seawards through **Gastoúni** **❽❼** to the hot springs and seaside resort of **Loutrá Killínis** **❽❽** (60 kilometers); a jumble of disproportionately large streets and hotels.

The nearby village of **Kástro** **❽❾** is dominated by the fortress of ***Hlemoútsi**, the best preserved Frankish fort in the Peloponnese, which stands on a hill above the plain. It was built by Geoffroy I de Villehardouin in 1223, and was known as Clairmont. Parts of houses and shops are still standing in front of the fortress. The keep was hexagonal, with vaulted galleries around an inner courtyard.

Killíni **❾⓿** (70 kilometers), ancient *Kylene*, was the main port of Élis in ancient times, and is now a ferry port for Zákinthos and Kefaloniá. After passing through **Leheniá**, you'll return to Highway 9, which leads through dull coastal country to Pátras (113 kilometers by the direct route from Olympia).

Excursion to Zákinthos

On the western side of **Zákinthos** **❾❶**, the most southerly of the Ionian Islands, steep cliffs drop to the sea from an 800-meter-high peak. On the other side of the mountain, the hills and valleys of a fertile farming area extend eastward. The island was Venetian from 1489 until 1797, and was called Zante and the "Flower of the East." Many of the island's inhabitants are Roman Catholics of Italian descent. The island has suffered many earthquakes – the most recent, in 1953, completely destroyed the town of **Zákinthos** **❶**. It has since been rebuilt to the old design, with its Italian arcades. The town lies on a wide, crescent-shaped bay with beaches; the Venetian **Kastro** looks down from the hill above the city. The rebuilt church of **Ágios Dionísios** contains the relics of the saint of the same name, pa-

Peloponnese

ZÁKINTHOS

0   10 km

tron saint of the island. The **museum** on Pl. Solomoú, by the harbor, displays mainly religious art; in the icons you can see the influence Italy had on post-Byzantine painting.

The **Solomós Museum** on Pl. Agíou Márkou is dedicated to the memory of Dionísios Solomós, Greece's poet laureate who was from Zákinthos. It stands above the mausoleum of Solomós and the poet Andréas Kálvos, who was also born on the island. A third 19th-century poet from the island, Ugo Foscolo, is one of the great figures of Italian literature.

Just eight kilometers from the town of Zákinthos is a massive beach in the bay of **Lagánas ❷**, which attracts many summer visitors.

Excursion to Kefaloniá

Kefaloniá ❷ is the largest of the Ionian Islands and has the most varied scen-

Right: A fisherman from the gulf coast sorts out his lines for the next catch.

ery. Its coast is wild. In the center of the island is the range of Mt. Enos, rising to 1,628 meters. Wine is made in the fertile uplands on its fringes. The ferry from Killíni arrives in the harbor of **Póros ❶**, in the southeast of the island. The island's other ports are Sámi in the central east coast, Fiskárdo in the north, and Argostóli, the island's capital, in the west.

Argostóli ❷ is situated on a spit of land projecting into a bay which cuts deep into the island. **Lixoúri**, Kefaloniá's second town, lies opposite Argostóli on the Palíki Peninsula. Both towns were rebuilt after the 1953 earthquake. The small **museum** in Argostóli contains mainly Minoan and Mycenaean objects.

Lord Byron lived in the village of **Metaxáta**, south of Argostóli, in 1823-24, before he went to Mesolóngion, where he died in 1824. The nearby hamlet of **Kástro**, which lies below a Byzantine **fortress**, was the island's ancient capital, known as Ágios Geórgios. On a hilltop above Kástro is the convent of **Ágios Gerásimos**, the island's patron saint.

At the northern tip of the peninsula of Argostóli, **sea-powered mills** once made use of the seawater rushing through subterranean channels – until the great earthquake. The water reappears in **Lake Melissáni ❸**, near Sámi on the opposite side of the island. The lake is part of a system of grottoes and **dripstone caves**. **Sámi ❹** is on a wide bay where the European fleet lay at anchor before the Battle of Lepanto against the Ottoman Turks in 1571. The resort of **Assos ❺** is attractively located on the northwest coast below a Venetian castle and on an isthmus between two bays. The small port of ***Fiskárdo ❻**, on the northern tip of Kefaloniá, is one of the few island villages that was not destroyed by the earthquake. Duke Robert Guiscard, a Norman, died in Fiskárdo in 1085; he was the first in a series of medieval conquerors to capture the island, which was in Venetian hands from 1500 until 1797.

Peloponnese

ACHAEA

Achaea occupies the north coast of the Peloponnese up to the middle of the Gulf of Corinth. Its only flat area is the marshy coast running towards the northwest tip of the Peloponnese at Cape Araxas. Everywhere else, mountains rise up directly from narrow strips of coastland. The interior of Achaea is bordered by the peaks of Mt. Erímanthos (2,224 meters) and the Aroánia Mountains (2,341 meters) – which are also called Hélmos after the range's main peak. Its coasts lie on the gulfs of Corinth and Pátras. The prefectural capital and capital of the Peloponnese region, Pátras is the third-largest city in Greece – behind Greater Athens and Thessaloníki – with a population of about 200,000.

Pátras

Pátras ⓕ (*Pátra*) is the main port of entry to Greece on the route across the Adriatic from Italy. The modern city was laid out after the War of Independence. Since World War II, its growth has been uncontrolled and it has become a charmless place. The only attractive thing about it is its location – beside the sea, beneath the peak of **Mt. Panahaïkó** (1,926 meters), snow-covered for several months of the year, and with a view of the coast of central Greece in the distance.

On the waterfront are docks for commercial shipping and ferries to Italy and the islands of Zákinthos, Kefaloniá and Ithaca. The city's main thoroughfare, Od. Agíou Nikoláou, leads uphill from **Platía tríon Simáhon**, a square in the middle of the waterfront. The third street on the left, **Od. Mézonos**, leads to **Pl. Olgas** and the city's **Archeological Museum**.

Gallery I: Fine Roman mosaic floor; portrait heads from the Classical period.

Gallery II: Displays of small finds from all periods; gold-work from the Classical and Hellenistic periods; and a rare fragment of blue window glass in a polygonal ivory frame from the 1st/2nd century A.D.

Od. Agíou Nikoláou ends in a flight of stairs. From here, Od. Agíou Georgíou, on the right, brings you to the **Odeion of Herodes Atticus** (A.D. 160); the present building is a modern reconstruction. The steps lead up to the **Kastro**, a fortified Byzantine citadel built on top of the ancient acropolis.

The church of **Ágios Andréas** (on the waterfront, at the western end of the docks) is probably the best example of the incredibly uniform disaster of modern Greek church architecture. The cathedral, dedicated to the city's patron saint, is a bombastic imitation of the Byzantine style. The largest church in Greece, it has been the repository of the skull of St. Andrew the Apostle, said to have been martyred in Pátras, since it was returned by Rome in 1964.

The Achaean Gulf Coast

The expressway, old highway and railroad run side by side, eastward along the narrow strip of coast at the foot of the mountains. At the start of the multi-lane expressway (E65) a broad access road branches left (seven kilometers from Pátras) towards **Río** 94. Here, the Ottoman maritime fortress of **Kástro Moréas** (15th century) guards the "Dardanelles of Greece," the strait between the Peloponnese and central Greece, which is only two kilometers wide. The ferries that ply across the gulf, day and night, carry more than two million vehicles annually. A suspension bridge across the strait is due to be completed in 2002.

The small town of **Egio** 95 has the most beautiful location on the entire Gulf of Corinth. Like ancient *Aigion* before it, the port (from which ferries leave for central Greece) looks out from a gently sloping plateau of rock which ends in a sheer cliff that drops 30 meters to the shore.

With its mixture of modern buildings, neoclassical merchants' houses and rustic cottages from the Ottoman period, Egio is

an interesting prototype of the Greek provincial town. A detour from here takes you through **Káto Melíssia** 96, through the delightful valley of the Selinoús River, to **Moní Taxiárhon** (Monastery of the Archangels) on the slopes of Mt. Panahaïkó (24 kilometer round trip).

Beyond Egio, the coastal strip widens into a plain which ends in **Diakoftó** 97. The hundred-year-old station on the ****Kalávrita narrow-gauge railway** – its track a mere 70 centimeters wide – is well worth a visit; a train journey into the mountains, with the toy-sized diesel locomotives and carriages, is a rare experience. The entire trip, both there and back (six departures daily with a 15-minute stop in Kalávrita), takes no more than two

Peloponnese

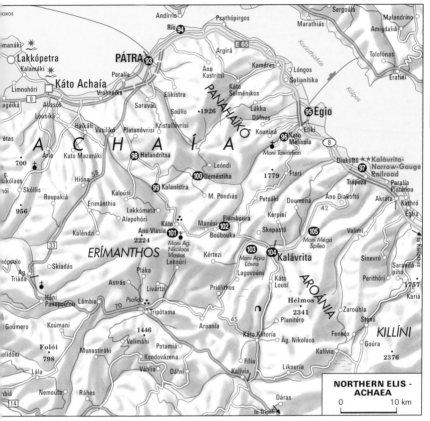

and a half hours. During the 68-minute journey the train climbs from sea-level to 720 meters. The route (23 kilometers) passes through the narrow tunnels of the **Vouraïkós Gorge**, where a mountain torrent cuts through the sheer cliff in a succession of waterfalls. On the steepest sections (14.5 percent gradient) the trains use rack-and-pinion traction, and even the longer adhesion sections have a gradient of 3.3 percent

The road to Kalávrita, and the Méga Spíleo and Agía Lávra monasteries branches off at **Trápeza**; it does not go through the gorge itself. The expressway leaves Achaea in **Dervéni** (72 kilometers) and continues to Corinth and Athens (129 and 206 kilometers from Pátras).

From Pátras to the Mountains

From **Pátras** (⓽③), the scenery of Achaea offers a beautiful tour through the mountains of the Peloponnese. The recommended route takes you in a wide arc through the triangle of the Panahaïkó, Erímanthos and Aroánia mountains to the coast of the Gulf of Corinth.

Follow Highway 33 (heading towards Trípoli) south through the hills above Pátras until the signposted turnoff for Kalávrita (after 13 kilometers). Beyond **Halandrítsa** ⓽⑧, once the seat of a Frankish barony, the beautiful mountain scenery begins. Outside **Kalanístra** ⓽⑨ a secondary road branches off towards **Deméstiha** ⓵⓪⓪, a village that has given its

name to the famous *Demestika* wine of Achaea.

The road then clings to the mountainside where goats graze, and climbs past abandoned hamlets to a height of 1,000 meters, where it crosses the slopes of **Mt. Erímanthos** (2,192 meters).

Perched on an egg-shaped hill near the twin villages of **Ano Vlasía** and **Káto Vlasía** ⑩ is the monastery of **Ágios Nikólaos Vlasías**. On the edge of the valley, below the villages, stood the ancient city of **Leontion**. Its excavated **theater** is hidden among the shrubs that cover the slopes of the valley.

After climbing through alpine scenery and pine forests to an altitude of 1,100 meters, the road descends into a high valley where the dilapidated villages have strange-sounding names, like **Boúbouka** and **Flámboura** ⑩. On a lonely hill, the **Heroon** (72 kilometers from Pátras) is an enormous memorial to the heroes of the Greek War of Independence.

Above: The Vouraïkós Gorge.

Not far away (74 kilometers) is the monastery of **Agía Lávra** ⑩, where, on March 25, 1821, Metropolit Germanós of Pátras proclaimed the Greek War of Independence from the Ottomans. The monastery, founded as a hermitage in A.D. 961, is one of the principal shrines of the modern Greek nation. The historic events associated with it are documented in the **museum**. The monastery you see today is a modern building; the previous one was reduced to ashes in 1943 during reprisals against the citizens of Kalávrita by the occupying German forces.

Kalávrita ⑩ lies at an altitude of 720 meters in the green valley of the Vouraïkós River beneath the Aroánia Mountains. Most Greek visitors come to the small town – not much more than a village – because it is the main ski resort on the slopes of the Aroánia's highest peak, **Mt. Hélmos** (2,341 meters). However, the shadow of the tragedy of December 13, 1943, still hangs over Kalávrita: After a German army unit had been attacked by partisans in the mountains nearby, the village's entire male population was herded together and shot by the Germans, who then proceeded to destroy the village. More than 1,400 men, women and children died that afternoon. The massacre is recalled by a memorial outside the village where the shootings took place. Ever since then, the clock on the left-hand tower of the village church has stood at 2:34, the moment when the slaughter began.

To the left of the road leading to the **narrow-gauge railway** station are the ruins of the late-Byzantine **palace** of Ekateríni Paleológina. Above Kalávrita, the ruined fortress of **Kastro Trémolo** takes its name from a Frankish baron, Humbert de la Tremouille.

The road to the coast climbs to the east of the Vouraïkós Gorge. The monastery of **Méga Spíleo** ⑩⑤ sits like an eagle's nest 950 meters up a sheer cliff face. The monastery of the Holy Virgin of the Great Cave was founded in the 6th century and rebuilt after a fire in 1934. From the entrance hall, steps lead down to the Great Cave, a sacred spring with a beautiful fountain where painted metal figures (life-sized) depict the legend of the monastery's origins: A shepherdess found an icon and with its help drove away the dragon which lived in the cave. The miraculous image of the Virgin can be seen to the right of the Holy Doors in the *templon* of the monastery's church; it is a Byzantine icon with miraculous powers which pious tradition attributes to St. Luke the Apostle. A small collection of beautifully illuminated Gospel manuscripts on parchment and valuable icons are displayed in the **museum**. The oldest dates from the 9th century.

Beyond the pass, before you reach the final descent to the coast, is a broad panorama across the Gulf of Corinth of the mountains of central Greece. At **Trápeza**, 108 kilometers from Pátras, you will rejoin the coastal road leading from Pátras to Corinth.

Peloponnese

LACONIA

AMYKLAI
🏛 **Archeological Site**, free access.

AREÓPOLI (☎ 0733)
▨ 😊😊😊 **Pyrgos Kapetanakou** (tower house), tel. 51233.
😊😊 **Mani**, tel. 51269.

DIRÓS (☎ 0733)
▨ 😊😊 **Dyros**, tel. 52306.

GERÁKI
🏛 **Byzantine Ruins**, free access.

GEROLIMÉNAS (☎ 0733)
▨ 😊 **Akrotaenaritis**, tel. 54205.

GÍTHIO (☎ 0733)
▨ ▨ 😊😊😊 **Laconis**, tel. 22666. **Cavo Grosso**, Mavrovouni, tel. 23488. **Belle Helène**, Vathi Ageranou, tel. 93001.
😊😊 **Kranae**, tel. 24394. **Laryssion**, tel. 22021. **Pantheon**, tel. 22284.
😊 **Aktaeon**, tel. 22294.
▣ *EXCURSIONS:* Ferries to the island of **Kíthira** depart several times a week from the harbor in Gíthio.
BEACHES: The beaches directly south of Gíthio, before the plain of **Mavrovoúni**, are nice.

ITILO (☎ 0733)
▨ 😊😊 **Itilo**, tel. 51300.

KÍTHIRA (☎ 0735)
▨ KÍTHIRA TOWN: 😊😊 **Margarita**, tel. 31711, beautiful hotel in a villa, central location.
KAPSÁLI: 😊 **Aphrodite**, tel. 31328, near the beach.

MISTRÁS
🏛 **Byzantine Ruins**, April 1-May 14 and Sept 1-Oct 31, daily 8 am-7 pm; May 15-Aug 31, daily 8 am-8 pm; Nov 1-March 31, daily 8 am -2:30 pm.

MONEMVASÍA (☎ 0732)
▨ 😊😊😊 **Ano Malvasia**, tel. 61113. **Malvasia II**, tel. 61323. **Panos**, tel. 61480. **Venetia**, tel. 61154. **Villa Trougakos**, tel. 61177. **Byzantino**, tel. 613 51.
😊😊 **Angela's House**, tel. 61418. **Minoa**, tel. 61209.
😊 **Akroyali**, tel. 61360. **Aktaeon**, tel. 61234. **Monemvasía**, tel. 61381.
▣ *BEACHES:* On the Laconian Peninsula, the best beaches are directly north and south of Monemvasía.

NEÁPOLIS (☎ 0734)
▨ 😊😊😊 **Limira Mare**, tel. 22208.
😊😊 **Aivali**, tel. 22287.
▣ *EXCURSIONS:* Ferries to the island of Kíthira depart daily from the harbor in Neápolis.
BEACHES: Neápolis is home to some of the finest beaches on the Laconian Peninsula.

PÓRTO KÁGIO

📩 *BEACHES:* There are many sandy inlets on the narrow southern tip of the Laconian Peninsula near Pórto Kágio.

PÍRGOS DIROÚ

🏛 **Dripstone Caves of Dirós**, Oct-May daily 8 am-2:45 pm; June-Sept daily 8 am-5:30 pm.

SPARTA (☎ 0731)

🛏 😊😊😊 **Lida**, tel. 23601. 😊😊 **Apollon**, tel. 22491. **Dioskouri**, tel. 28484. **Sparta Inn**, tel. 21021. 😊 **Cecil**, tel. 24980. **Laconia**, tel. 28951. **Panellinion**, tel. 28031.

🏛 **Acropolis**, free access; **Archeological Museum** (Od. Dionysíou), Tue-Sun 8:30 am-3 pm.

VAFIO

🏛 **Domed Grave**, free access.

VÁTHIA (☎ 0733)

🛏 😊😊😊 Traditional **Tower Houses**, central reservations, tel. 55244.

MESSENIA

📩 *BEACHES:* The best sand beaches on the Messenian Peninsula are in **Koróni** (south of town) and **Methóni**. Further north, the **west coast** offers many other fine sand beaches, including the popular resort of **Kiparissía**.
There are many good beaches along the coast of Outer Mani; popular resorts include **Kardamíli** (pebble) and **Stoúpa** (sand).

ÁGIOS ANDRÉAS (☎ 0725)

🛏 😊😊 **Akroyali**, tel. 31266. **Longas Beach**, tel. 31583.

ÁGIOS AVGOUSTINOS (☎ 0722)

🛏 😊😊😊 **Club Aquarius San Agostino Beach**, tel. 22151.

BASSAE

🏛 **Temple of Apollo**, Tue-Sun 8 am-2:30 pm.

EPÁNO ENGLIANÓ

🏛 **Nestor's Palace**, Mon-Sat 8:45 am-3 pm, Sun 10 am-3 pm.

FILIATRA (☎ 0761)

🛏 😊 **Limenari**, tel. 32935.

HÓRA

🏛 **Museum** (Nestor's Palace), Wed-Sat 9:15 am-3:30 pm, Sun 10 am-3 pm. **Fort Palékastro**, free access.

KALAMÁTA (☎ 0721)

🛏 😊😊😊 **Elite**, tel. 25015. **Filoxenia**, tel. 23166. 😊😊 **Galaxias**, tel. 86002. 😊 **George**, tel. 27225. **Plaza**, tel. 82590. **Nevada**, tel. 82429.
📩 *BEACH:* The beach (sand and pebble) in Kalamáta is several kilometers long.

KALO NERO (☎ 0761)

🛏 😊😊😊 **Oasis** (apartments.), tel. 72561. 😊 **Akroyali**, tel. 71345.

KARDAMÍLI (☎ 0721)

🛏 😊😊😊 **Kalamitsi**, tel. 73131. 😊😊 **Esperides**, tel. 73173. **Kardamíli Beach**, tel. 73180. **Patriarcheas**, tel. 73366. **Theano**, tel. 73222.

KIPARISSÍA (☎ 0761)

🛏 😊😊😊 **Kiparissía Beach**, tel. 24492. 😊😊 **Apollon**, tel. 24411. **Ionion**, tel. 22511.

KORÓNI (☎ 0725)

🛏 😊😊😊 **Auberge de la Plage**, tel. 22401. 😊 **Diana**, tel. 22312. **Marinos**, tel. 22522.

MESSÉNE (Neohori)

🏛 **Ancient Ruins**, free access. **Ithome Hill Fortress** and **Vourkánou Monestary**, free access.

MESSÉNE (☎ 0722)

🛏 😊😊 **Messiní**, tel. 23002.

METHONI (☎ 0723)

🛏 😊😊😊 **Amalia**, tel. 31193. **Methoni Beach**, tel. 31544. **Odysseas**, tel. 31600.
😊😊 **Alex**, tel. 31219.
😊 **Albatros**, tel. 31160. **Dionyssos**, tel. 31317. **Finikas**, tel. 31390. **Rex**, tel. 31239.
🏛 **Fortress**, daily 8:30-3 pm. **Ágios Ioánnis Monastery** in the **Koróni Fortress**, daily 9 am-1 pm and 5-7 pm.

PÍLOS (☎ 0723)

🛏 😊😊😊 **Karalis Beach**, tel. 23021. 😊😊 **Galaxy**, tel. 22780. **Karalis**, tel. 22960. 😊 **Navarinon**, tel. 22291. **Nilefs**, tel. 22518.
🏛 **Museum**, Tue-Sun 8:30 am-3 pm; **Kastro**, Tue-Sun 8:30-3 pm.

STOÚPA (☎ 0721)

🛏 😊😊 **Maistrali**, tel. 54595. **Stoupa**, tel. 77308.

ÉLIS

AMALIADA (☎ 0622)

🛏 😊😊 **Hellinis**, tel. 28975.

ANDRÍTSENA (☎ 0626)

🛏 😊😊 **Theoxenia**, tel. 22219. 😊 **Pan**, tel. 22213.

ARKOUDI (☎ 0623)

🛏 😊😊 **Arkoudi**, tel. 96480. **Lintzi**, tel. 96483.

GLIFA (☎ 0623)

🛏 😊😊 **Kypriotis**, tel. 96372.

KAIAFAS (☎ 0625)

🛏 😊😊 **Kaiafas Lake**, tel. 32954. **Jenny**, tel. 32252. 😊 **Arini**, tel. 31710. **Xenon A**, tel. 31710.
📩 *BEACH:* Narrow beach lined with pine trees.

KÁSTRO (☎ 0623)

🛏 😊😊😊 **Robinson Club Hotel**, tel. 95205. 😊😊 **Chryssi Avgi**, tel. 95224. **Paradise**, tel. 95209.

KATÁKOLO (☎ 0621)
⌷ ⊜⊜ **Ionio**, tel. 41494.
◤ *BEACH:* Fine sand beach.

KILLÍNI
◤ *EXCURSIONS:* Ferries depart for the islands of **Zákinthos** (up to six times daily) and **Kefaloniá** (at least twice a day) from the harbor in **Killíni.**

KOUROUTAS (☎ 0622)
⌷ ⊜⊜⊜ **Akti Kouroutas**, tel. 22902.

LIGIAS (☎ 0623)
⌷ ⊜⊜⊜ **Helidonia**, tel. 96393.

LOUTRÁ KILLÍNIS (☎ 0623)
⌷ ⊜ **Ionion**, tel. 92318. **Xenia**, tel. 96275.
◤ *BEACH:* Fine sand beach before Vartholomio's large woodland area.

MIRTIA (☎ 0621)
⌷ ⊜ **Zorbas**, tel. 94233.

OLYMPIA (☎ 0624)
⌷ City Information Center, Od. Praxitélous Kondíli, tel. 23125.
⌷ ⊜⊜⊜ **Altis**, tel. 23101. **Amalia**, tel. 22190. **Antonios**, tel. 22348. **Apollon**, tel. 22522. **Evropi**, tel. 22650. **Olympic Village Hotel**, tel. 22211.
⊜⊜ **Ilis**, tel. 22547. **Kronion**, tel. 22502. **Olympiaki Dada**, tel. 22668. **Phedias**, tel. 22667. **Xenia**, tel. 22510.
⊜ **Hermes**, tel. 22577.
⌷ **Archeological Site** and **Museum**, April 1-May 14 and Sept 1-Oct 31 8 am-7 pm; May 15-Aug 8 am-8 pm; Nov 1-March 31 8 am-2:30 pm. **Ancient City of Élis**, free access. **Hlemoútsi Fortress**, Mon-Sat 9 am-3:30 pm, Sun 10 am-3 pm. **Olympic Games Historical Museum**. Mon-Sat am-3:30 pm, Sun 9 am-4:30 pm.

PÍRGOS (☎ 0621)
⌷ ⊜⊜ **Ilida**, tel. 28046. **Pantheon**, tel. 29746.

VARTHOLOMIO (☎ 0623)
⌷ ⊜⊜ **Alfa**, tel. 41707. **Fegarognemata**, tel. 41222.
⊜ **Ilida**, tel. 41266.

VRANAS (☎ 0623)
⌷ ⊜⊜ **Taxiarhis**, tel. 41440.

ACHAEA

AKRATA (☎ 0696)
⌷ ⊜⊜ **Akrata Beach**, tel. 31180.

AROANIA (☎ 0692)
⌷ ⊜ **Tartaris**, tel. 61213.

BOZAITIKA (☎ 061)
⌷ ⊜⊜ **Achaía Beach**, tel. 99180.

DAFNÍ (☎ 0692)
⌷ ⊜ **Dafni**, tel. 71217.

DIAKOFTO (☎ 0691)
⌷ ⊜⊜ **Chris-Paul**, tel. 41715.
⊜ **Chelmos**, tel. 41236. **Lemonies**, tel. 41229.

EGIO (☎ 0691)
⌷ ⊜⊜ **Telios**, tel. 28200.

FTERI (☎ 0691)
⌷ ⊜ **Fteres**, tel. 98233.

KALÁVRITA (☎ 0692)
⌷ ⊜⊜ **Chelmos**, tel. 22217. **Villa Kalávrita**, tel. 22712. **Filoxenía**, tel. 22422.
⊜ **Megas Alexandros**, Kapota, tel. 22221.

KALOGRIA (☎ 0693)
⌷ ⊜⊜ **Christina Beach**, tel. 31469. **Kalogria Beach**, tel. 31276.
◤ *BEACH:* Wide sandy beach south of Kalogria.

KAMINIA (☎ 061)
⌷ ⊜⊜ **Possidon**, tel. 678602.
⊜ **Posidon**, tel. 671602.

KÁTO ALISSOS (☎ 0693)
⌷ ⊜⊜ **Tarantella**, tel. 71205.

KÁTO ZAHLOROU (☎ 0692)
⌷ ⊜ **Romantzo**, tel. 22758.

LAKOPETRA (☎ 0693)
⌷ ⊜⊜⊜ **Lakopetra Beach**, tel. 51394.
⊜⊜ **Ionian Beach** (bungalows), tel. 51300.
◤ Beaches between Lakopetra and Káto Achaea.

LONGOS (☎ 0691)
⌷ ⊜⊜ **Long Beach**, tel. 71296.

NIFOREIKA (☎ 0693)
⌷ ⊜⊜ **White Castle**, tel. 23390.

NIKOLEIKA (☎ 0691)
⌷ ⊜⊜ **Poseidon Beach**, tel. 81400.

PÁTRAS (☎ 061)
⌷ ⊜⊜⊜ **Astir**, Od. Agíou Andréou 19, tel. 277502.
⊜⊜ **Acropole**, Od. Óthonos 39/Amalias, tel. 279809. **Marie**, Od. Goúnari 6, tel. 331302. **Olympic**, Od. Agíou Nikoláou 46, tel. 224103. **El Greco**, Od. Agíou Andréou 145, tel. 272931. **Ránnia**, Pl. Kolokotróni, tel. 220114.
⊜ **Hellas**, Od. Agíou Nikoláou 14, tel. 273352. **Metropolis**, Pl. tríon Simáhon, tel. 277535. **Mediteranee**, Od. Aghíou Nikoláou 18, tel. 279602. **Rannia**, Od. Ríga Feréou 53, tel. 220114.
✕ **Lavírinthos**, Poukevil 44, traditional Greek meals, unusual preparation.
⌷ **Archeological Museum**, Pl. Vasilís Ólgas, Tue-Sun 8:30 am-3 pm. **Odeion**, Tue-Sun 8:30 am-3 pm.
◤ Daily ferries to Kefalonía, Ithaca and Corfu.

PSATHOPIRGOS (☎ 061)
⌷ ⊜⊜ **Florida** (motel), tel. 931279.

RÍO (☎ 061)
⌷ ⊜⊜⊜ **Pórto Río**, tel. 992102.
⊜⊜ **Georgios**, tel. 992627.

RODIA (☎ 0691)
⌷ ⊜⊜ **Eden Beach**, tel. 81195.

SELIANITIKA (☎ 0691)
⌷ ⊜⊜ **Kanelli**, tel. 72442. **Panayotis**, tel. 71840.

A GASTRONOMIC ODYSSEY
WITH MR. P.

In Greece, eating and drinking is more than the mere act of taking in nourishment. It is an occasion for being sociable; it takes time and dedication, but also helps you to relax. To give an idea of how this works, let us spend an evening with the imaginary Mr. Papadópoulos, accompanying him on his tour of Greek gastronomy during a long, leisurely evening at the end of a hot summer day.

After waking from an afternoon nap at around six o'clock, Mr. P.'s first visit is to a *kafenío*, where a strong coffee revives his spirits. He can drink his coffee black (*skéto*), medium-sweet (*métrio*), very sweet (*varí glikó*), or prepared in any of a dozen other ways.

After a little gossip, Mr. P. heads for his local bar, where he regularly meets his

Above: Succulent Greek specialty – spring lambs on the spit. Right: An old recipe for baking bread into hard biscuits.

paréa, his inner circle of friends. Every evening they sit together in the *ouzerí*, with glasses of *oúzo* or *tsípouro*. They are served *mezédes* (appetizers) with their aniseed-flavored spirits, and with every round of drinks the waiter takes care to bring a new side dish, such as *htapódi* (grilled octopus), pieces of cheese, tomato or cucumber, olives, *dolmadákia* (vine leaves filled with rice), *garídes* (prawns), *kolokithákia* (fried slices of zucchini) or *marídes* (grilled sardines).

After nine o'clock, Mrs. P. and her women friends appear, possibly with several children. The large party then moves on to a *taverna*. Once there, the choice of starters is quickly made: *taramosaláta* (fish-roe spread), *tzatzíki* (yoghurt with cucumber and garlic), *gígantes* (broad beans), *htapódi saláta* (marinated octopus), *féta* (sheep's cheese), *spanakópites* (spinach pie) or *kreatópites* (meat pie) with flaky *phyllo* dough. Salads are brought to the table at the same time, and include a bit of everything: *maroúli* (green salad), *lahanosaláta* (cabbage salad), and *angourodomotosaláta* (mixed cucumber and tomato salad).

The *horiátiki saláta* (country salad) is something for the tourists. Mr. P. would not be satisfied with the little bit of olive oil the cook has sprinkled over it; when *he* dips fresh bread into his salad bowl, he wants it to be soaked in oil. Also, at Mr. P.'s table each person is not served his own individual portion: everyone naturally takes a little of everything.

Assuming that Mr. P.'s party is large enough for dishes to be chosen right across the menu, they might be served *souvlákia* (meat kebab), *païdákia* (lamb cutlets), *arní foúrnou* (roast lamb) and *kotópoulo krasáto* (chicken in wine sauce). In addition, everyone helps themselves to *giovétsi* (beef in a clay stew-pot, with semolina noodles), *kokkinistó* (braised beef in a tomato sauce), *soutzoukákia* (meatballs with cumin in tomato sauce), *biftékia* (stuffed meatballs), *pastítsio* (macaroni casserole), *stifádo* (braised beef with onions) and *mousakás* (potato and eggplant casserole topped with béchamel sauce).

And don't forget the fish: *barboúnia* (red mullet), *sinagrídes* or *lithrínia* (seabream), *gópes* (pilchards) and *bakaliáros me skordaliá* (dried cod with a garlic and potato paté). Regardless of what is ordered and eaten, there is always room on the table for some side dishes, such as *patátes foúrnou* (baked potatoes), *fasolákia* (steamed beans), *gemistés* (stuffed peppers) and *melitzánes* (braised eggplant).

Everyone at Mr. P.'s table drinks wine; preferably *retsina*, a wine flavored with resin straight from the *krasí híma*, (barrel). But even the bottled wines are not to be sneezed at: fresh white *Porto Carras* from the Halkidikí, sparkling light red *Rombóla* from the island of Kefaloniá, mild dark red *Náoussa* wines from Macedonia, or the Greek everyday table wine called *Deméstika*, which comes from the Peloponnese.

Eating and Drinking

It is almost midnight and fruit is brought to the table. Mr. P. and his companions sample some iced *karpoúzi* (watermelon) and *pepóni* (honeydew melon). There are also *síka* (fresh figs) and *stafília* (grapes). The fruit is followed by some *kefalotíri* or *anthótiro* (strong country cheeses). Finally, the party breaks up.

Mr. P. and his family may well need something to fortify them after this long and strenuous evening, so they go into the nearest *zaharoplastío* (pastry shop) to try a little *pásta* (cream cake), some *kadaïfi* (honey cakes), *rizógalo* (rice pudding with cinnamon), and *krem karamél* (caramel pudding).

Mr. P. takes leave of his wife and children and hurries to the *kafetéria*, where his friends are waiting for him once more. There, the leisurely evening is rounded off in Greek style, with a decent Scotch whisky. With his drink, Mr. P. nibbles some *passatémbi* (sunflower seeds) and *fistíkia* (pistachios), because drinking without having something to eat would, in his book, just be boozing.

METRIC CONVERSION

Metric Unit	US Equivalent
Meter (m)	39.37 in.
Kilometer (km)	0.6241 mi.
Square Meter (sq m)	10.76 sq. ft.
Hectare (ha)	2.471 acres
Square Kilometer (sq km)	0.386 sq. mi.
Kilogram (kg)	2.2 lbs.
Liter (l)	1.05 qt.

TRAVEL PREPARATIONS

Climate / Travel Season

Expect hot, dry weather in the six summer months; and the damp, mild winters that characterize Greece's subtropical climate. From May – sometimes as early as April – through September there is virtually no rainfall in the south and on the central mainland. A short, but violent rainy season occurs at the end of the summer, followed by a period of stable weather, often lasting until the turn of the year – similar to an extended Indian summer. Heavy winter rains in the months of January and February turn into snow in the mountainous interior. Spring arrives in Greece by stages – from the south northwards and from the sea up into the mountains – in March and April. May and June, already summer, are the best months for traveling in Greece.

The temperature of the sea rises only gradually, from about 17 to 19°C in May up to about 24 to 27°C in August, and remains pleasantly warm until October. The air temperature in July and August normally has a daytime range of between 25 and 32°C.

Clothing

In the spring and autumn you should be prepared for fluctuations between summer heat and cool, rainy days. In July and August you only need to pack cool, light clothing: shorts and cotton shirts are the most useful items of apparel for both sexes.

Long pants for men and a skirt or dress for women are required when visiting churches or monasteries, and will also come in handy for trips into rural towns. A lightweight sweater is always useful. Even for short walks in the stony countryside you need strong shoes and long pants to protect you from the bushes.

Arrival / Customs

For citizens of the European Union, an identity card is sufficient for entry into Greece. Everyone else needs a valid passport.

For private travel and personal use within the EU, most goods are not restricted. The following are restricted and only the given amounts may be brought from other EU countries into Greece: 800 cigarettes, 400 cigarillos, 200 cigars, 1 kilogram of tobacco, 10 liters of spirits, 20 liters of other alcoholic beverages (maximum 22 percent alcohol content), 90 liters of wine (maximum 60 liters of sparkling wine), 110 liters of beer.

People arriving from non-EU countries may bring up to 10 kilograms of food and non-alcoholic beverages, 200 cigarettes or 250 grams of tobacco, and 1 liter of spirits or 2 liters of wine into Greece.

The same limits apply to goods bought from duty-free shops (airports, ferries) in a non-EU country before arrival in Greece, as well as from duty-free shops in Greece before arrival in a non-EU country. There has been no duty-free shopping on journeys between countries of the EU free-trade zone since 1999.

Old icons and relics may not be taken out of Greece. Anyone caught trying to do so will be heavily fined.

Currency / Exchange

There is no limit to the amount of foreign currency you may bring into Greece, either in cash or travelers checks. Cash sums of more than US $1,000, or the equivalent in other currencies, must be declared on entry and no more than the declared sum may later be taken out of the country. Importation of Greek Drachma (GRD) is limited to 100,000 drachma, and export to 20,000 drachma. Changing foreign currency into drachma is considerably more favorable in Greece than abroad. Eurochecks and travelers checks are accepted in all banks, but post offices only accept travelers checks.

At international ferry ports and airports, banks keep their exchange offices open only during arrival hours. In Athens, they are open 24 hours a day. In holiday resorts you can exchange money at the official rate at private exchange desks (e.g., travel agents, hotels), as well as in the exchange booths on all ferries to and from Italy. The Greek drachma circulates in coins with denominations of 1, 2, 5, 10, 50 and 100 drachmas and in notes of 50, 100, 500, 1,000, 5,000 and 10,000 drachmas.

At the time of publication the exchange rate was:

1 US$. . . . . 336 GRD
1 GB£. . . . . 547 GRD
1 Euro. . . . . 331 GRD

Health Precautions

No special precautions are necessary either before starting your trip or, as far as eating and drinking are concerned, in Greece itself. In case of illness, you will receive the best medical attention in Athens; the quality of medical services declines rapidly as you get further into the provinces, especially as regards equipment for emergency treatment.

In the chief town of each district there is a state-run health center, and every prefectural capital has a hospital. Most places, down to the larger villages, have plenty of pharmacies; unfortunately, no pharmacological expertise is required of the people who run them.

TRAVELING TO GREECE

By Plane

Athens, Thessaloníki and Corfu (for visits to Epirus) are served by scheduled flights to Greece from abroad. Charter flights to Athens, Thessaloníki, Kavála, Corfu, Préveza, Pátras, Kalamáta and Skiáthos (for visits to Pílion and Thessaly) are also available.

Olympic Airways provides international service to Greece as well as operating an extensive network of domestic links. You can get information through any Greek Tourist Board (EOT) office (see "Addresses," p. 91). In the US, call 1-800-223-1226 or (212) 838-3600; in the UK, (0171) 409 3400 (11 Conduit St., London W1R 0LS).

As state-run Olympic's monopoly relaxes, new airlines have been starting up. Cronus Airlines, for example, offers direct flights from Munich, Frankfurt and London (98 Wigmore Street, London W1H 9DR, tel. 0171-3317090, fax. 3317091).

By Car

Because of the tensions and wars that have plagued the former Yugoslavia since 1991, and especially since the war in Kosovo, it will be a long time before the land route to Greece can be used. It is best to arrive by ferry via Italy.

By Ship

The Greek ports of Igoumenítsa and Pátras are linked to several ports in Italy by dozens of different ferries. The most important Italian ports are Venice, Ancona, Trieste, Bari and Brindisi. Travel agents and automobile clubs can inform you about schedules and prices. There are different classes of travel on all crossings, from deck passage to luxury class. On some, passengers with motor homes may spend the night in their vehicles.

Taking a ferry from Venice to Igoumenítsa takes 25 hours (35 hours to Pá-

Guidelines

85

tras), from Ancona to Igoumenítsa 16 hours (19-22 hours to Pátras), and from Bari to Igoumenítsa 9-12 hours (15.5 hours to Pátras). Following is a short selection of ferry lines:

Superfast Ferries, daily service from Ancona, Amalias 30, 10558 Athens, tel. (01) 331-3252, fax. 331-0369; in the US: 757 Deep Valley Drive, Rolling Hills Estates, CA 90274, tel. (310) 544-3551. Internet: www. superfast.com; e-mail: sffathens@superfast.com.

Strintzis Lines, from Venice, Bari and Ortona to Pátras (the last two via Corfu) Akti Poseidonos 26, Piraeus, tel. (01) 422-5010, fax. 422-5265. Internet: www. strintzis.gr; e-mail: sales @strintzis.gr.

Ventouris Ferries, from Bari, Pireos 91 and Kithiron 2, 18541 Piraeus, tel. (010) 482-8001, fax. 483-2919.

Minoan Lines, from Venice and Ancona. Central office: Leoforos Kifisias 64B, 15125 Maroussi, tel. (01) 689-8340. Internet: www.minoan.gr; e-mail: booking-eta@minoan.gr.

By Train

There has been no direct rail connection through the former Yugoslavia since 1991. Travelers wishing to avoid car and airplane travel should take the train to one of the Italian ports, and then take the ferry from there.

TRAVELING IN THE PELOPONNESE

By Plane

Olympic Airways (Athens, tel. 01-9269111 / 9369111; fax 9219933) flies three times a week to Kalamáta.

By Train

The rail network of the Greek Railroad Company OSE only amounts to around 2,500 kilometers of predominantly single tracks. With its appalling track maintenance, aged trains and dilapidated stations, it is like a Third World railroad. On the other hand, all this, as well as 1,000 kilometers of associated narrow-gauge lines, make Greece an Eldorado for railroad history buffs. Attempts at modernization are being made. Comfortable express trains operate between Athens, Pátras and Kalamáta.

At the Peloponnese Station (*Stathmós Pileponísou*) in Athens the narrow-gauge southern route begins, running through Piraeus to Corinth, and on into the Peloponnese. A spur runs from Corinth to the seaside resort of Loutráki. The Peloponnesian Line describes a circle around the peninsula; from Corinth to Pátras (from Diakoftó there is a rack-and-pinion line to Kalávrita), southwards through Pírgos (branch line to Olympia), to Kiparisía, then inland via Megalópoli (with a branch to Kalamáta) and Trípoli to Argos and back to Corinth.

By Bus

Buses are the most important mode of public transport in Greece. Long-haul services are organized into regional cooperatives (KTEL). They function quite smoothly, are safe and inexpensive, and reach almost every village in Greece; all the larger provincial towns and cities are linked with Athens. From Athens, buses to the Peleponnese leave from Terminal A, Kiffissou 100.

From the regional capitals and larger urban centers, you can reach any town in that region. The prefectural capitals are the hub of a network that gives you access to the surrounding villages. The yellow-and-green KTEL long-distance buses depart from the central bus stations.

On long-haul routes, running parallel with the main rail lines, gray buses are also operated by the railroad company. You should keep in mind that the buses leave their departure points punctually, to the minute, and that timetable information can only be obtained at the bus stations – not from travel agents or other sources.

By Ship

For information on domestic shipping lines in Greece (Athens), call (01) 411-4785 or the Port Authority of Piraeus, (01) 451-11311. Some of the companies listed on page 86 also provide service within Greece during the high season.

Rental Cars

The major international rental car companies are represented in most of the larger towns and cities, and at the international airports. Local Greek rental car companies can be found in all provincial capitals and in the tourist centers along the coasts. These firms also offer a wide range of four-wheel-drive vehicles, motorcycles, scooters and mopeds. In holiday resorts, bicycle rentals are becoming increasingly popular.

Many car rental companies are quite specific about what kind of roads you may attempt: a sensible concern in many places where only the main arteries are paved and the rutted tracks to the beaches can wreak havoc on a chassis. It would be foolhardy to try to navigate many of these roads in anything less than a four-wheel-drive vehicle in any case; if you are planning to do some active exploring, rent a jeep.

Speed Limits: 50 kmh within city limits (motorcycles 40 kmh); 110 kmh outside city limits (motorcycles 70 kmh); 120 kmh on highways and expressways (motorcycles 90 kmh).

Blood-Alcohol Limit: 0.5 ppm.

Additional Traffic Regulations: Yellow lines on the edge of the roads in Athens, and the "street with right-of-way" sign, also mean "no parking."

In order to drive a motorcycle with an engine up to 50 cc, even tourists must have a Class 1 driver's license. (It may look fun to ride without a helmet, but don't!)

While driving, cell and mobile phones may only be used in connection with a hands-free speaker system.

PRACTICAL TIPS FROM A TO Z

Accommodation

Greek hotels are classed in six categories: Luxury and A to E. In our experience, qualitative differences between categories B, C and D are often negligible. In category C hotels one is usually well looked after, but the accommodation, equipment and service standards do not bear comparison with those in northern Europe. A price list (governed by a state-imposed schedule of prices) must be displayed in every hotel room, even in licensed private guestrooms.

Hotel reservations from abroad: At good travel agents or directly through the Greek Hoteliers Association, XENEPEL, Od. Stadíou 24, GR-Athens 10564, fax 01-3312535.

A recommended form of accommodation is a stay in one of the historic houses restored by the EOT in the following traditional villages: Váthia and Areópolis (Mani). Details from branches of the EOT. Vacation homes are increasingly being offered for rent (agents advertise in the major daily newspapers).

The accommodation categories in the *INFO* sections (at the end of each chapter) are as follows:

☺☺☺ Double room with breakfast from 25,000 GRD; in the off-season from 16,000 GRD. ☺☺ Double room with breakfast from 15,000 GRD; in the off-season from 12,000 GRD. ☺ Double room without breakfast from 7,000 GRD; in the off-season from 5,000 GRD.

Banks

Banks are open Monday-Thursday 8 a.m. to 2 p.m., Friday 8 a.m. to 1 p.m.; sometimes longer hours in the city centers of Athens, Piraeus and Pátras. Cash machines, used with credit or EC cards and PIN number, are common; depending on your credit line, you may withdraw up to 100,000 GRD a day. User fees are high for credit cards, quite low for EC cards.

Guidelines

Business Hours

Opening hours are no longer regulated by the government, but most places of business still follow the old hours which are: Monday, Wednesday and Saturday from 8:30 a.m. to 2:30 p.m.; Tuesday, Thursday and Friday from 8:30 a.m. to 1:30 p.m. and 5 to 8 p.m. Shops catering to tourists are usually open all day.

The kiosks (*períptero*) can be a great blessing; Greece's miniature department stores, they will supply your most urgent needs 24 hours a day – not only cigarettes, but everything from cans of iced tea to stamps and condoms.

Credit Cards

Almost all credit cards are accepted in the larger hotels, better restaurants and many shops in cities and major towns. They are increasingly accepted at gas stations in towns and on the main highways.

Crime

"Greeks don't steal," said an Englishwoman, leaving her purse lying on a café table when she went off to get something from her house. Still, caution is advisable in tourist centers. As for Athens: Keep a tight hold on your purse. Women, the Greeks say, should be especially careful. The late 1990s saw something of a crime wave. Greeks blame it on the huge influx of Albanians who started pouring in when their country's borders opened.

Eating and Drinking

Greeks themselves don't eat breakfast, or if they do then only something very light. In simple hotels there is usually nothing offered, or only the basics. Larger tourist hotels, on the other hand, often offer beautiful buffets; expensive hotels meet international standards. Coffee houses, snack bars and cafés are a good alternative for those staying in simpler accommodations.

It is not customary among Greeks to have lunch before 2 p.m., however, Greek restaurants are getting used to serving crowds of hungry tourists from northern climes at an earlier hour.

The evening meal, which is the main meal of the day, is normally not eaten by Greeks until after 9 p.m. Consequently, most restaurants stay open at least until midnight. Coffee houses (*kafenéion*), cafeterias, patisseries and bars stay open longer, often until 2 a.m. in holiday resorts and elsewhere.

In holiday resorts, at least, the menus are normally set out bilingually in Greek and English. Even so, the old Greek custom of leading baffled customers into the kitchen, to indicate by sign-language which of the simmering pots takes their fancy, has persisted. If you want to eat well and cheaply, you should observe the following rule of thumb: Go where the locals go. In the towns, the market district is where you will always be able to find simple but good well-established restaurants and tavernas.

Electricity

The electric current in Greece is 220 volts. Since the sockets are often still three-pin, unlike those of many countries, it is advisable to bring a plug-adapter with you, just in case.

Emergency Phone Numbers

First Aid. 166
24-hour medical service
(Athens). 331-0310
Police 100
Fire Department. 199
Breakdown Assistance 104
Forest Fire Center. 191
Tourist Police 171
(24-hour, year-round information in English, German, French and Greek.)
U.S. Citizens
Emergency Aid 721-2951

Festival Calendar

January 1 (New Year's Day): Many Greeks spend New Year's Eve playing cards or dice for high stakes. Children go from door to door singing carols (*kálanda*) to St. Basil (*Ágios Vasílios*), whose festival falls on New Year's Day. Everyone in the family gets a slice of the New Year's cake (*vasilópita*). A coin is hidden inside, bringing good luck to the finder.

January 6: At this Epiphany festival, the baptism of Christ is celebrated in seaside towns with processions down to the harbor. The priest blesses the water and throws a cross into the sea, which is fished out by young divers.

Carnival: In the weeks and particularly the last few days before the beginning of Lent, dances and balls are put on with great merrymaking. But only a few towns have carnival processions. The largest is held in Pátras.

March 25: A national holiday to celebrate the 1821 outbreak of the rebellion against the Turks, with military and school parades throughout the country.

Good Friday: The figure of Christ is carried through the streets in a procession.

Holy Saturday: Shortly before midnight the lights in the churches go out, the priest lights a big candle and speaks the words: "Come ye hither and take the light from a light that knows no evening!" With a cry of *Hristós anésti!* (Christ is risen!), the congregation lights the candles they have brought with them from the newly lit candle, and take them home. Outside the church fireworks are let off, firecrackers are thrown or effigies of Judas burnt. Afterwards, the family gathers for a late meal of *magirítsa* (a soup made from lamb's offal).

Easter Sunday: Easter is the Orthodox Church's supreme festival and the most important family celebration of the year. The traditional Easter meal is mutton or lamb, which is roasted either over glowing coals or in the oven.

The date of the Orthodox festival is governed by a calendar calculation that differs from the Latin one by as much as seven weeks, corresponding to the beginning of Lent and Whitsun. The next dates for Orthodox Easter are April 30, 2000 and April 15, 2001.

April 23: St. George (*Ágios Geórgios*).

May 1: Even though this is International Workers Day, it is also celebrated as a spring festival. Families go out into the countryside and weave garlands of flowers with which they decorate first their cars, then their front doors.

May 21: St. Constantine and St. Helena (*Ágios Konstandínos / Agía Eléni*).

June 24: Birth of John the Baptist (*Ágios Ioánnis Pródromos*).

June 29: St. Peter and St. Paul (*Ágios Pétros / Ágios Pávlos*).

July: Beginning of the Athens Summer Festival in the Odeion of Herodes Atticus (through September) and the Festivals of Epidauros in the ancient theater (until August). Wine festival in Dafní, near Athens (through August). Wine festival in Pátras (through September).

July 26 : Agía Paraskeví.

July 27: Ágios Panteleḯmonas.

August 6: Transfiguration of Christ (*Metamórfosis tou Sotíros*).

August 15: The bodily ascension of the Virgin Mary is not recognized by Orthodox doctrine, so the great national Ascension Day holiday is dedicated to the "Dormition of the Mother of God" (*Kímisis Theotókou*).

August 29: Beheading of John the Baptist (*Ágios Ioánnis Pródromos*).

October 26: Ágios Dimítrios.

October 28: The national holiday to commemorate the "No" given by the dictator Metaxás, in 1940, to Mussolini's request that Italian troops be allowed to enter Greece unopposed.

December 6: St. Nicholas (*Ágios Nikólaos*).

Christmas: This festival is not celebrated with the same traditional piety as Easter, nor is it a time for annual family get-togethers as it is in northern Europe and North America.

Guidelines

Hiking and Climbing

Information about mountain climbing and hiking can be obtained from the Greek Mountaineering and Skiing Association EOXO, Od. Karageórgi Servías 7, GR-Athens 14121, tel. 01-3234412.

Maps

Local tourist offices generally offer – often, sell – maps; but even the ones that cost money tend to be rather crude and lacking in detail. The key distinction between paved and dirt roads, for instance, often indicated by lines of different thicknesses or colors, can prove to be misleading, which is something you may not want to discover when you're confronted with an uphill road of scree in the semi-trackless mountains somewhere.

If you plan to do any serious exploring, and especially if you want to hike, it's worth investing in some decent ordinance survey maps, either before you go or in Athens. Streets and roads may not be widely known by their official names, so visitors sometimes encounter blank stares when they're asking directions to a specific address. Addresses in Greece are given with the street name first, the number second. *Odos*, the word for "street," is seldom included in the address.

Photography

All international brands of film are available, but the prices are relatively high – so bring an ample supply with you. Before photographing a local person, you should ask them for permission, which is usually granted. In museums photography with a flash or tripod is only permitted after payment of a fee. You should remember to be careful to observe the strict ban on photography at military installations (indicated by a sign with crossed-through camera).

Post and Telephone

Local post offices in cities are open Monday through Friday 7:30 a.m. to 6 p.m., Saturday to 1 p.m.; the main post offices in large cities stay open until 7 p.m. (9 p.m. on Saturday); in Athens (Od. Eólou 100) until midnight. Post offices in large villages are open from 7:30 a.m. to 1 p.m. (closed Saturday).

For telephone offices (look for the OTE sign) the same hours apply. You can use a phone card at countless phone booths. You can also make international calls from almost any kiosk, and in the villages from the general store, which serves as a public telephone and postage counter.

The country code for Greece is +30. When calling from overseas, include the town's area code without the 0.

Press

International newspapers can be bought year-round at kiosks in the center of Athens after 2 p.m. on the day of publication, and in other cities and holiday resorts – the latter only during the tourist season – the day after publication.

Public Holidays

National public holidays are: January 1, January 6, March 25, Good Friday, Easter (Sunday and Monday), May 1, Whitsun (Sunday and Monday), August 15, October 28, and December 25-26 (Christmas).

At a local level, additional church festivals are held on the day recognizing the saint to whom the church is dedicated (see "Festival Calendar," pp. 88-89). In places whose names begin with *Ágios* or *Agía* (male or female saints) you can be sure that on the relevant day a church festival (*panigíri*) will be held, with traditional dancing in the marketplace and music all night long.

Shopping

The range of souvenirs specifically aimed at tourists is mostly kitsch and is not worth mentioning. Items that can be recommended include jewelry, the well-made and good-value leatherware (bags, belts, backpacks, etc.), and cotton garments of all kinds. The wide choice of jewelry that is available everywhere runs from simple silver rings and bangles to gold necklaces. The craftsmanship of Greek gold- and silversmiths is based on a tradition of high quality. There is also no shortage of good pottery.

Shoes can be bought rather more cheaply than in the rest of Europe, as can furs. For your kitchen you can stock up on olive oil, cheese (*kefalotíri* or *anthótiro*) wine, ouzo and brandy, wild herbs, including some for herbal teas, even strings of garlic – all quite cheap.

Sports

Tennis courts are pretty rare in Greece and are almost only to be found on the grounds of large hotels. The coastal waters are ideal for all forms of water sports. In many places, windsurfing boards can be rented, and there are windsurfing and waterskiing schools in most resort areas. The possibilities for sailing are inexhaustible, and the waters below the cliffs are good for snorkeling.

Time

Greece is one hour later than Central European Time (Paris), 2 hours later than GMT (London); 7 hours later than Eastern Standard Time (the eastern US and Canada); 10 hours later than Pacific Time (California, British Columbia).

Summer time runs from March 26 to October 29, 2000, and from March 25 to October 28, 2001.

ADDRESSES

Internet

The Foreign Ministry has launched an English-language "news" site on the Internet with business, political and cultural information, updated daily, at www.cthesis.com.

The *Athens News* also updates its site daily: www.athensnews.dolnet.gr

Embassies and Consulates in Athens

AUSTRALIA: D. Soutsou 37, tel. (01) 644-7303.
CANADA: I. Genadiou 4, tel. (01) 727-3400.
IRELAND: Vasiléos Konstantinou 7, tel. (01) 723-2771.
NEW ZEALAND: Xenias 24, tel. (01) 771-0112, 748-6667.
UK: Ploutarhou 1, tel. (01) 723-6211.
US: Vassílissis Sofiás 91, Athens, tel. (01) 721-2951, 721-8401.

Breakdown Assistance

Greek Automobile Club (ELPA), Leof. Mesogíon 2-4, Athens, tel. 01-7791615. During the holiday season, ELPA operates a scattered chain of advice points along the main coastal routes. Failing this, there is a dense network of repair shops with a towing service, operated by two private companies: **Express Service** and **Hellas Service**. These are found on the main highways and on the outskirts of all towns.

Greek National Tourist Organization (EOT) Offices Abroad

AUSTRALIA / NEW ZEALAND: 51 Pitt St., Sydney, NSW 2000, tel. (00612) 241-1663, fax. 235-2174.
CANADA: 1300 Bay St., Toronto, Ontario M5R 3K8, tel. (416) 968-2220, fax. 968-6533; 1233 de la Montagne, Suite 101, Montreal, Quebec H3G 1Z2, tel. (514) 871-1535, fax. 871-1498.
UNITED KINGDOM AND IRELAND: 4 Conduit St., London, W1R ODJ, tel. (0171) 4999758, (0181) 734-5997, fax. 287-1369.
UNITED STATES: 645 Fifth Ave. (Olympic Tower), New York, NY 10022, tel. (212) 421-5777, fax. 826-6940; 168 North Michigan Ave., Suite 600, Chicago, IL 60601, tel. (312) 782-1084, fax. 782- 1091; 611 W. 6th St., Suite 2198, Los Angeles, CA 90017, tel. (213) 626-6696, fax. 489-9744.

Guidelines

EOT in Greece

Head Office: Amerikis 2, Athens, tel. (01) 322-3111, fax. 322-2841.

Information Desks: National Bank of Greece, Sindágma Square, Karageorgi Servias 2, Athens, tel. (01) 322-2545, 323-4130; General Bank of Greece, Ermou 1, Athens, tel. (01) 325-2267.

THE GREEK LANGUAGE

Greek is the oldest spoken language in Europe, although Modern Greek has evolved a long way from Ancient Greek. It's worth your while to pick up at least a few phrases and the alphabet; knowing the latter will give you confidence in dealing with buses, trains and road signs (although the latter are transliterated into Roman characters). And even if your attempts at producing Greek phrases are lamentable, people will be pleased that you're making the effort.

The 24 letters of the Greek alphabet may be difficult, but at least the pronunciation is logical. There are a few "false friends" among the consonants: b and d are pronounced "v" and like a voiced "th," while x is like the "ch" in German "ach," also transliterated as "h." In Greek, a "b" sound is spelled "mp," while an English "d" is "nt." You can see signs for snack bars called "Mpampis": "Bobby's." "G" is usually soft (Gianni is pronounced, as pop fans know, Yanni). Two gs together are "ng"; "angel" derives from the Greek αγγελοσ.

The diphthongs reduce to a relatively limited number of vowel sounds: a is "ah" (father), e and ai are "ay" (as in hay), o is "oh" (clove), and ou is "oo" (toucan). This leaves ei, h, i, oi, and u, all of which are pronounced "ee" (as in he).

The Greek Alphabet

Letter		Name	Transliteration
A	a	**alpha**	*a*
B	β	**beta**	*v*
Γ	γ	**gamma**	*g*
Δ	δ	**delta**	*d*
E	ε	**epsilon**	*e*
Z	ζ	**zeta**	*z*
H	η	**eta**	*ee*
Θ	θ	**theta**	*th*
I	ι	**iota**	*ee*
K	κ	**kappa**	*k*
Λ	λ	**lamda**	*l*
M	μ	**miu**	*m*
N	ν	**niu**	*n*
Ξ	ξ	**xi**	*x*
O	o	**omicron**	*o*
Π	π	**pi**	*p*
P	ρ	**rho**	*r*
Σ	σ/ς	**sigma**	*s*
T	τ	**tau**	*t*
Y	υ	**upsilon**	*y*
Φ	φ	**phi**	*f*
X	χ	**chi**	*ch, kh*
Ψ	ψ	**psi**	*ps*
Ω	ω	**omega**	*o*

GLOSSARY

good day, hello	*kaliméra*
good afternoon	*kalispéra*
hello (lit. "your health")	*yássou*
hello (polite form)	*yásass*
excuse me	*signómi, oríste*

(the first can be used in the sense of "I'm sorry"; the second, politely to get someone's attention)

Where is...?	*Pú íne...?*
the bus	*to leoforío*
the boat	*to plío*
the beach	*i paralía*
here, there	*ethnó, ekí*
When...?	*Póte...?*
What time is it?	*Tí óra íne?*
What's your name?	*Pos sas léne?*
today, tomorrow	*símera, áwrijo*
morning, night	*proí, vrádi*
What is...?	*Tí íne...?*
How much does it cost?	*Pósso káni aftó?*
alright / okay	*endáxi*
good	*kaló*
bad	*kakó*
Do you have...?	*Échete...?*
I want...	*Thélo...*
I would like...	*Tha íthela...*

I don't want... . . . . *Then thélo...*
that . . . . *aftó*
a room. . . . . *éna thomátjo*
a glass. . . . . *éna potíri*
wine . . . . *krasí*
water . . . . *neró*
the check . . . . *o logariasmós*
Do you speak English? . . . . . *Omilaté*
                                Angliká?
church . . . . *eklissía*
monastery . . . . *monastíri*
pharmacy . . . . *farmakío*
doctor . . . . *iatrós*
hospital . . . . *nossokomío*
I don't understand . . *Then katalawéno*
what . . . . *pós*
please . . . . *parakaló*
thank you . . . . *efcharistó*
one . . . . *éna, miá*
two . . . . *thío*
three . . . . *tría*
four . . . . *téssera*
five . . . . *pénde*
six . . . . *éksi*
seven . . . . *eftá*
eight . . . . *ochtó*
nine . . . . *ennjá*
ten . . . . *théka*
twenty . . . . *íkossi*
one hundred . . . . *ekató*
two hundred . . . . *thiakósses*
one thousand . . . . *chíljes*
two thousand . . . . . . *thío chiljáthes*

Notes on transliteration: The transliteration from Modern Greek as used in
this book follows the internationally accepted standards. In certain cases this
transliteration differs from the pro-
nuncation as shown in the glossary: the
letter *g* before *e* and *i* is pronounced as a *y*
("Geórgios" is pronounced *Yeóryios*;
"Agía" *Ayía*); *s* is always pronounced as
in "sock," not "rose"; *h* is always *ch* (as in
Scottish "loch"); the unvoiced *th* (as in
"thin") is represented in the transliteration by "th," but the softly "lisping" *dh* is
simply "d." Accents are used in all cases
except in single-syllable words or when

the stress falls on a capital letter at the beginning of a word ("Ágios," for example,
is pronounced *áyios*).

AUTHORS

Anne Midgette is a freelance writer on
music, art and travel. An opera and art
critic for *The Wall Street Journal, The
New York Times, Newsday, Opera News*,
and *Opern Welt*, she has written or contributed to travel guides to Germany, the
United States, France and the United
Kingdom for a variety of publishers. She
first traveled to Greece while working toward her degree in Classical Civilizations
from Yale University, and has been a
devotee of the islands ever since ("Athens
– Ancient and Modern Capital").

Wolfgang Josing studied medieval
and modern Greek philology, Byzantine
culture and ancient history. For over 30
years he has traveled extensively
throughout Greece, and he lived there for
several years. His deep understanding of
Greece has been the source of several
books that he has written or edited ("The
Isle of Pelops," "A Gastronomic Odyssey
with Mr. P.").

PHOTOGRAPHERS

Guidelines

INDEX